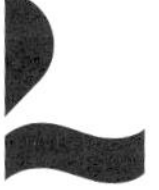

In loving memory of Robert

HAPPY TATTOOS

The Best Fun-Loving Tattoo Artists

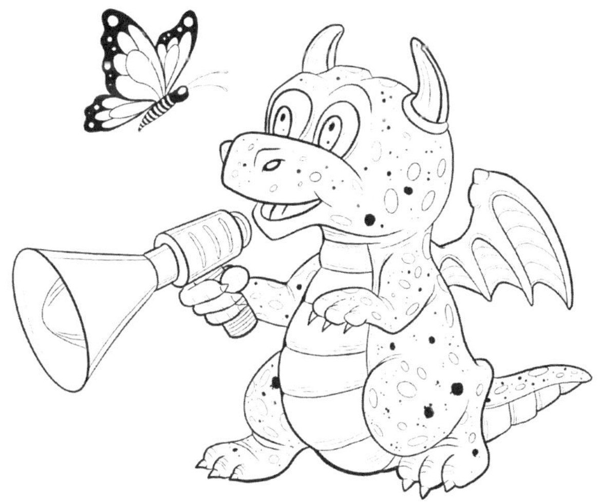

SVEN RAYEN & TI RACOVITA

Lannoo

FOREWORD

— SVEN RAYEN

Happy tattoos are serious business. As they should be.

Tattoos can give you strength, help you grieve, or simply serve as a reminder of who you are and - over time - once were. What you cared about, what made you laugh, what risks you took, what you found comfort in. They're personal archives written in ink, as intimate and permanent as memory allows.

To the casual observer, a silly tattoo might look like the result of an impulsive decision. But even a velociraptor on a skateboard or a farting skunk can carry genuine emotional weight. Humour is layered. And tattoos - even the ones that make you laugh - are often rooted in something more than just a punchline.

In this third volume of our series, we've put together a carefully curated selection of tattoo artists from around the world who specialise in joyful, funny and flat-out happy artwork. These tattoos aren't just jokes on skin - they're small, permanent celebrations. They capture memories, honour moments, or simply reflect someone's

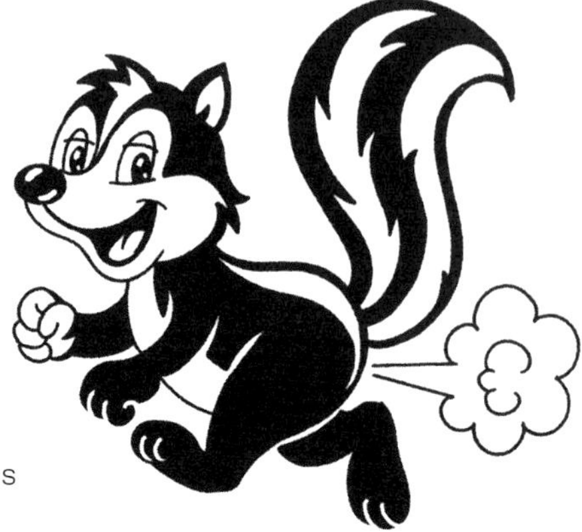

way of facing the world with a grin. There's beauty in choosing to be light-hearted in a world that often feels heavy.

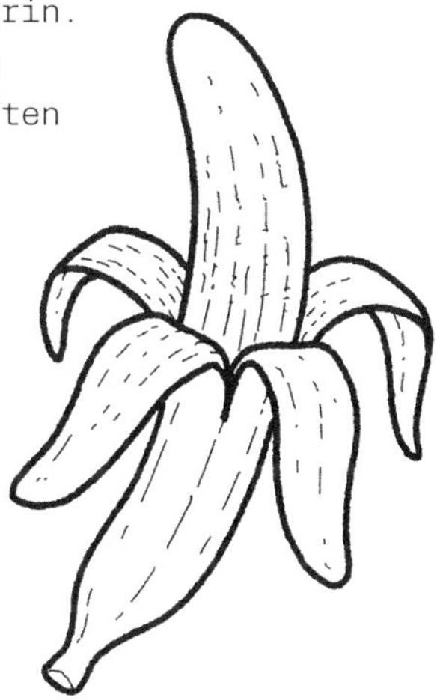

When you tattoo someone regularly over the years, you start to get a sense of their life. Every session - short or long - adds a new piece to the puzzle. With some clients, we've seen partners come and go, parents pass away, and little bundles of joy arrive on the scene. As a tattoo artist, it's a privilege to be trusted with something that personal and to help mark those milestones.

At Studio Palermo, my colleague Ti and I spend quite a bit of time on consultations before the actual tattooing begins. For us, it's about understanding the motivation behind the idea, giving certain projects the attention they deserve. It was no different with one young man in 2021.

The sporadic consultations with Ti and tattoo sessions with me slowly turned into a friendship. Robert had a natural warmth, a kind of quiet charm. Over time, we learnt that Robert was sick, and had been for a while. To the extent that the hope of a full recovery was growing thin. Nonetheless, Robert was most joyful and warm of character.

As his treatments got more intense, he didn't stop getting tattoos. In fact, he started choosing funnier and funnier designs. It was as though the worse things got, the harder he leaned into joy. One of the last pieces we gave him was a peeled banana on his forearm - small and simple, but an iconic symbol of slapstick comedy and of not taking anything too seriously, even when everything around you seems to suggest you should.

Near the end, he was spending most of his time in a hospital bed. His tattoos, he said, were all he had left to express himself. And if that banana could make the nurses smile? That was enough for him.

Robert passed away in early 2022. Not long after, we got a message from his family, whom we'd never met, inviting us to his memorial. Robert had spoken about his tattoos with such love and pride that they felt we were part of his story.

Sometimes, a happy tattoo isn't about being funny. Sometimes, it's a quiet, powerful act of defiance. A choice to laugh. A declaration of joy - even when joy is hard to find.

HAPPY REBELLION

If there's one constant running through this book, it's this: people often get happy tattoos not just because they feel joyful, but because they strive to be. Uplifting images, nostalgic cartoons, absurd characters and vibrant colours act like little emotional anchors. Symbols that say: 'This is who I want to be in the world.'

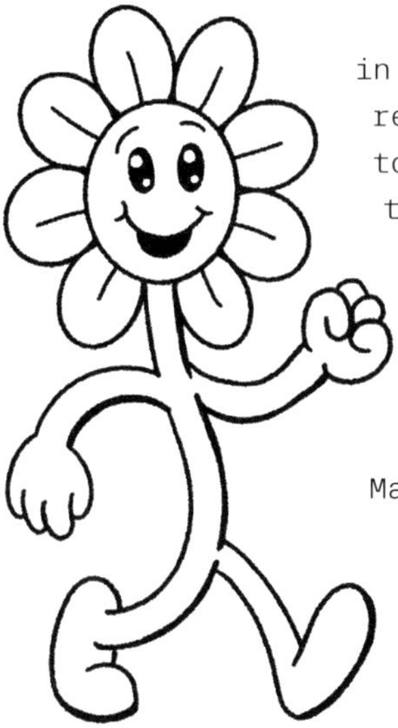

Happy tattoos are affirmations in ink. Sometimes they're reminders to not take life too seriously. Sometimes they're reminders that the person survived something. Sometimes they're just reminders to laugh, even if it's through gritted teeth.

Artists like Woozy Machine or Mr. Heggie have made dark and cynical humour their signature style. Their tattoos walk a fine line between the hilarious and the haunting - absurd designs with goofy captions that border on the philosophical. Their work is smart, strange and often laugh-out-loud funny. Jolly, but never lightweight. Their pieces are loaded with meaning, and often come from a place of deep feeling.

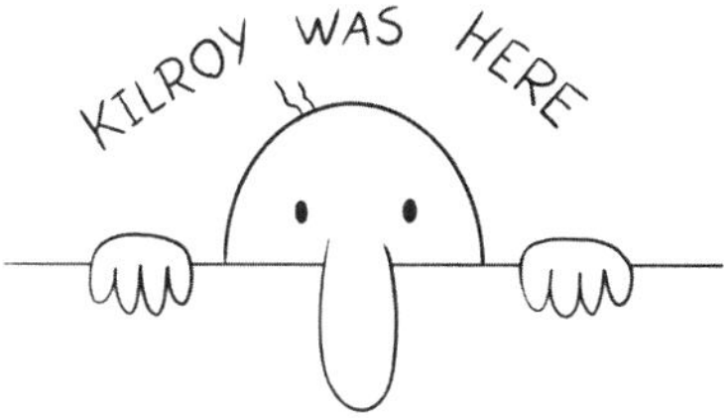

In a world that often rewards seriousness and superficiality, choosing joy can feel like rebellion.

WHEN DID TATTOOS BECOME HAPPY?

Ask someone what the first intentional act of art was, and they'll probably say cave paintings, some of which date back 45,000 years. But body modification - tattooing, scarification, piercing - may be just as old.

Archaeologists point to etched patterns on Upper Palaeolithic figurines, like the Löwenmensch (lion-man) or the Venus of Hohle Fels, as early representations of tattooing. Ötzi the Iceman - Europe's oldest known natural mummy - had over sixty tattoos, many on pressure points, possibly for pain relief. Tattoos were mostly marks of status, symbols of spirituality, forms of medicine, even tools of punishment. There was little room for humour.

So when did we start tattooing jokes on ourselves?

That's much harder to pin down, but it likely emerged with the rise of modern and postmodern individuality, and possibly with 19th-century circus culture. In those spaces, tattoos were both performance and rebellion. They were a sign of otherness, but also pride.

One early example mentioned sex workers in the early 1900s with tattoos like 'Keep off the grass' or 'Admission: 50 cents' tattooed on their pubic area.

Or the 'Kilroy was here' doodle, which emerged during World War II as a ubiquitous form of graffiti among American servicemen. Though the exact origins of the symbol remain debated - often attributed to ship inspector James Kilroy or variations of British and Australian doodles - it quickly became an iconic marker of American presence across the globe. Scrawled on walls, military equipment and in the ruins of battlefields from Europe to the Pacific, the phrase served both as a humorous declaration and a morale-boosting sign that 'Kilroy', meaning the United States military, had been there.

The symbol also became a popular tattoo theme among soldiers. Often etched onto arms, shoulders or other parts of the body, the Kilroy figure served as a personalised badge of identity, camaraderie and shared experience. These tattoos reflected not only a soldier's physical journey through wartime landscapes but also their emotional connection to the broader culture of resilience and gallows humour that sustained troops during the hardships of combat.

'Kilroy was here' continues to resonate as a symbol of historical memory, with new generations adopting the motif in tribute to its layered meanings - blending nostalgia, defiance and solidarity.

THE SELF AS CANVAS

In modern society, identity was still tied to roles, institutions and grand narratives - you were defined by your job, class, religion or nation. Postmodern society, by contrast, celebrates the individual as a fluid, self-defined being. Authenticity, personal expression and the freedom to construct one's own identity take centre stage. The self becomes a canvas - sometimes literally, in the form of tattoos

- reflecting the shift from collective meaning to personal significance.

It is in that perspective that happy tattoos come into play. Fashion designer Marc Jacobs famously has a SpongeBob SquarePants cartoon tattooed on his arm as a tribute to whimsy in an industry known for taking itself far too seriously. And *Jackass* star Steve-O has a full back tattoo of his own smiling face and two thumbs up. It's so absurd, it loops back into a strange kind of sincerity. Whether it's a grinning frog with sunglasses, a slice of pizza with angel wings, or a cartoon shouting nonsense - tattoos like this live in a space between humour and seriousness, unimaginable 50 years ago.

The artists featured in this volume understand something crucial: joy is a craft. It takes real skill to make someone laugh, especially when that laugh has to live on skin forever. Creating happy tattoos is not about dismissing seriousness, but about expanding the emotional range of what tattooing can express. These artists understand that the world is complicated. Because grief exists. Because burnout is real. Because joy can be fleeting, and choosing to hold on to it, to mark it permanently, is a brave thing.

So, whether it's a rainbow cowboy boot, a raccoon eating spaghetti, or a badly drawn potato saying something profound, these tattoos are monuments to being human. They're weird and wonderful and deeply necessary.

So here's to the peeled bananas. The googly eyes. The misspelled words. The silliness. The rebellion. The joy.

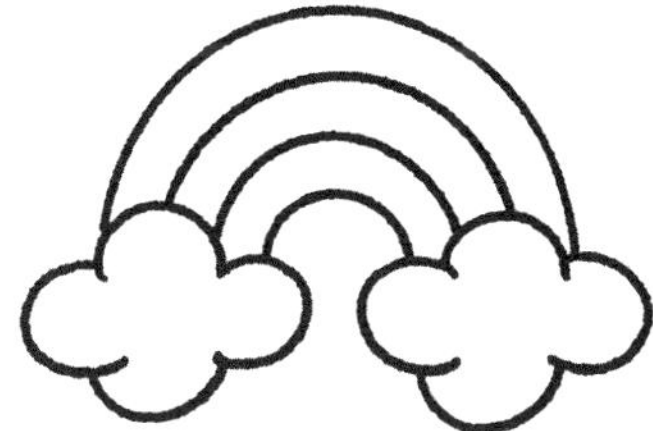

INDEX

TATTOO ARTISTS

88WORLD

South Korea / worldwide

88world is a South Korean pixel tattoo artist who travels the world sharing unique designs inspired by cartoons, video games and pop culture.

Since the start of his tattoo career in 2018, 88world has specialised in pixel art, bringing iconic characters and scenes to life through a nostalgic and playful lens. Each tattoo blends the charm of retro gaming and classic animation with the precision of tattoo craftsmanship, creating pieces that resonate with fans of all ages.

More than just body art, 88world's tattoos are personal tributes - capturing memories, emotions and stories that have shaped each client's world. With every design, 88world brings joy, whimsy and a sense of comfort to the skin, turning nostalgia into a permanent, wearable experience.

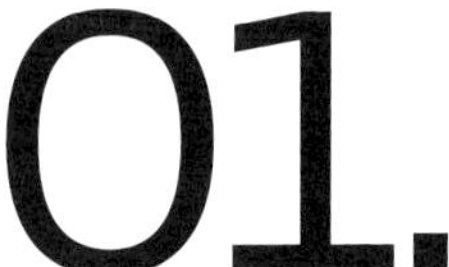

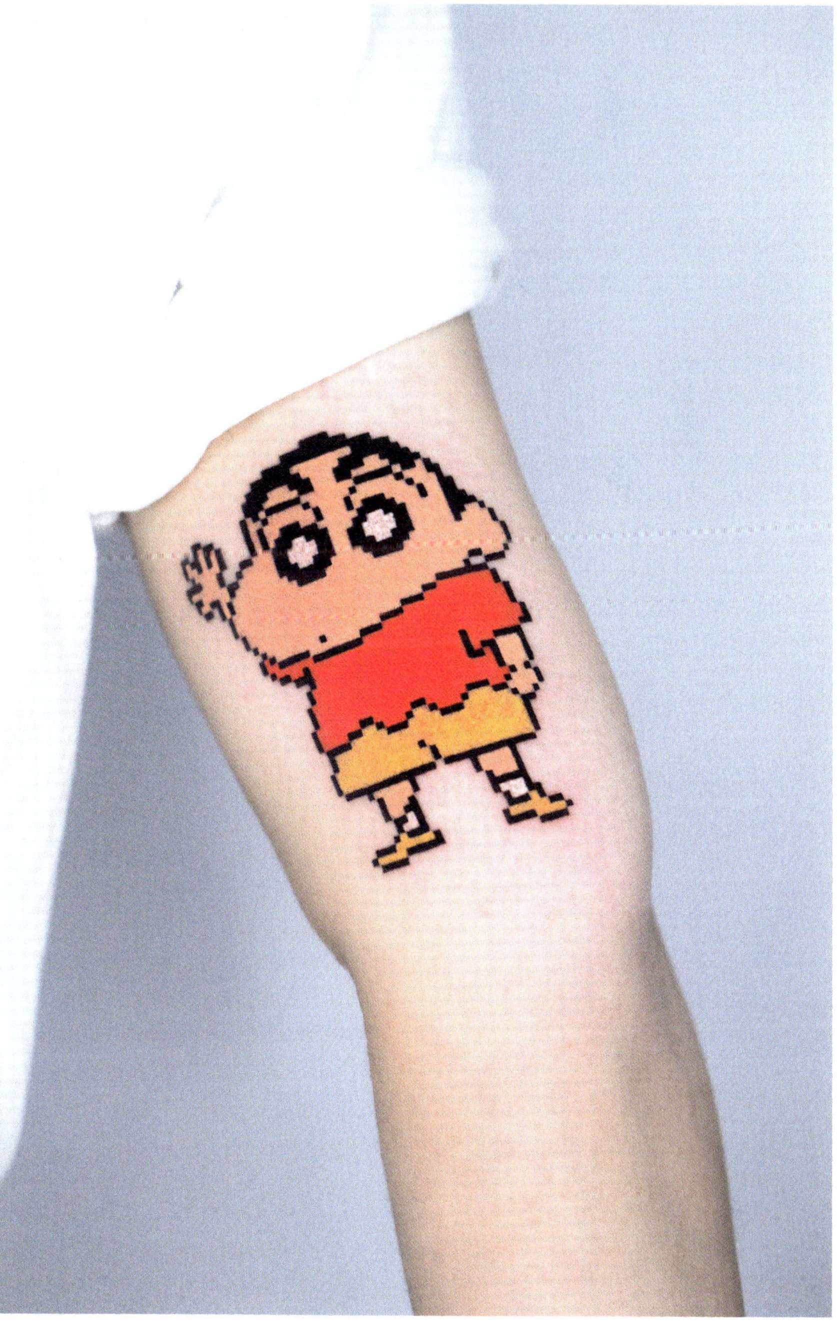

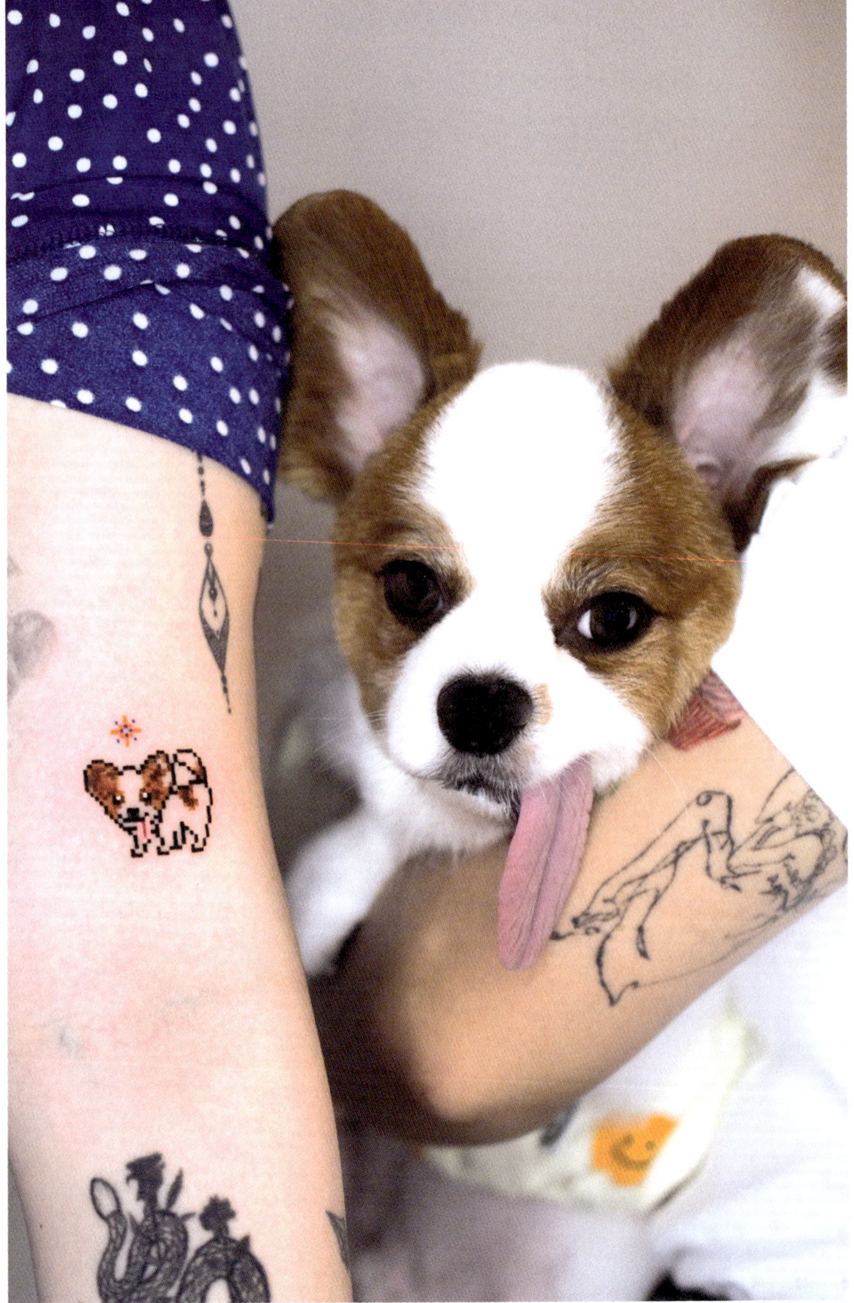

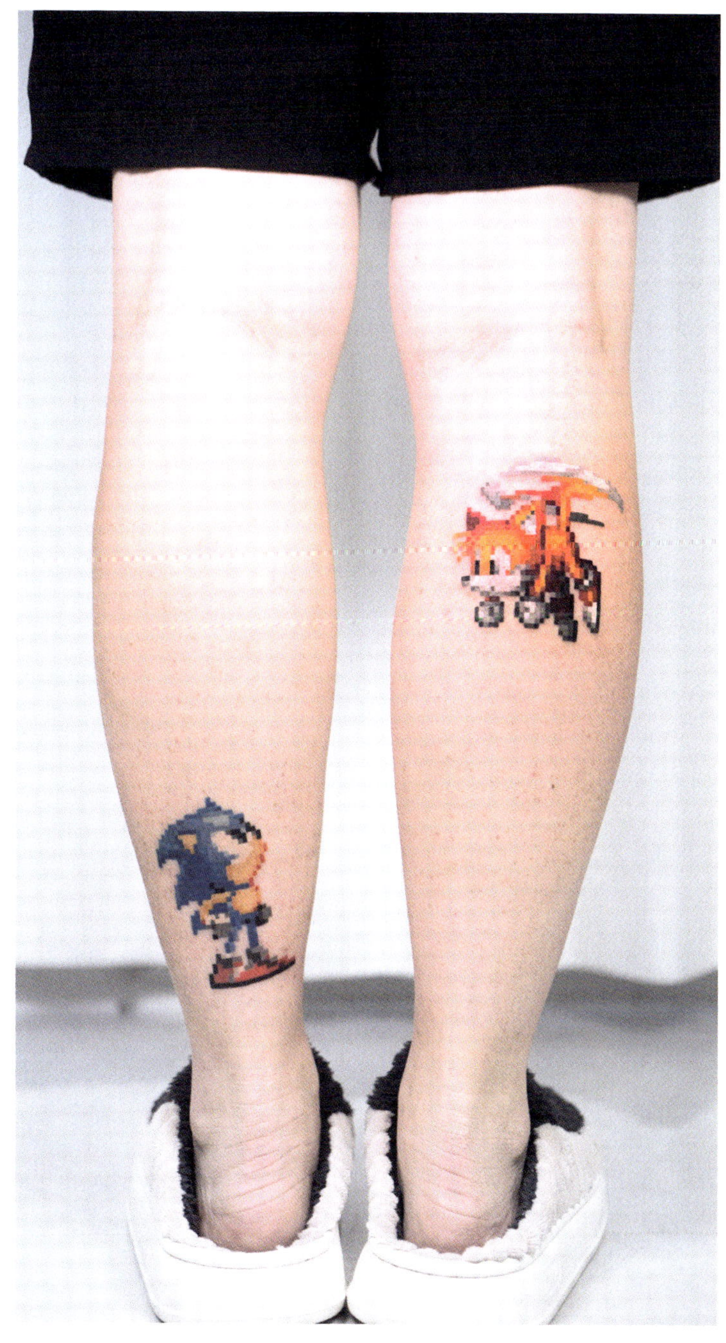

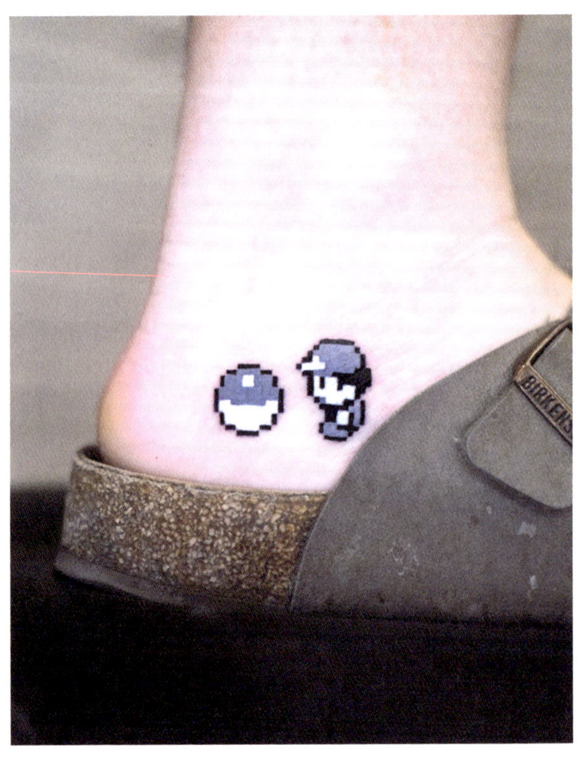
BIRKENS

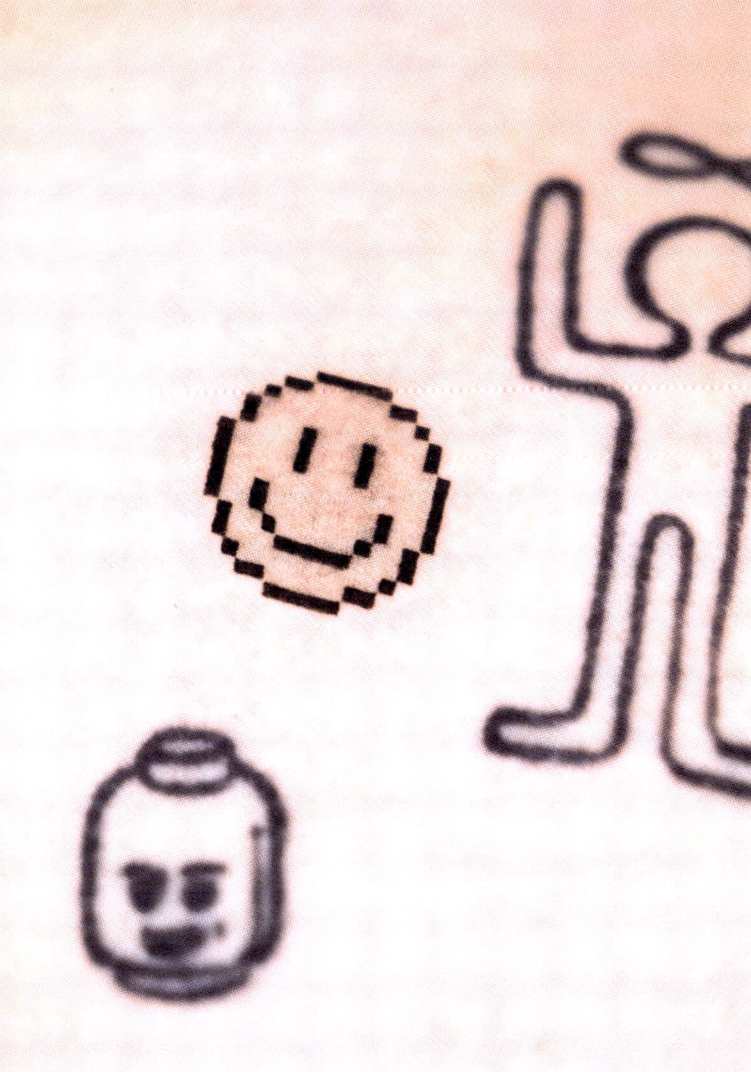

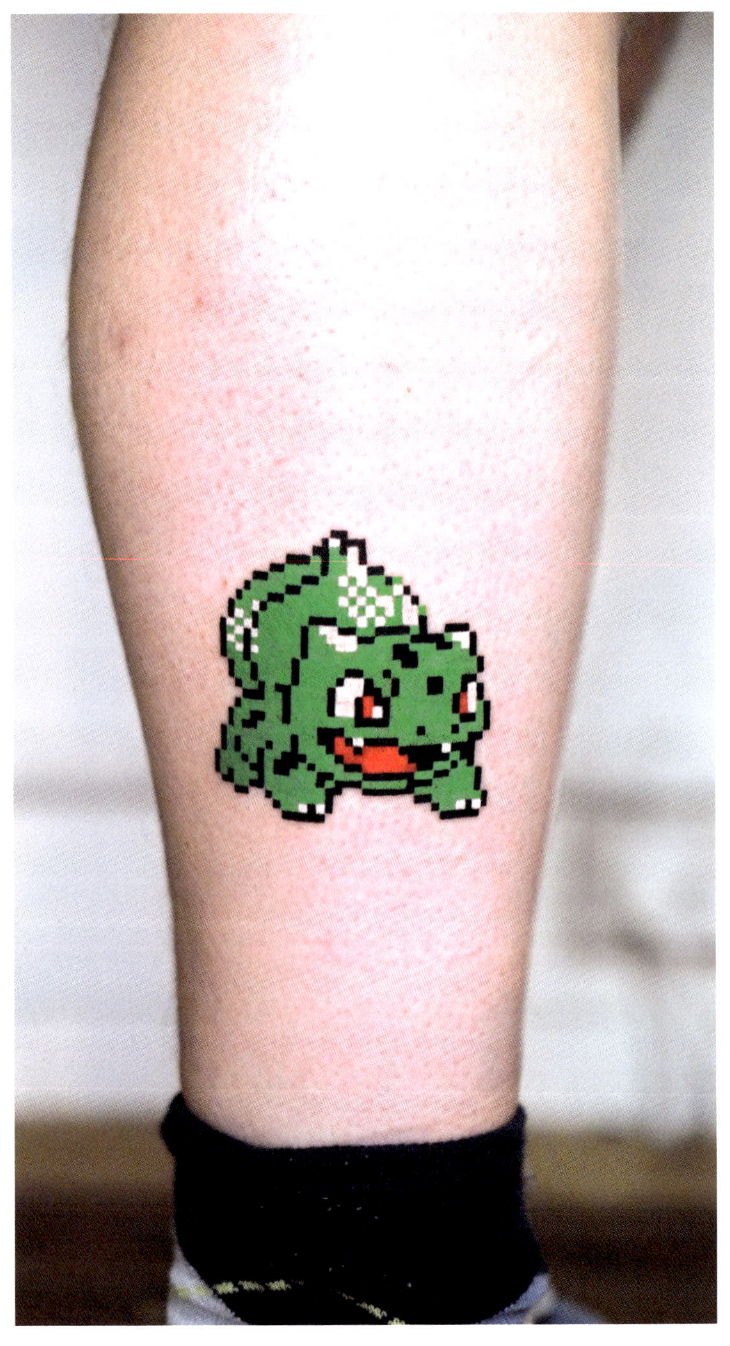

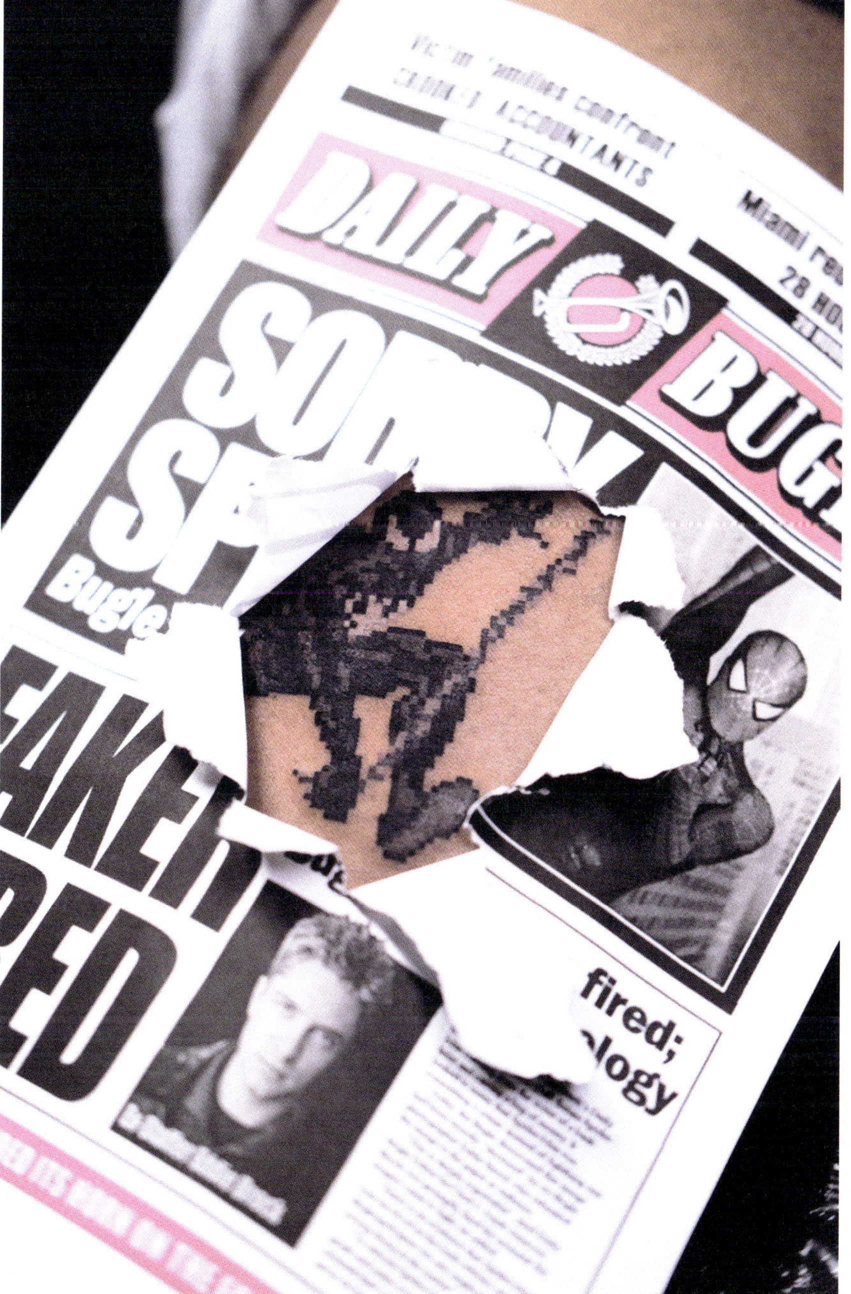
DAILY
Bugle
fired;

AGATARIS

Porto, Portugal

Ágata Gonçalves, professionally known as Agataris, is a Portuguese tattoo artist based in Porto. Since 2016, she has been working from her private studio, Lusco Fusco, developing a distinct visual language defined by bold colours, abstract forms and a focus on one-of-a-kind compositions. Each tattoo is created as a singular piece, designed to be worn by one person.

Entirely self-taught in tattooing, Agataris draws inspiration from painting, photography, music and travel. With a background in textile and fashion design, her work reflects a deep understanding of structure, texture and visual rhythm.

Rather than imposing fixed meanings, Agataris approaches her practice intuitively, allowing space for personal interpretation. Her work exists in the connection between image and body - where memory, emotion and aesthetics meet.

02.

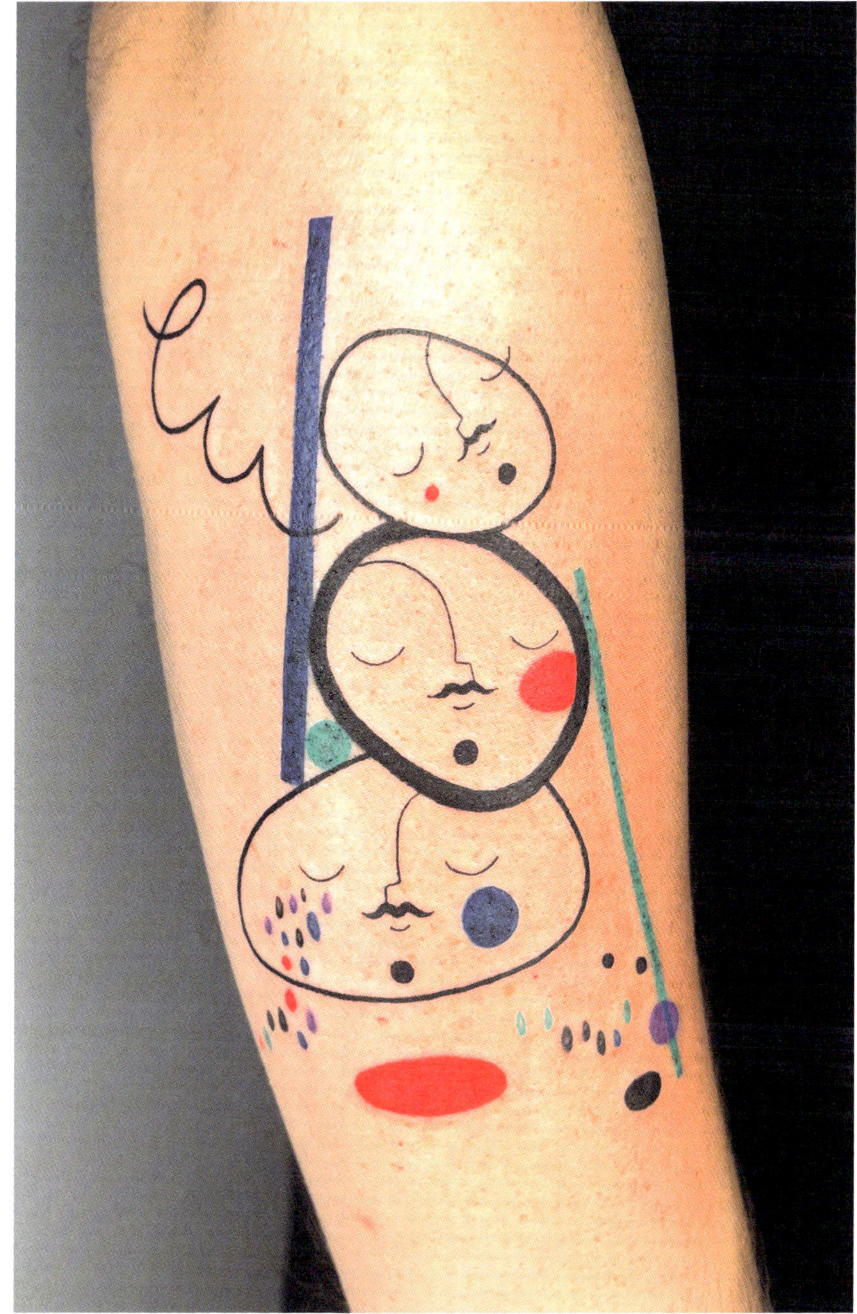

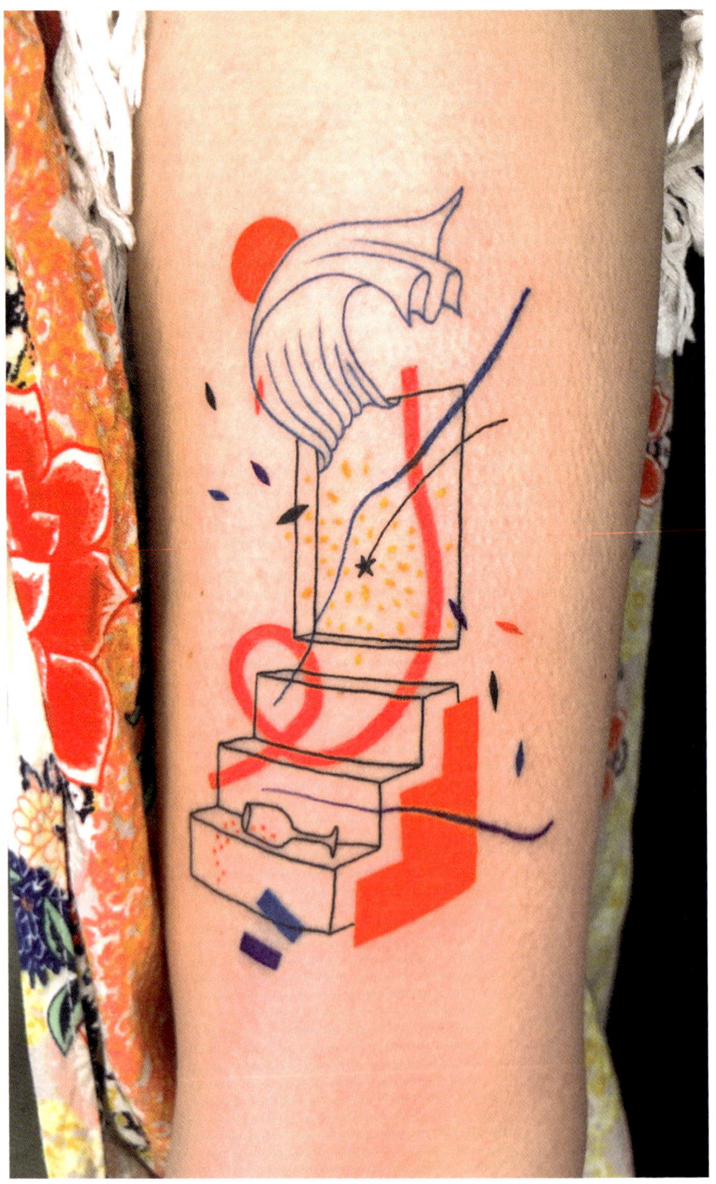

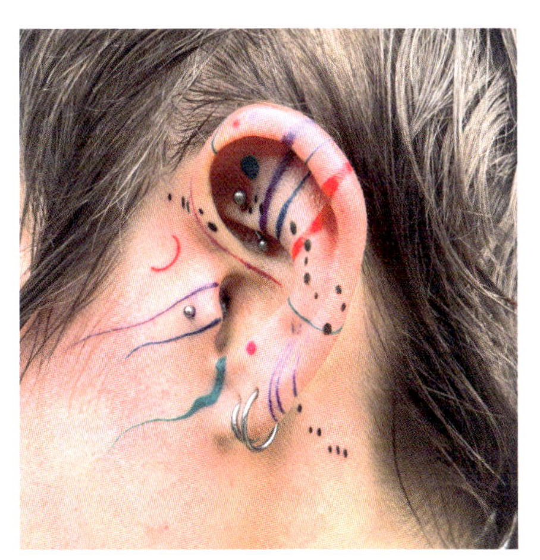

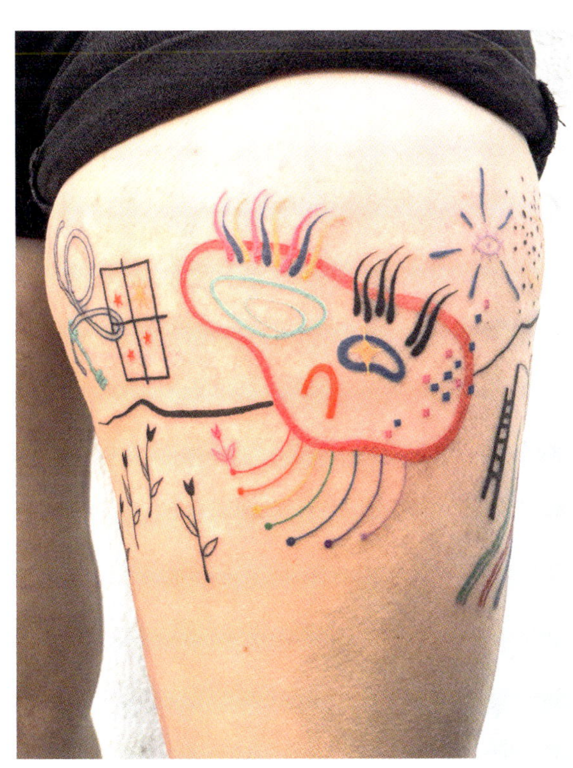

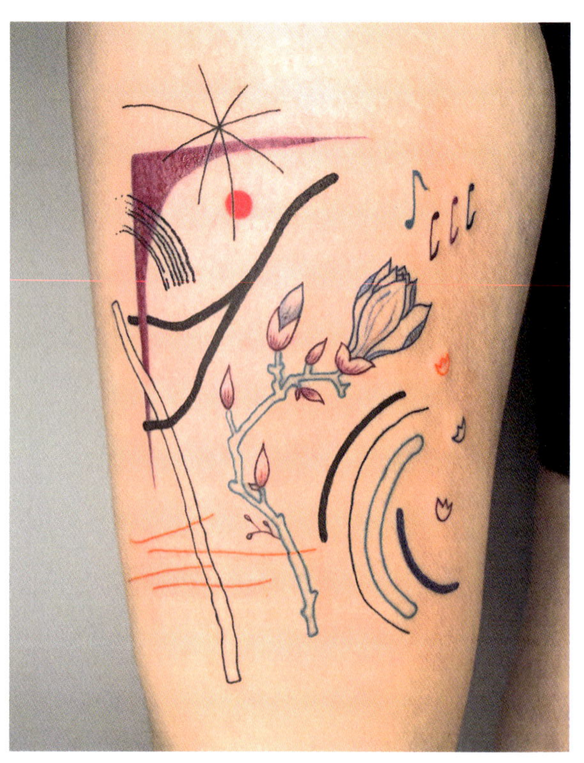

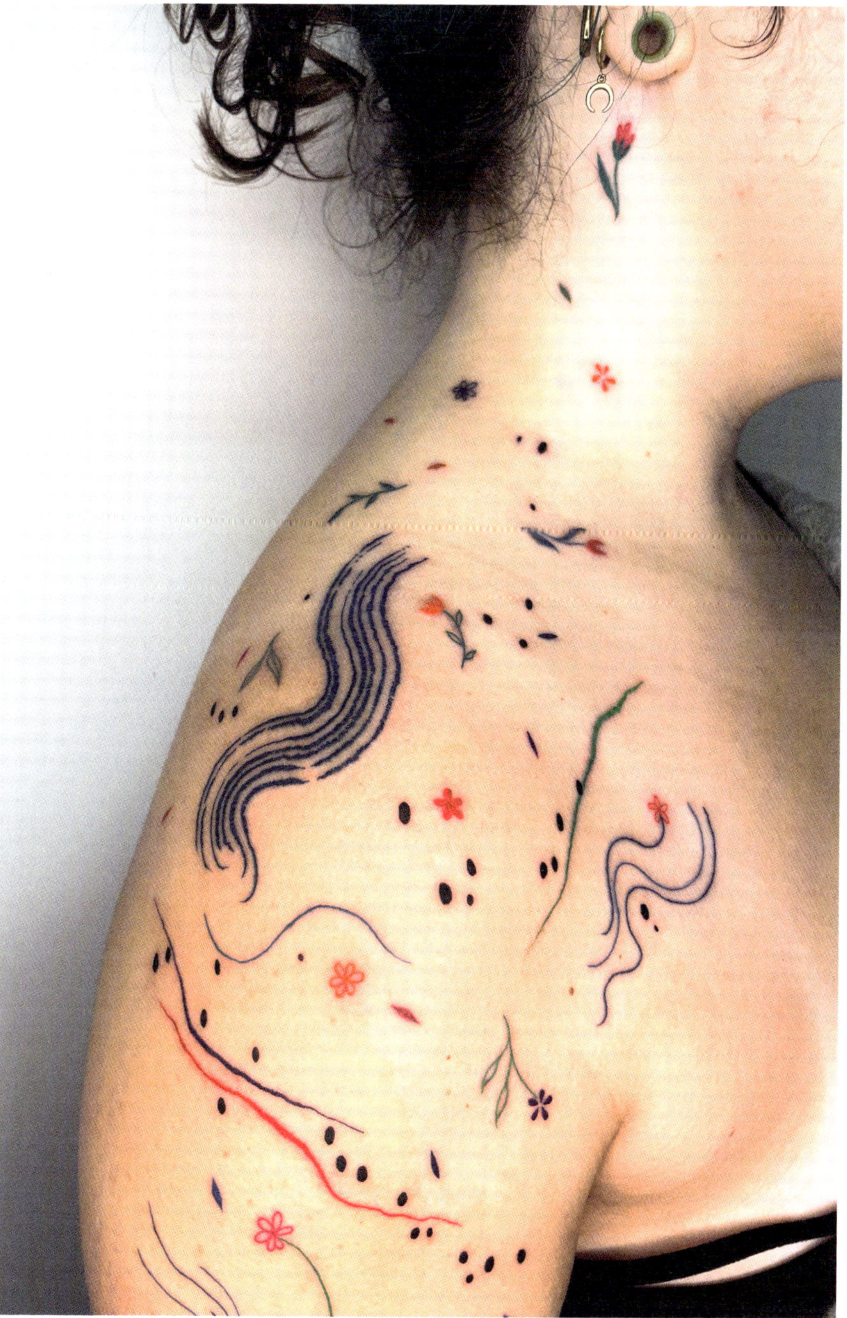

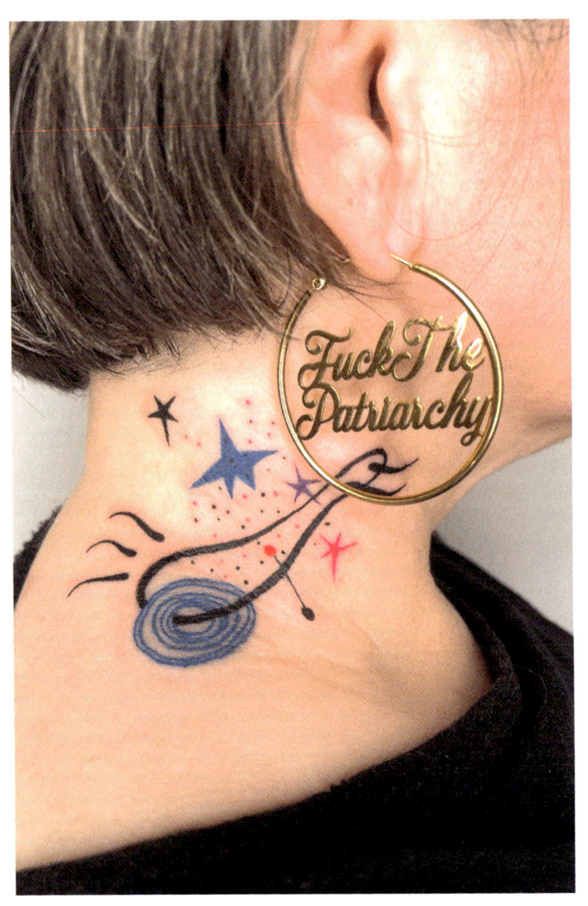
Fuck The
Patriarchy

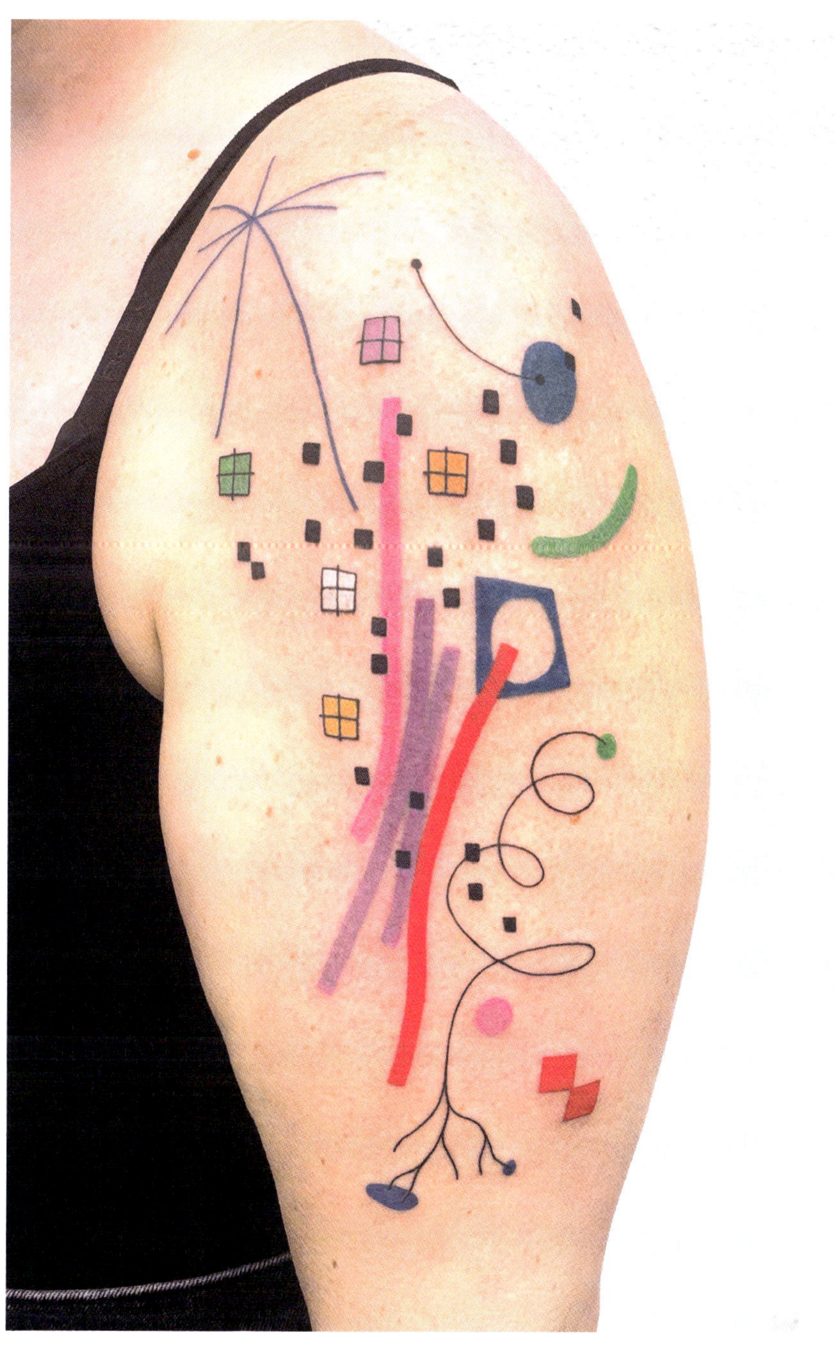

ANSHIN ANSHIN

Brighton, UK

Based in Brighton, UK, Will Barbour-Brown - known professionally as Anshin Anshin - is a highly skilled tattoo artist and illustrator with over 15 years of experience. His distinctive style is defined by bold line work and a striking colour palette, creating visually compelling designs that leave a lasting impression.

Will began his tattooing journey in 2010 with a traditional apprenticeship at Blue Dragon Tattoo Studio, Brighton's longest-running tattoo shop, established in 1989. Before tattooing, he studied illustration at Southampton Solent University, graduating in 2009. Inspired by fashion, movie and video game character design, and concept art, Will continues to evolve his artistic approach. Beyond his work in Brighton, he has travelled extensively across Europe and Japan, refining his craft and building an international clientele.

While tattooing takes up most of his time, he still pursues illustration projects and commissions that excite him.

03.

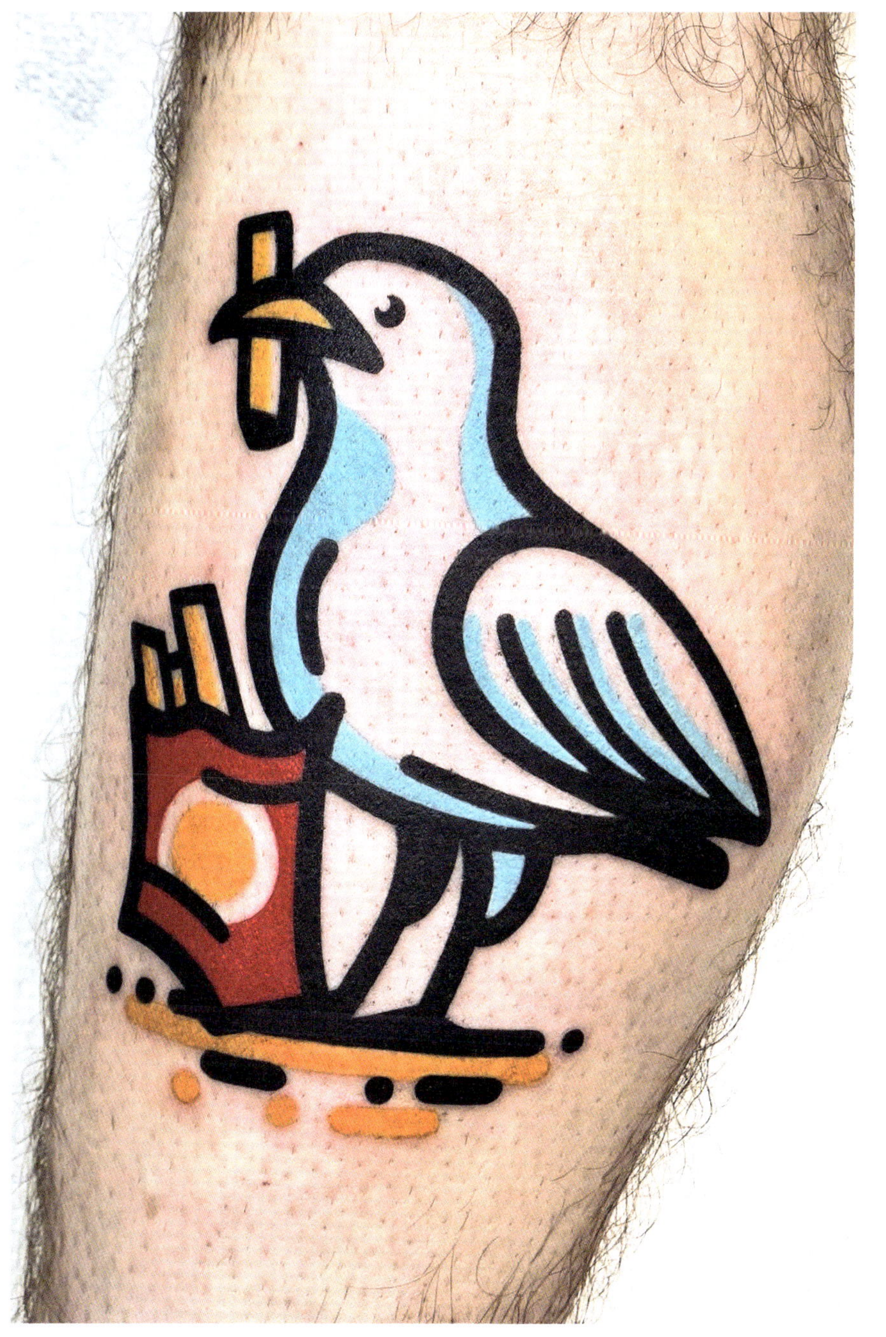

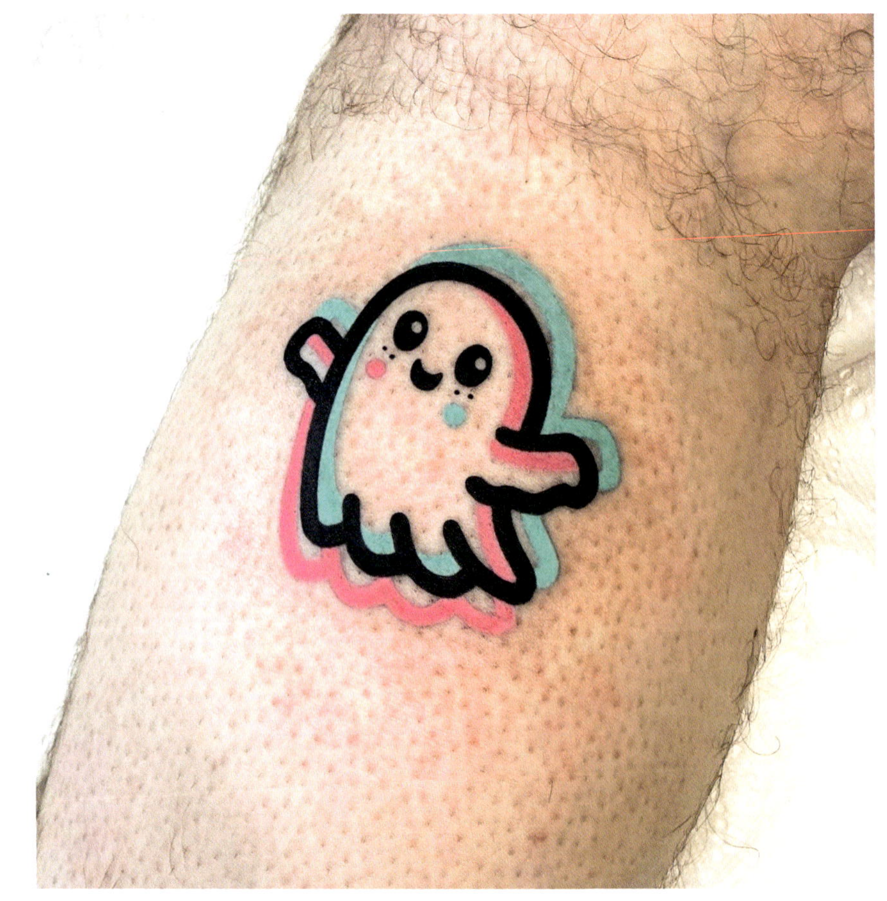

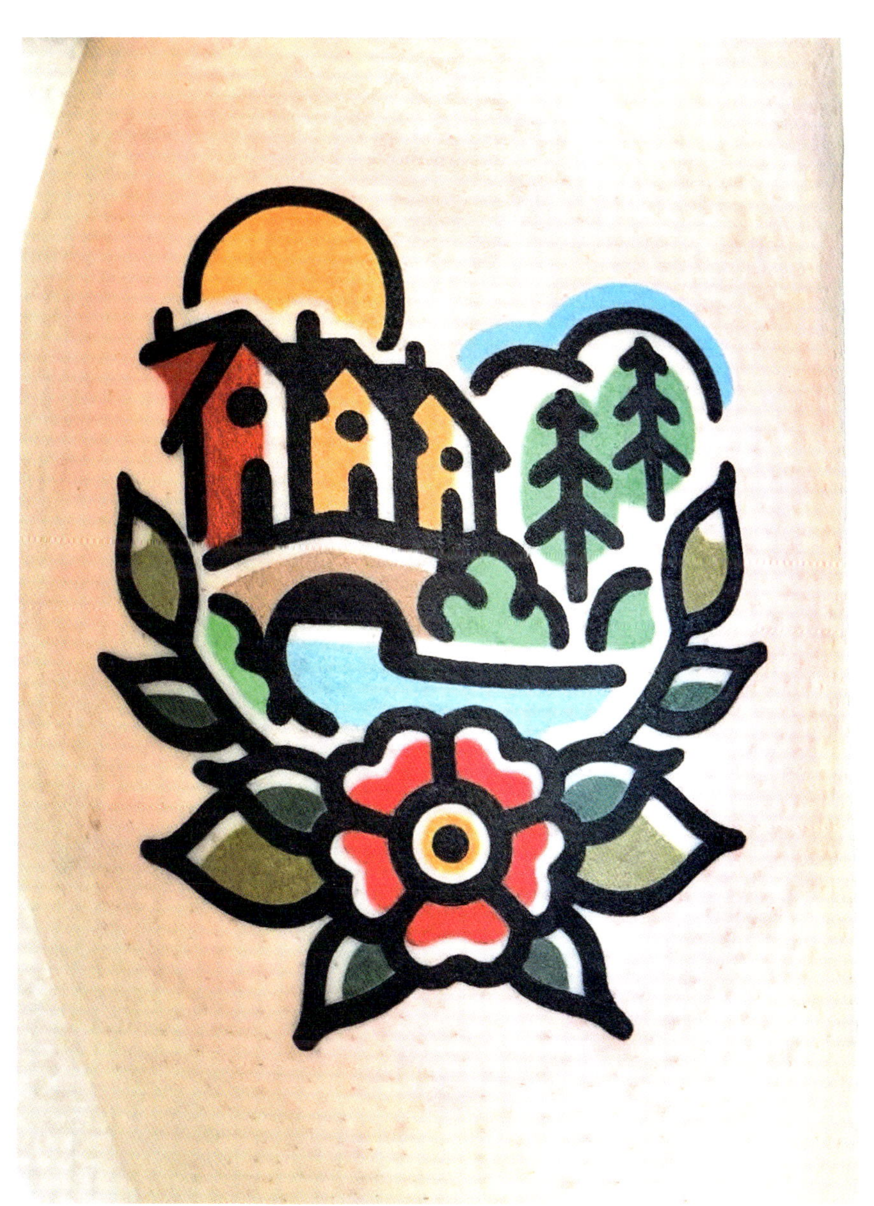

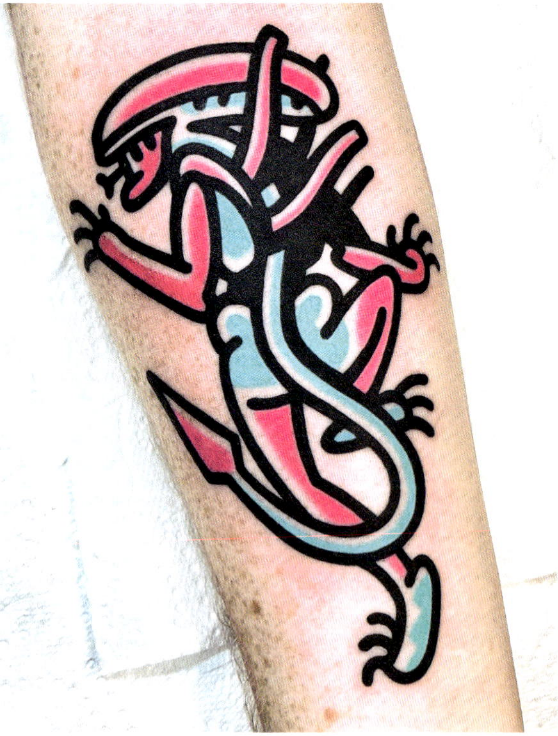

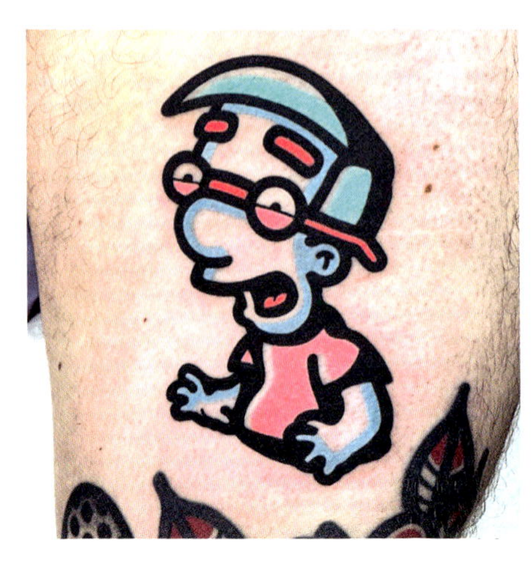

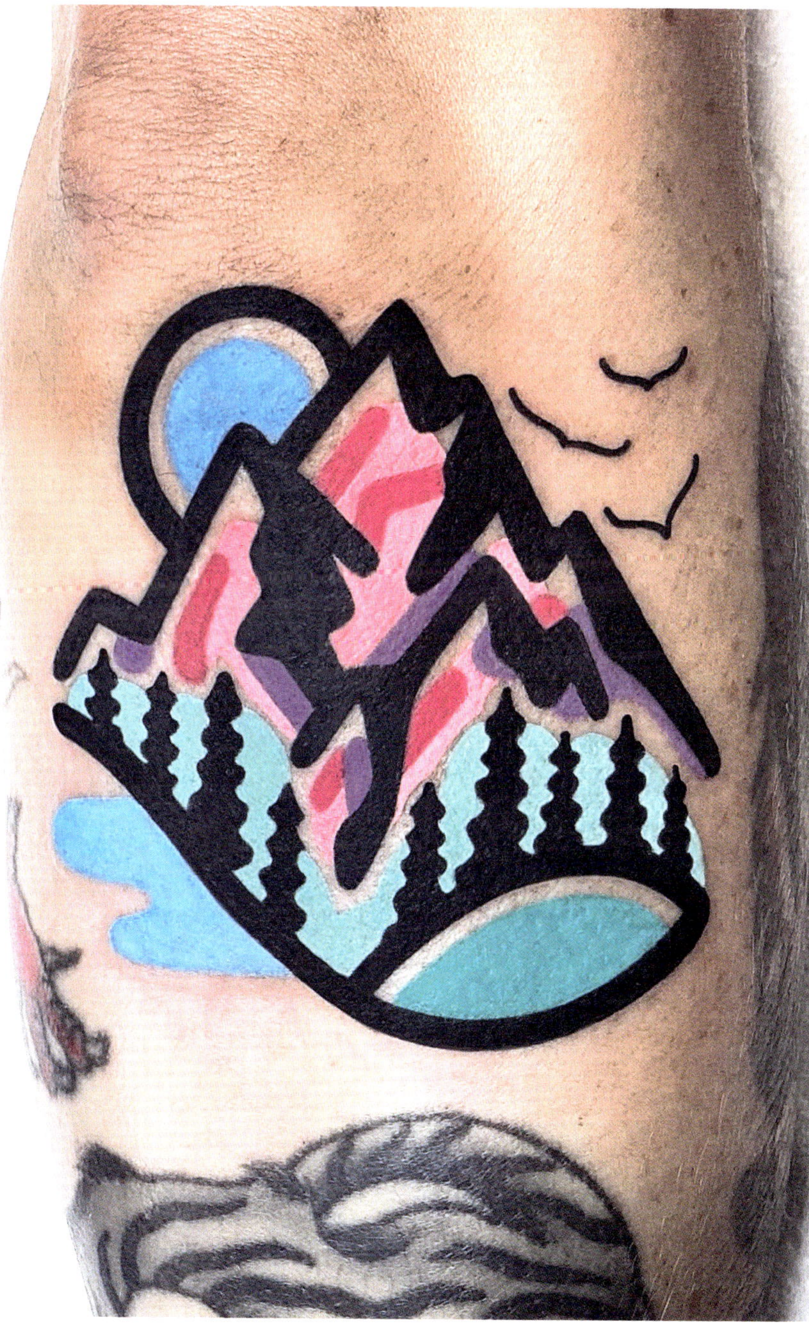

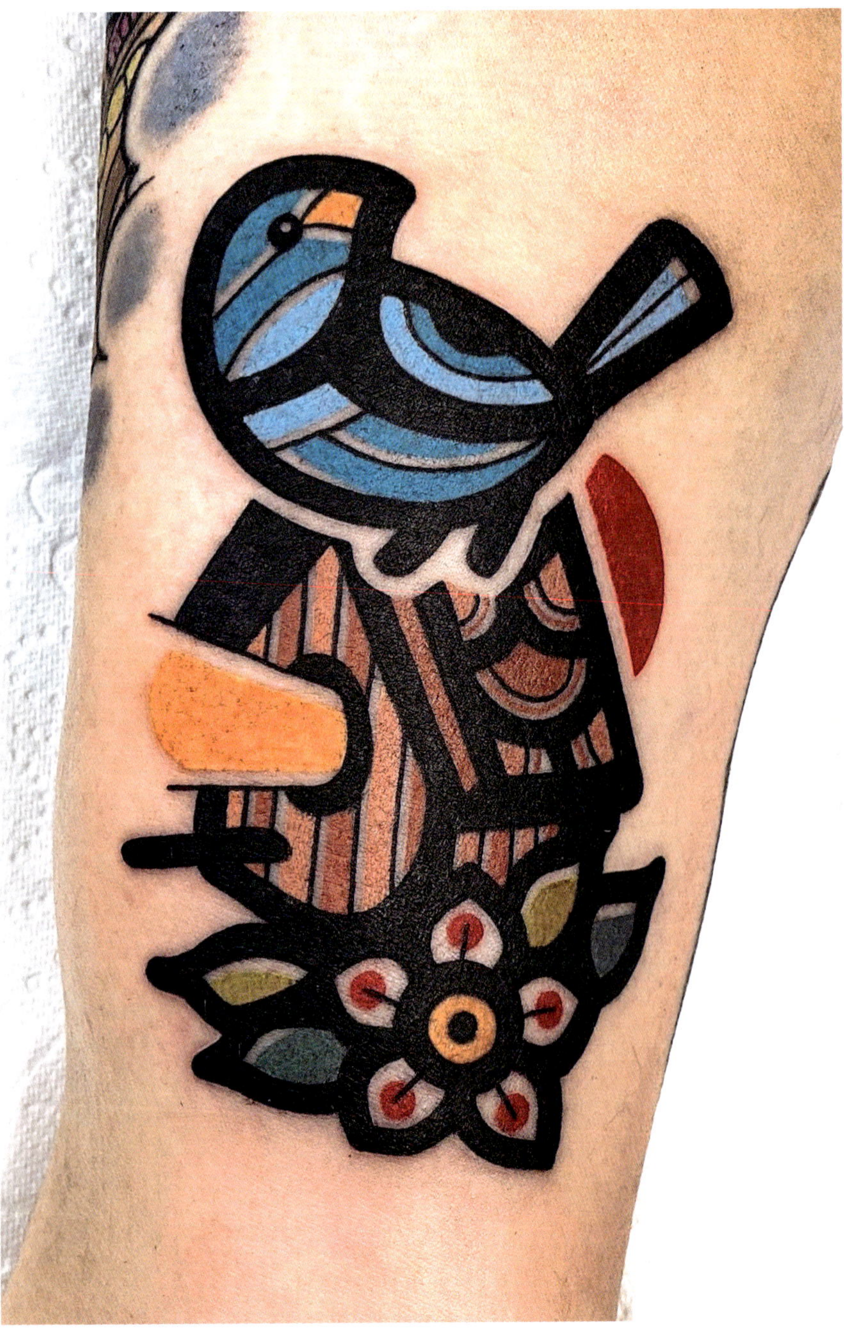

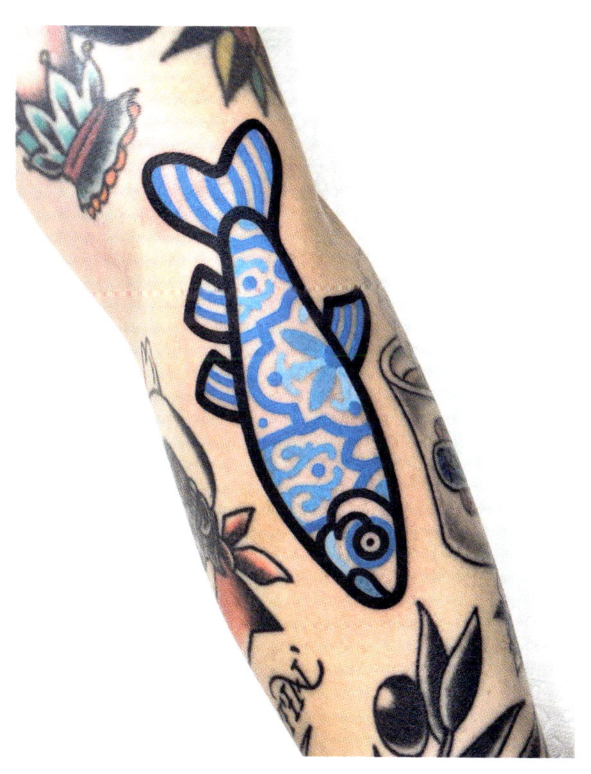

BABY ASTEROID

Lisbon, Portugal

Mariana Julieta, known artistically as Baby Asteroid, is a Lisbon-based tattoo artist with a passion for creating whimsical, joyful designs. With five years of professional experience, her love for tattooing began in childhood, inspired by tattoo magazines and television shows that fuelled her creativity from the age of eight.

Specialising in endearing illustrations, Baby Asteroid brings to life a world of charming characters, cheerful animals in party hats and vibrant floral compositions. Her work is an extension of her imagination - a colourful, playful space filled with confetti, glitter, pink trees and orange clouds, where animals dance freely.

She draws inspiration from everyday moments - whether it's her dog in a headscarf, a cat caught mid-bath, or a shop assistant carefully arranging products by colour. Finding beauty in life's small, delightful details, Baby Asteroid strives to create tattoos that bring warmth, humour and a touch of magic to her clients' lives.

04.

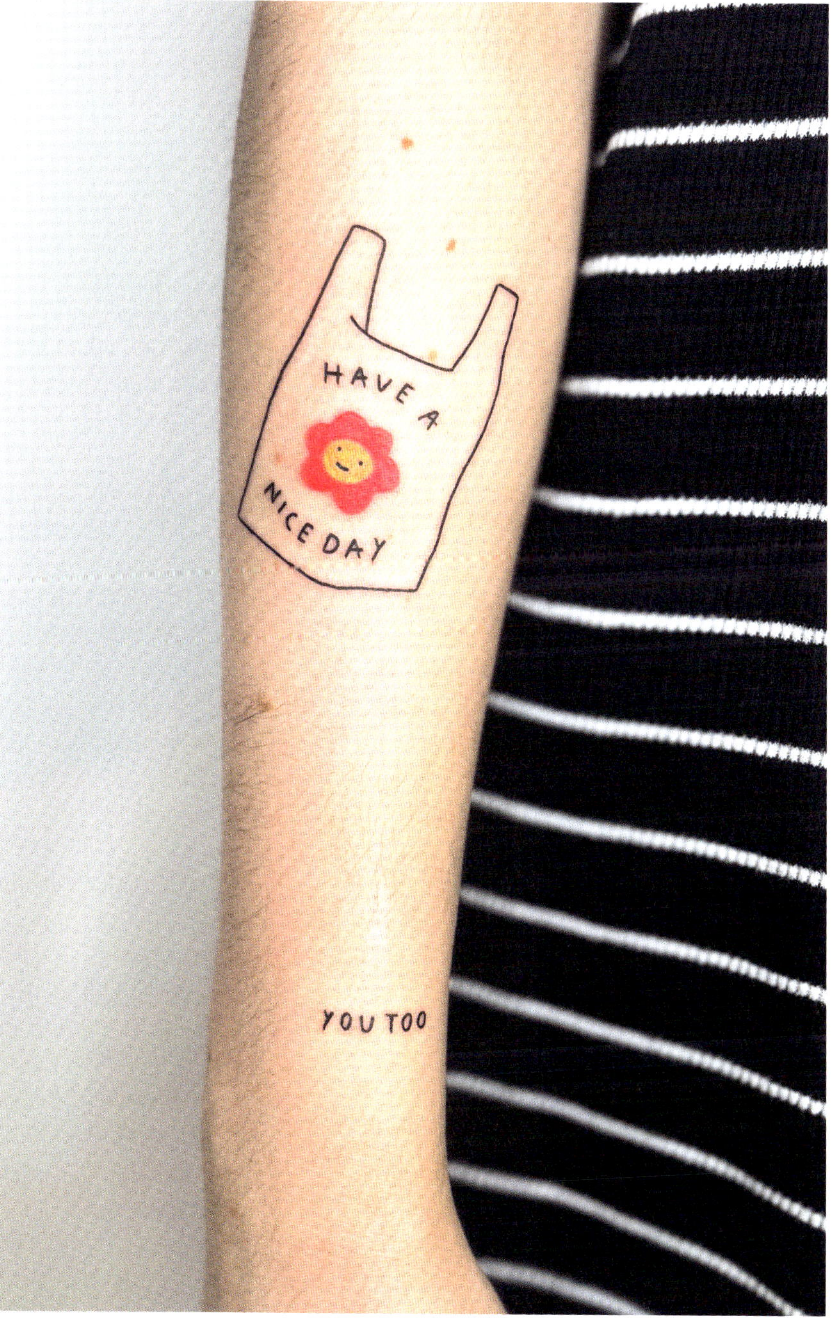
HAVE A
NICE DAY
YOU TOO

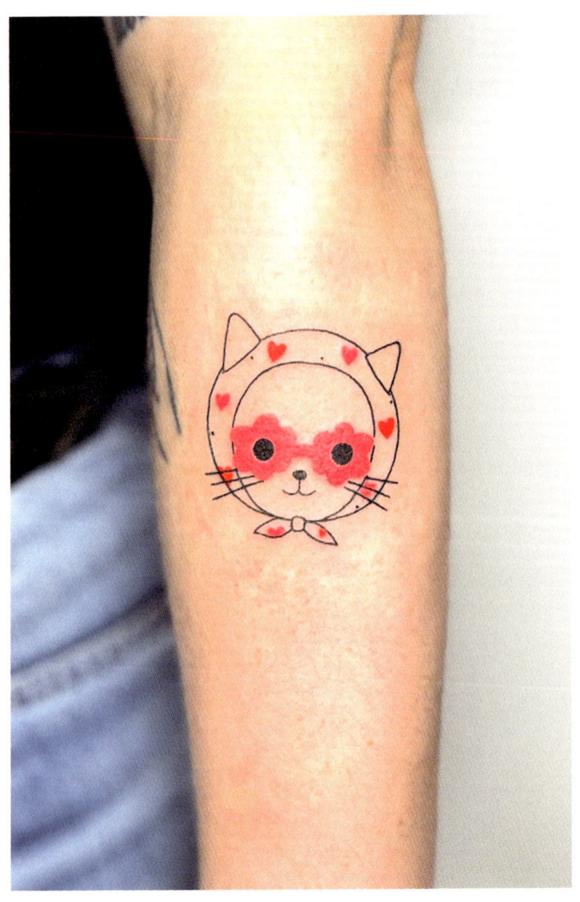

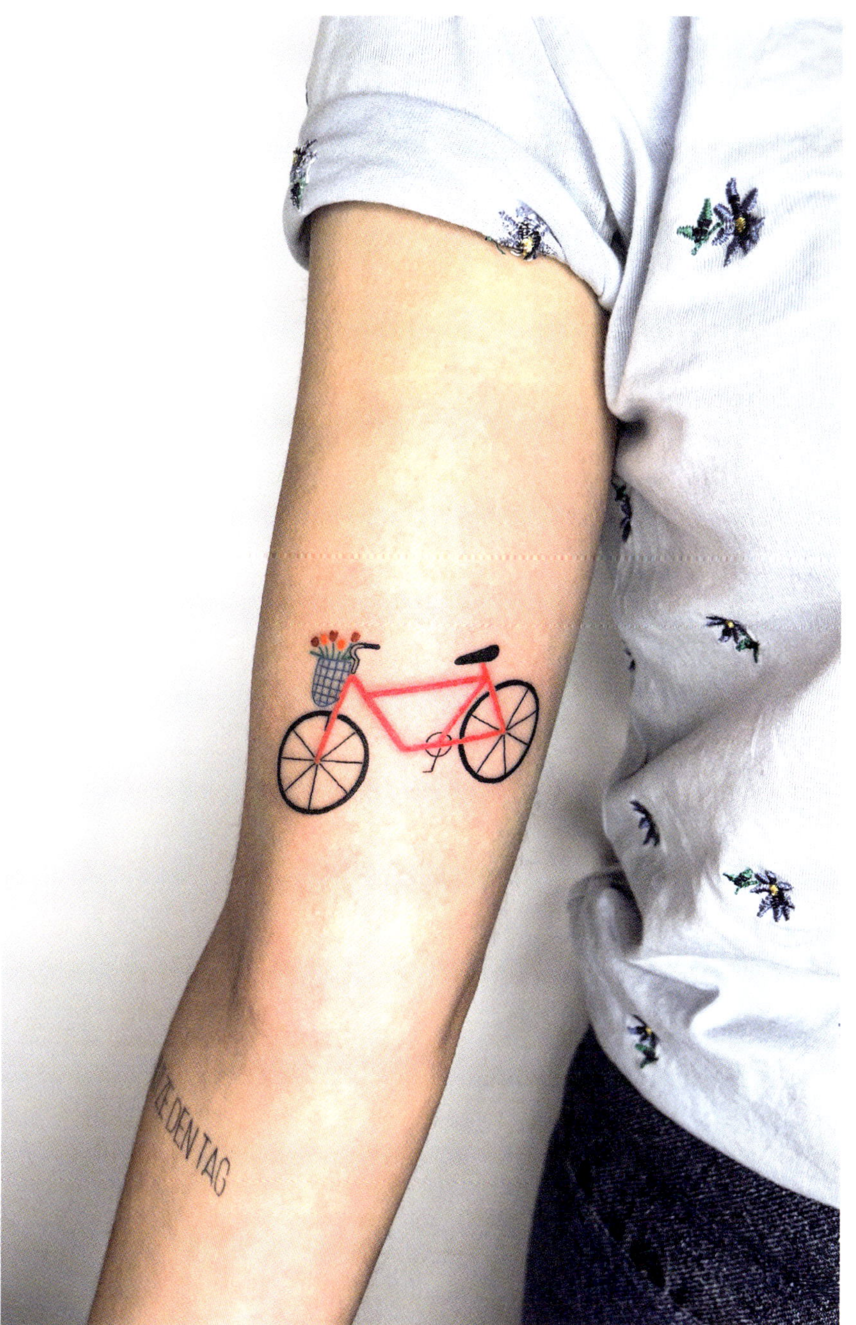
ZE DEN TAG

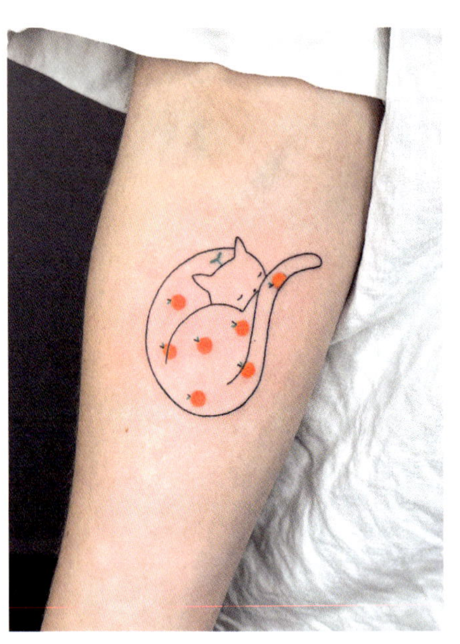

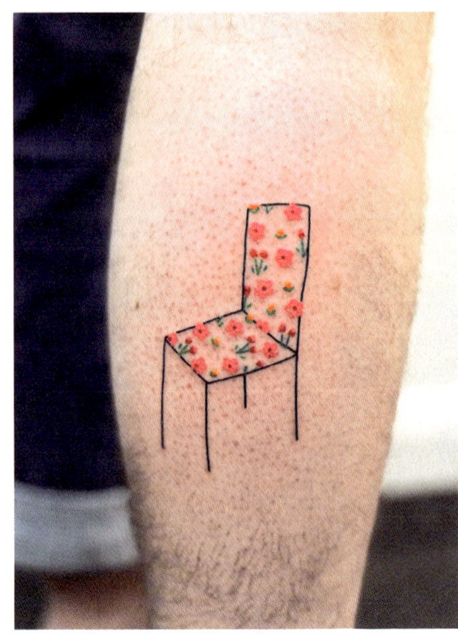

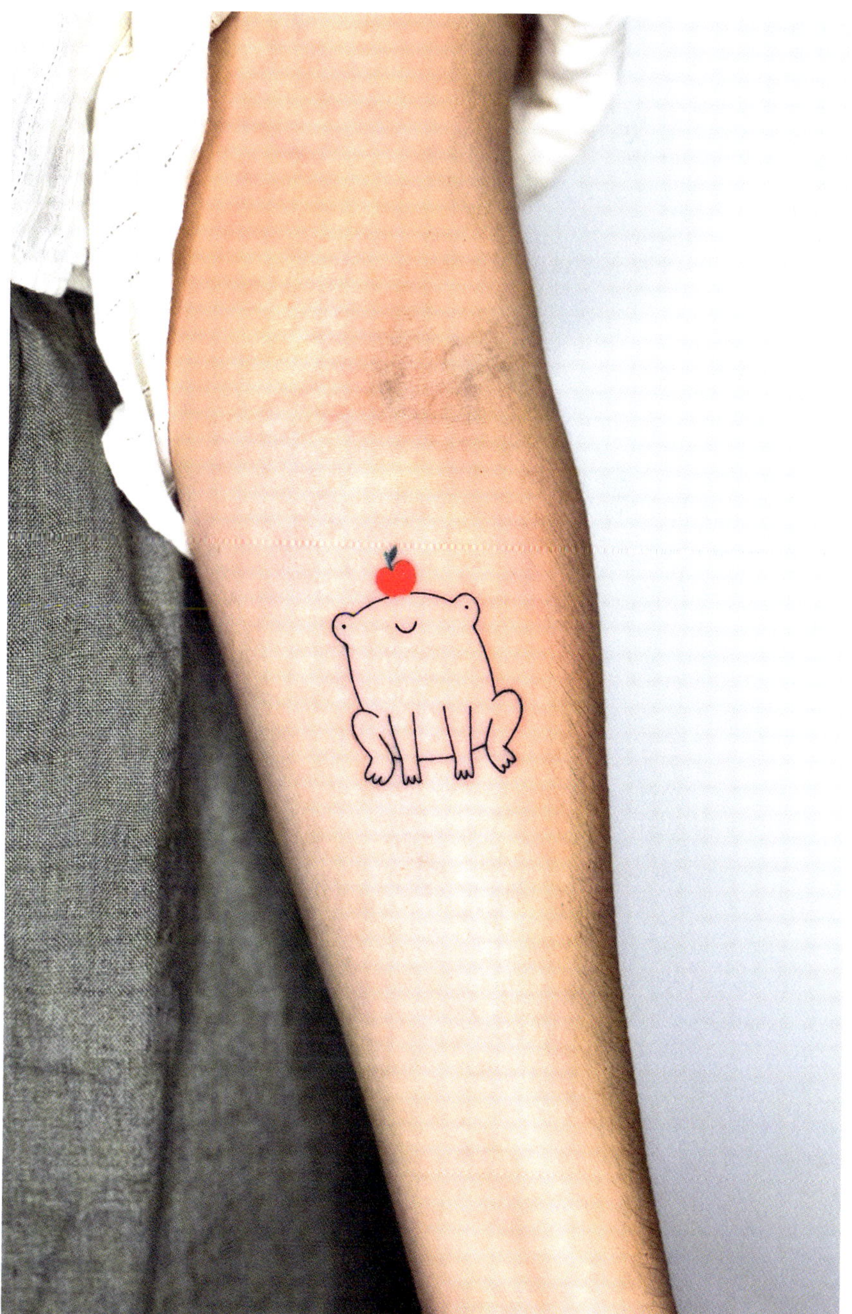

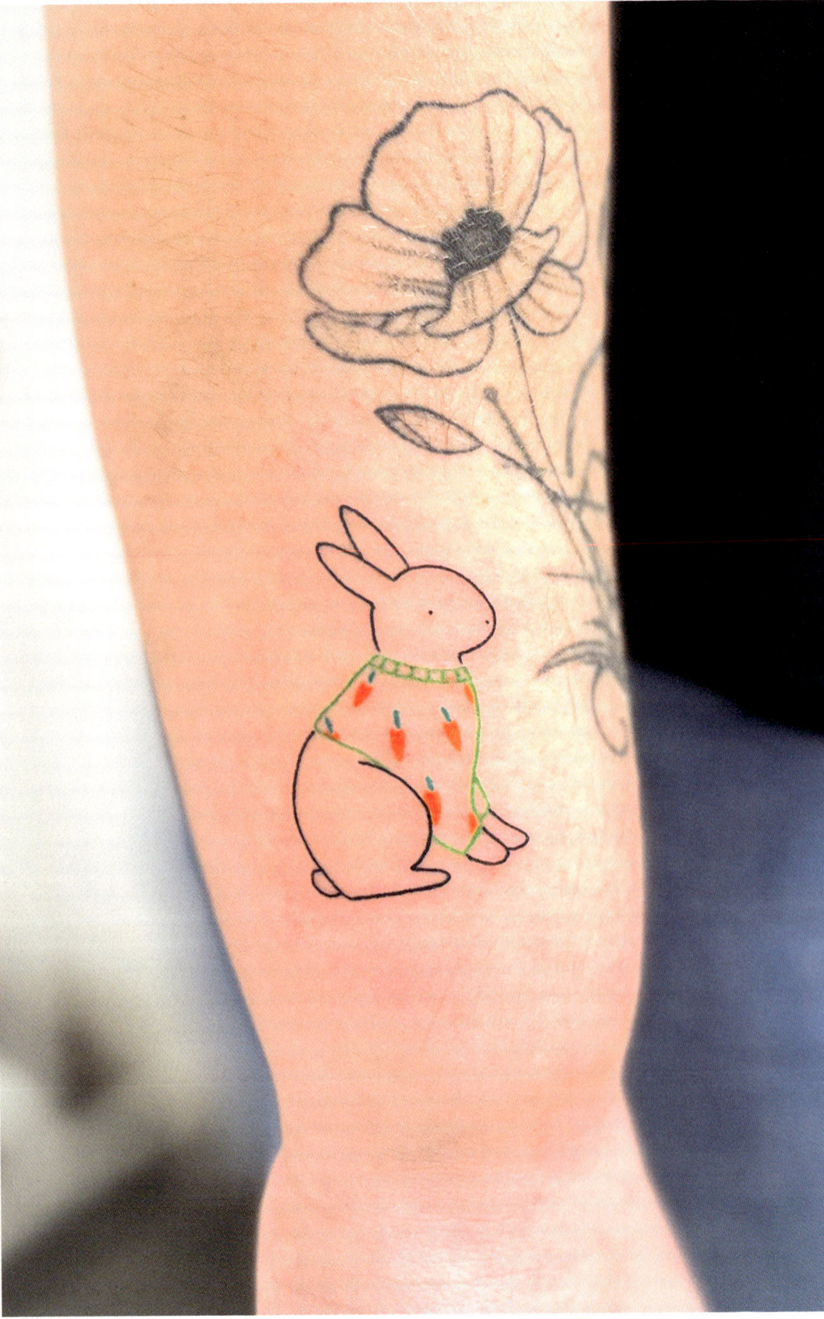

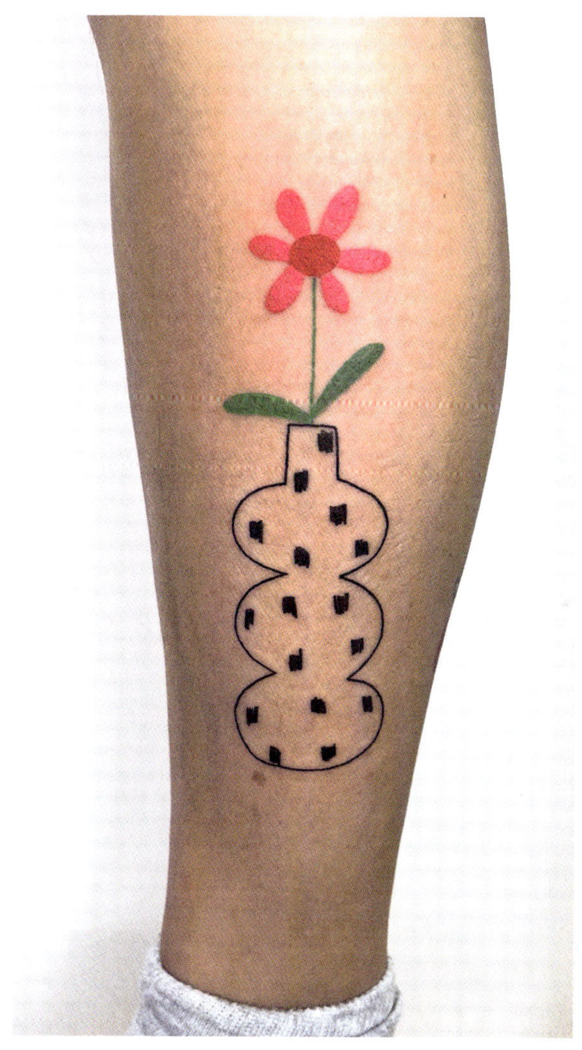

BEHIND THE TATTOO

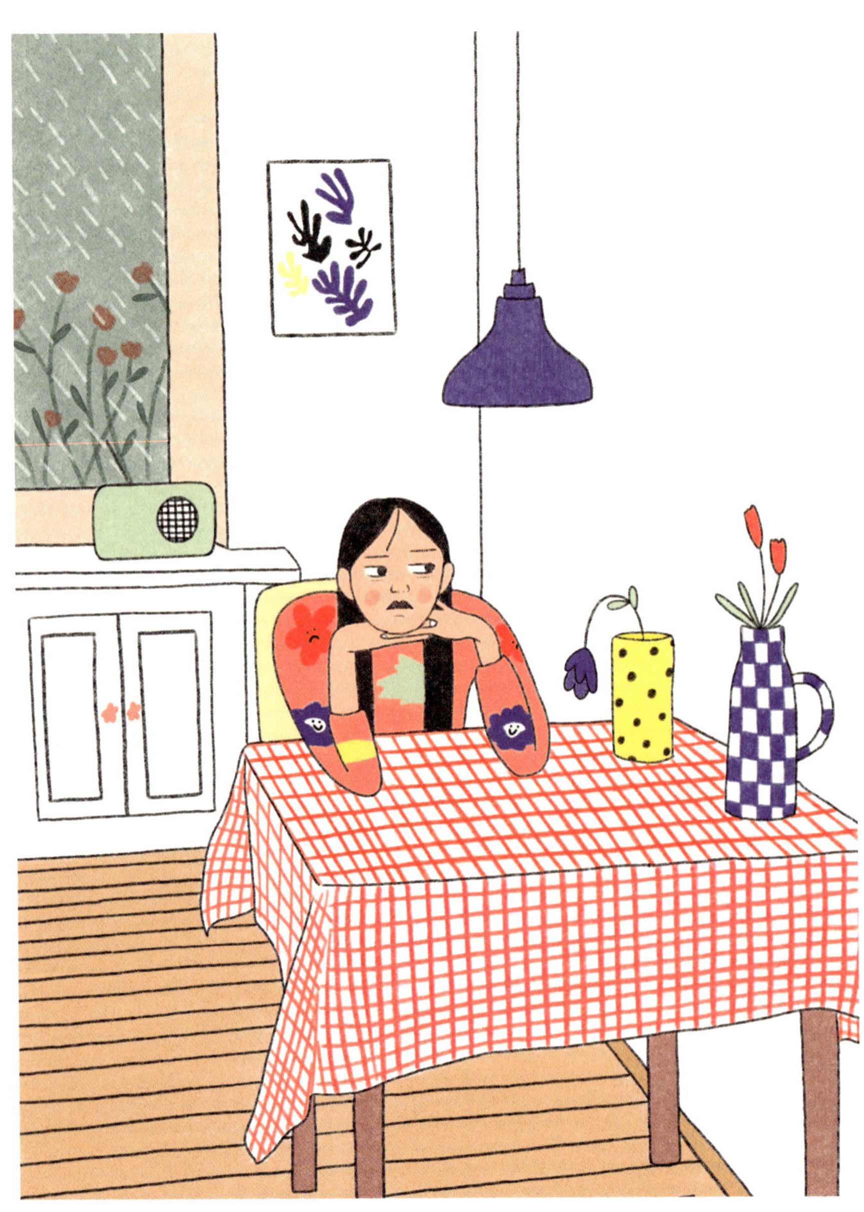

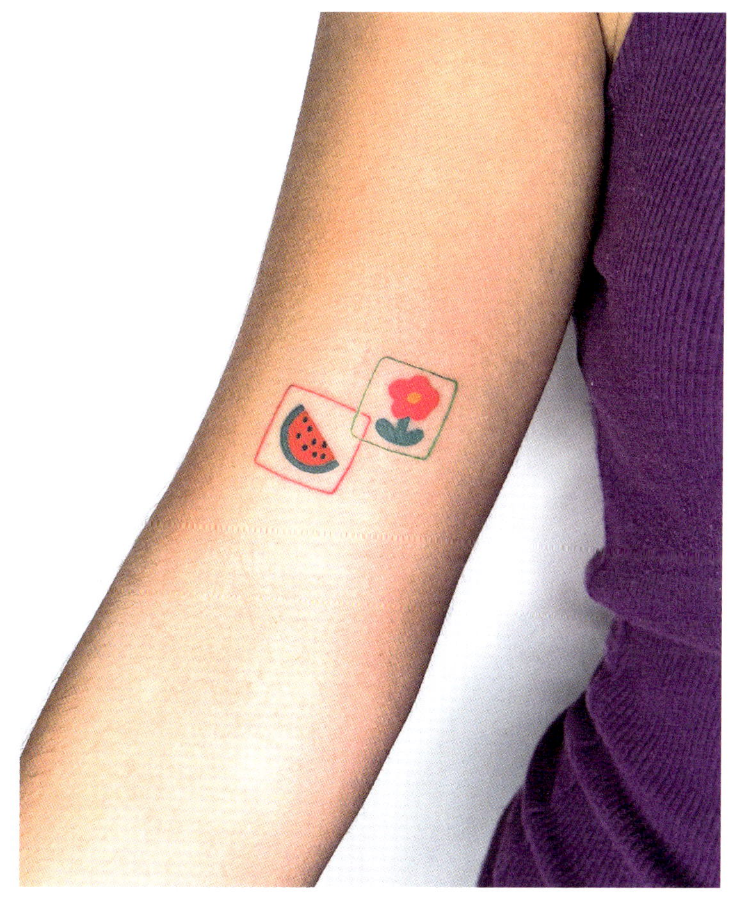

'I enjoy staying in, doing nothing in particular, just being with myself and drawing. There's something special about taking your time, letting your mind wander, noticing the simple things... That quiet space – where you're not rushing, just existing – can open up a whole fantasy world. And often, that's where the most honest creativity begins.'

— BABY ASTEROID

BUOY THE FISHLOVER

Vancouver, Canada

Originally from South Korea, Buoy The Fishlover currently lives and works in Vancouver, Canada, after previously tattooing at Studio Temple in Seoul. After obtaining a major in sculpture at Hongik University, Buoy began tattooing in September 2018 and has since built a growing international clientele. Buoy describes his designs as dumb, funny and harmless, and his work features playful, light-hearted depictions of animals in silly, endearing situations. With a focus on bringing joy through art, Buoy creates feel-good designs that are both unique and uplifting, making people smile wherever they go.

05.

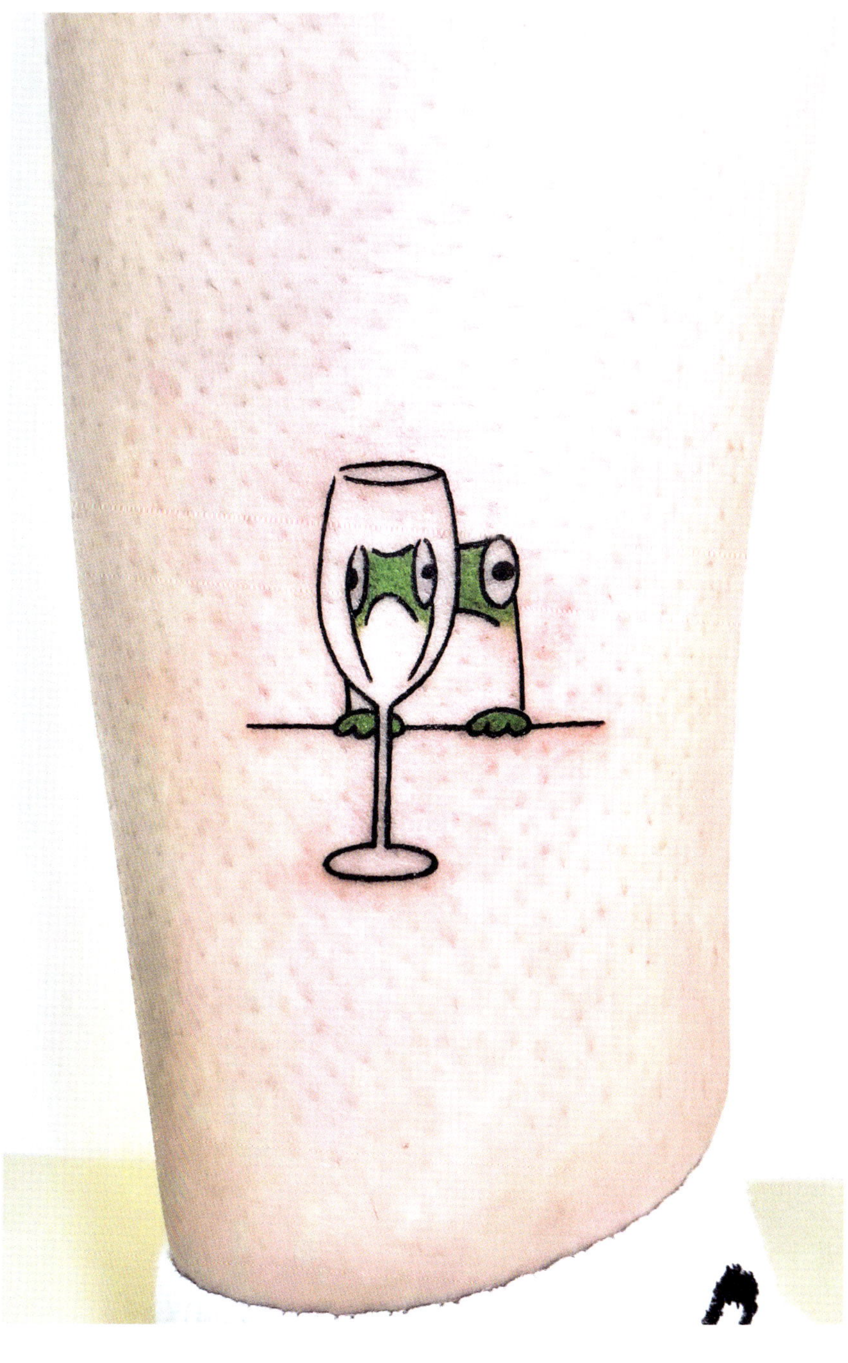

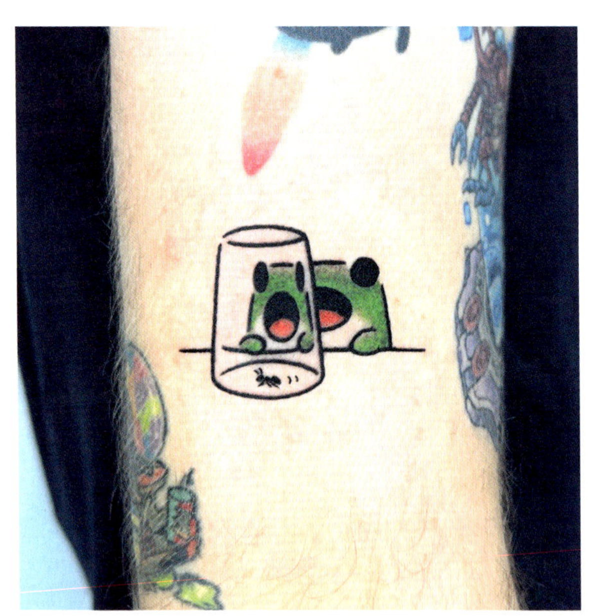

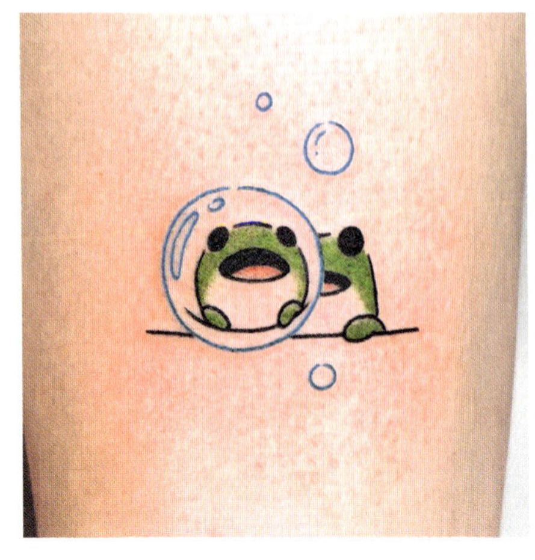

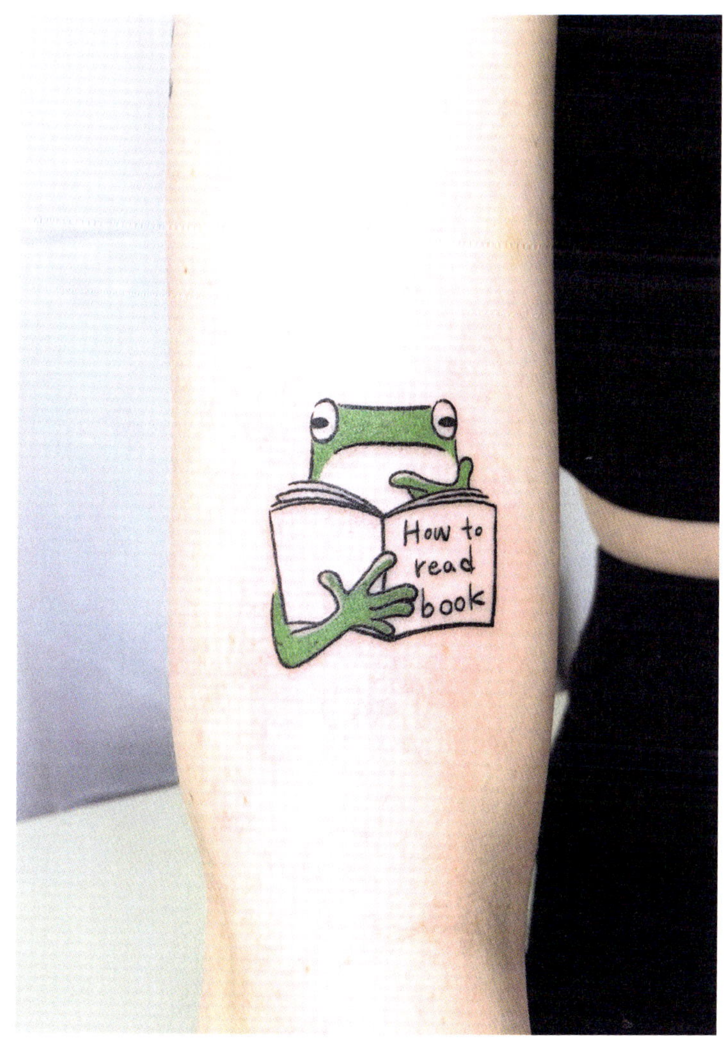
How to
read
book

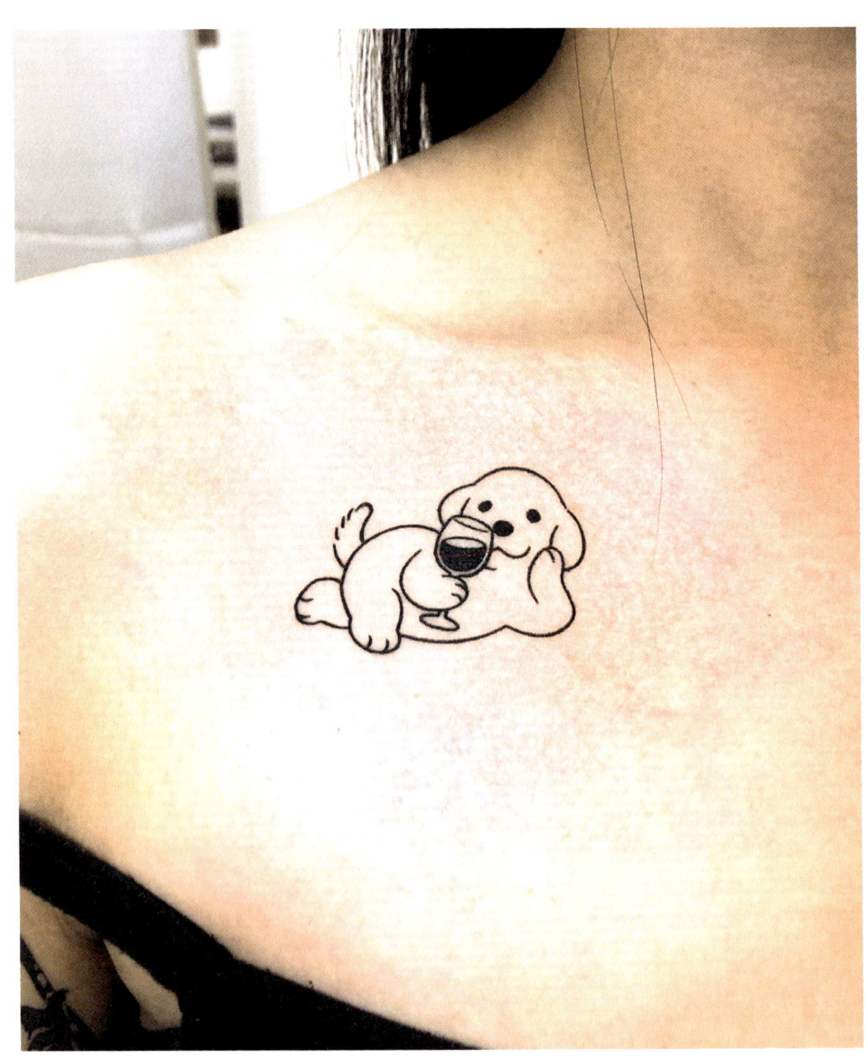

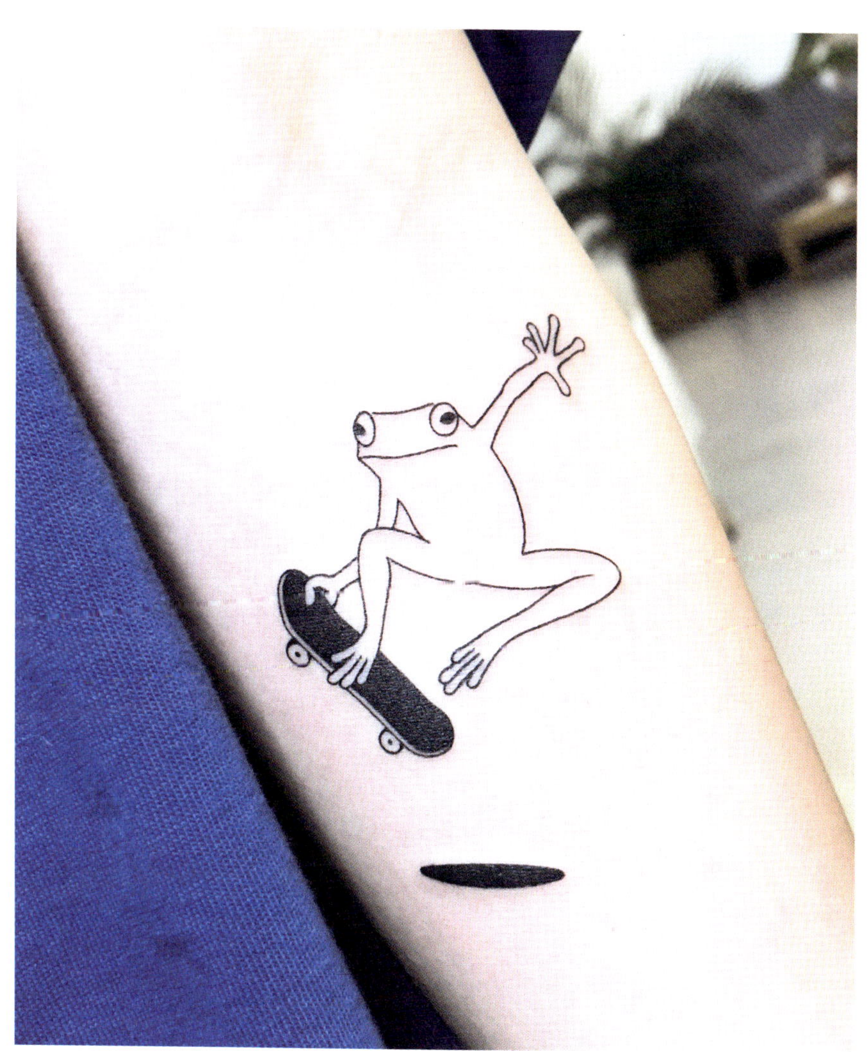

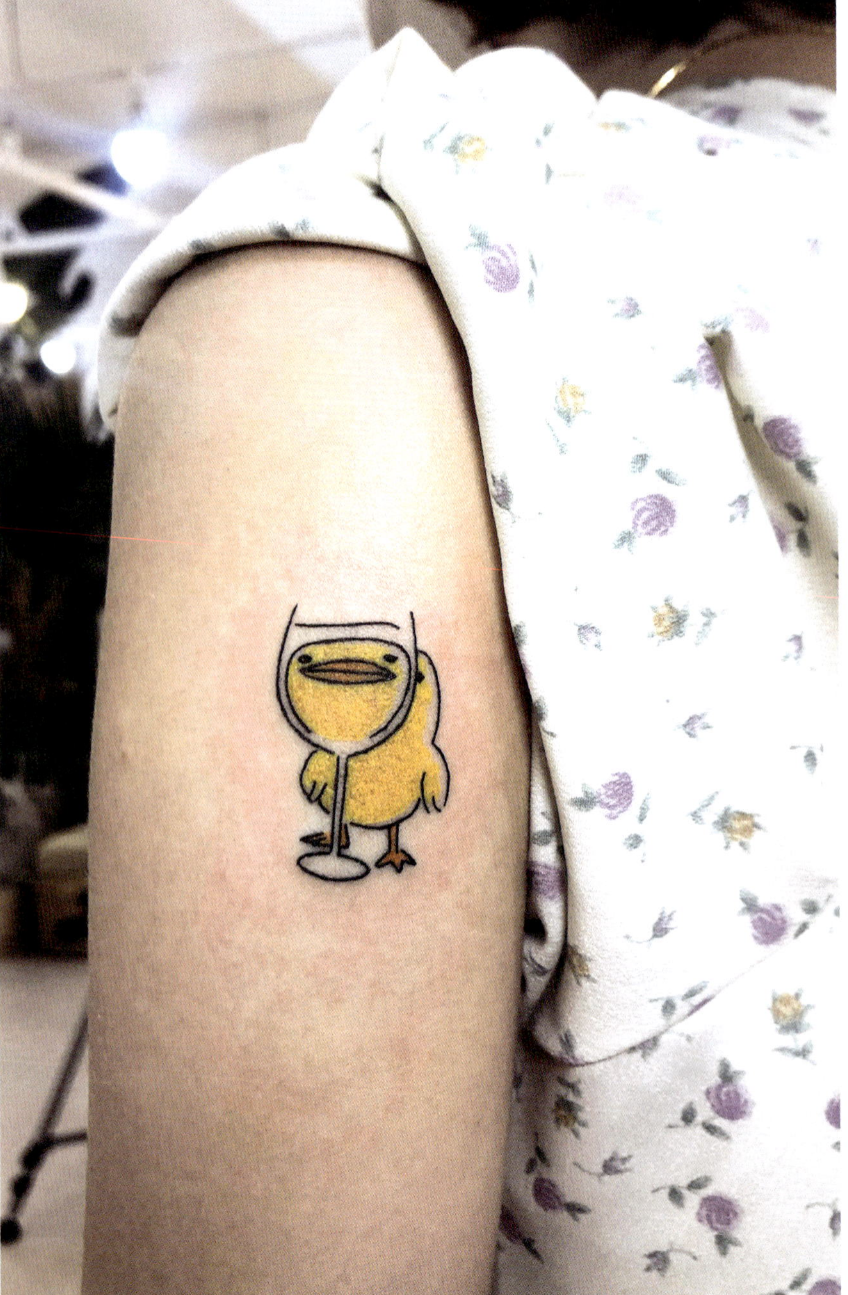

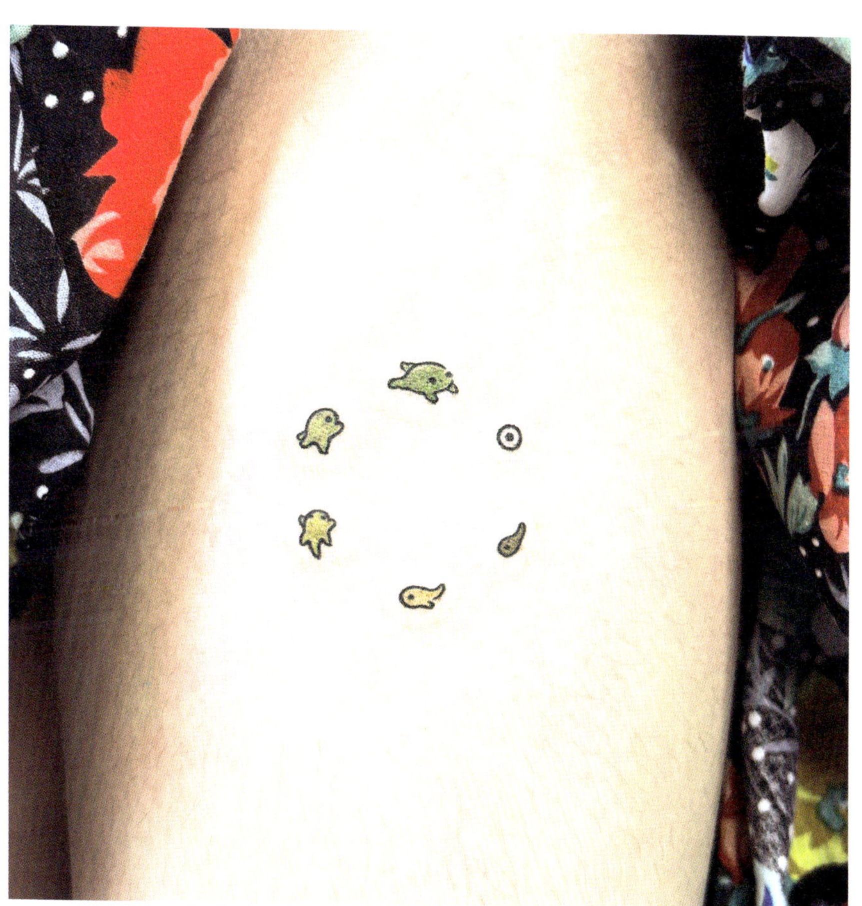

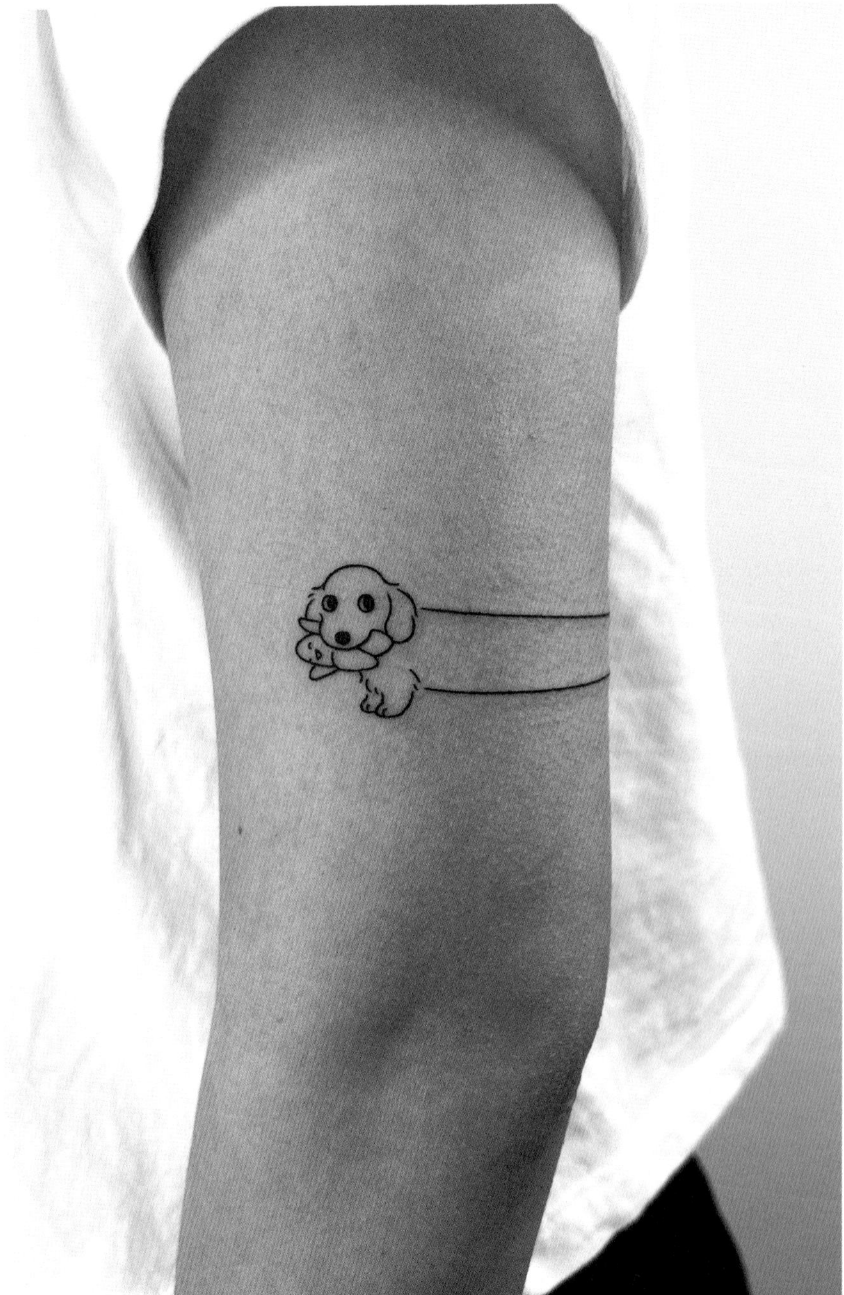

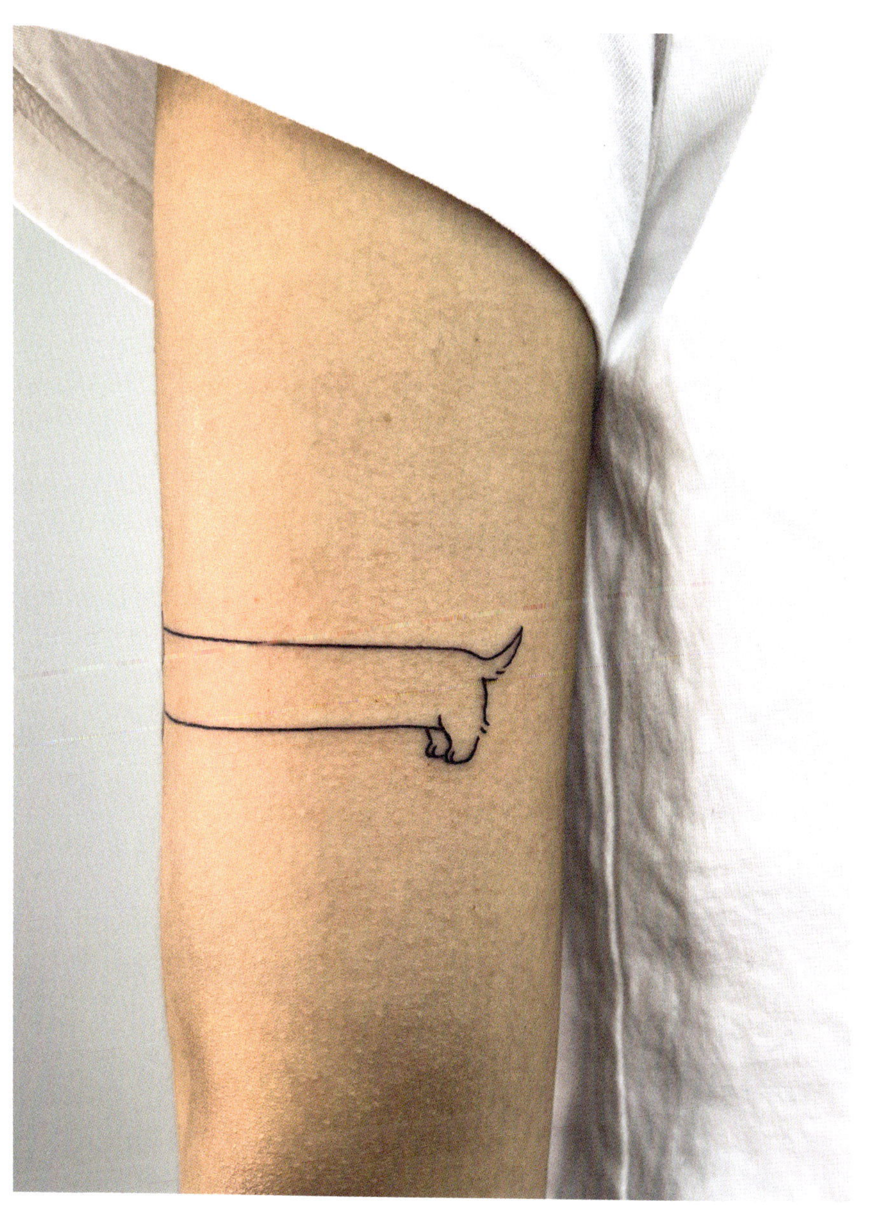

055

DENNIS BEBENROTH

Braunschweig, Germany

Dennis Bebenroth is a tattoo artist and owner of Sorry Mom Tattoo in Braunschweig (Brunswick), Germany. Renowned for seamlessly blending traditional tattoo styles with contemporary influences, his work preserves the timeless appeal of classic designs while incorporating fresh, modern elements that make each piece unique.

His passion for tattooing first emerged while studying communication design at the School of Art in Braunschweig, eventually leading him to pursue a formal apprenticeship in 2002. Over the past 23 years, he has honed his craft, developing a distinctive style that reinterprets tribal motifs in bold and unexpected ways. By merging well-known comic characters with tribal aesthetics, he creates humorous and unconventional compositions that captivate fans worldwide.

As an artist constantly pushing creative boundaries, Dennis thrives on crafting imaginative mash-ups that fuse seemingly unrelated worlds, resulting in one-of-a-kind artistic expressions.

06.

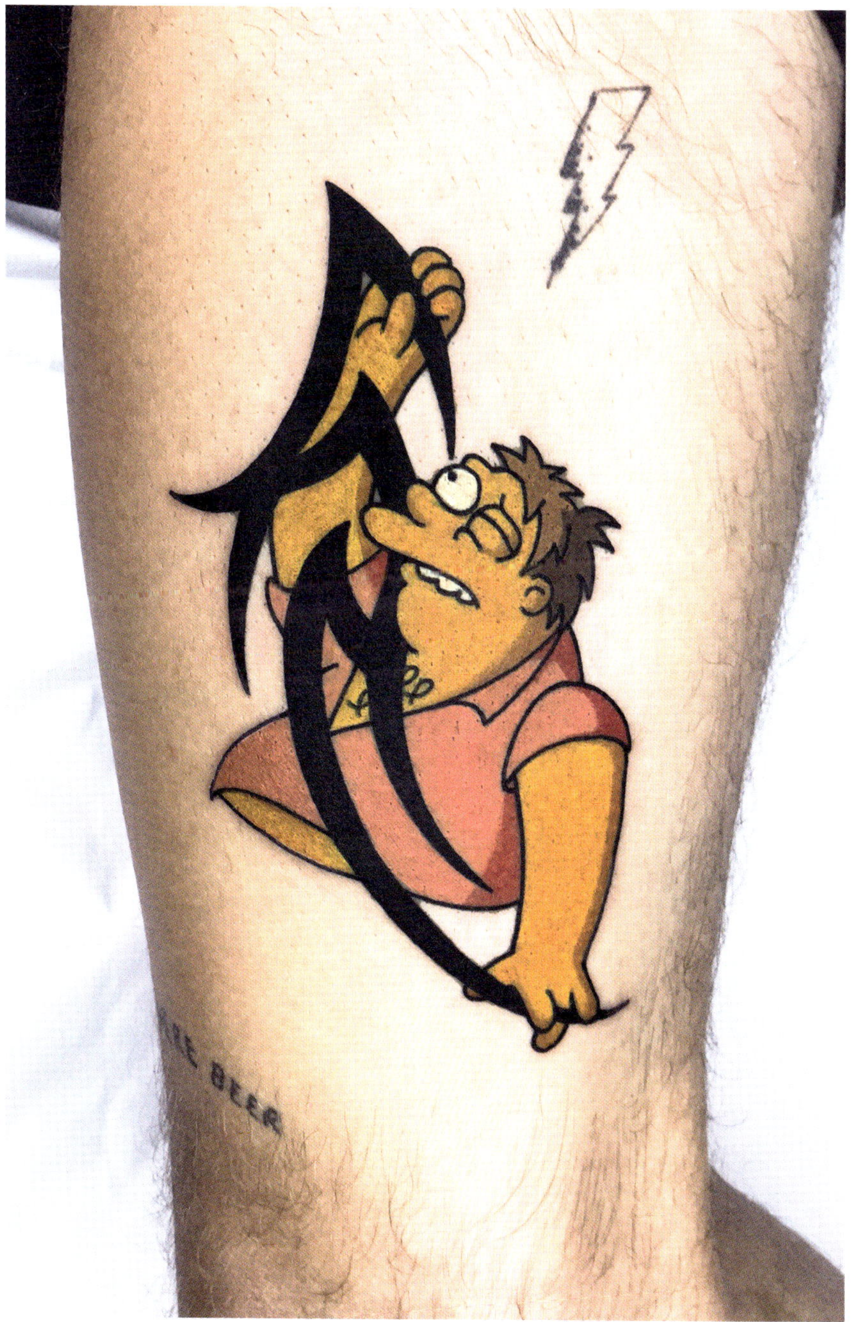
BEER

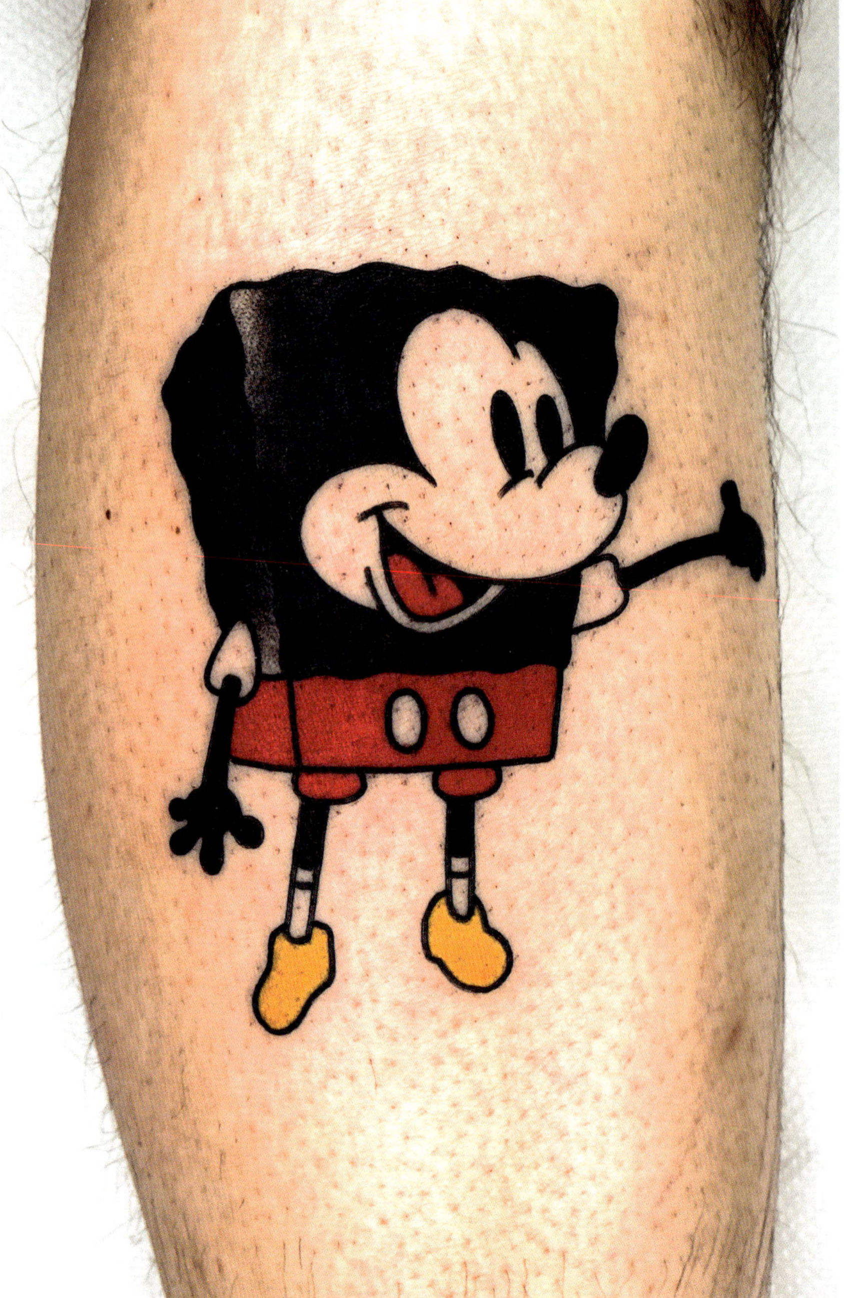

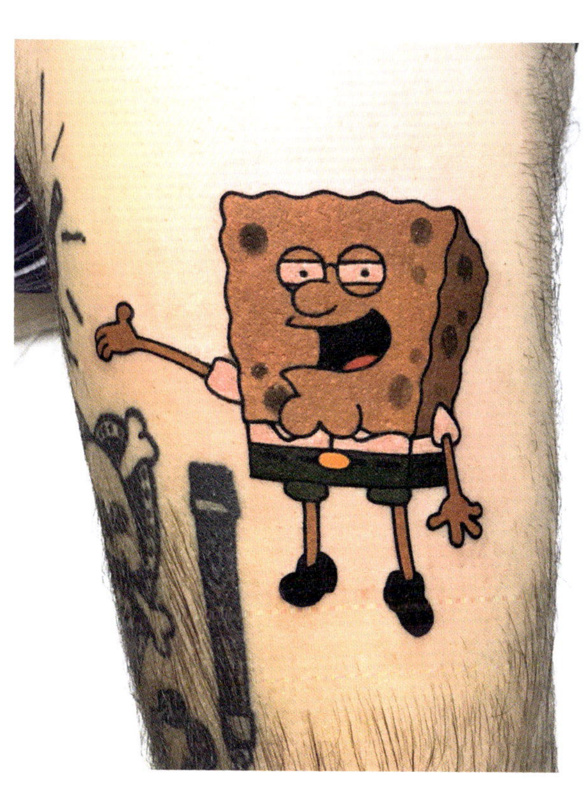

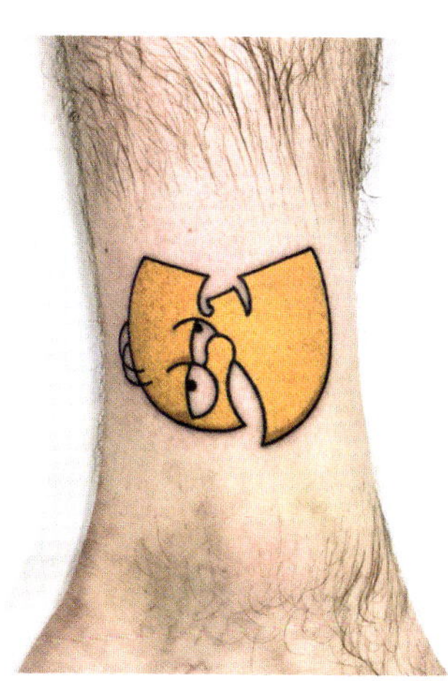

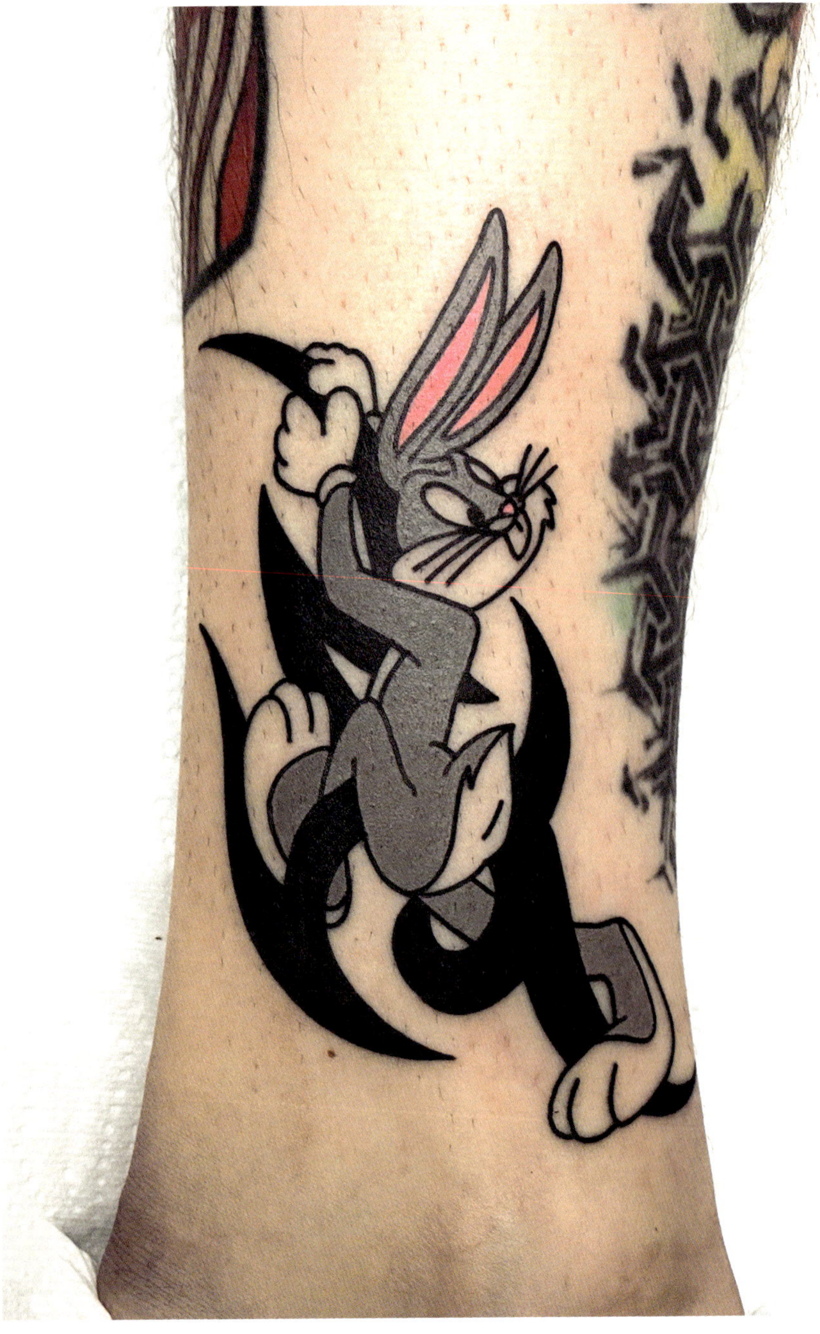

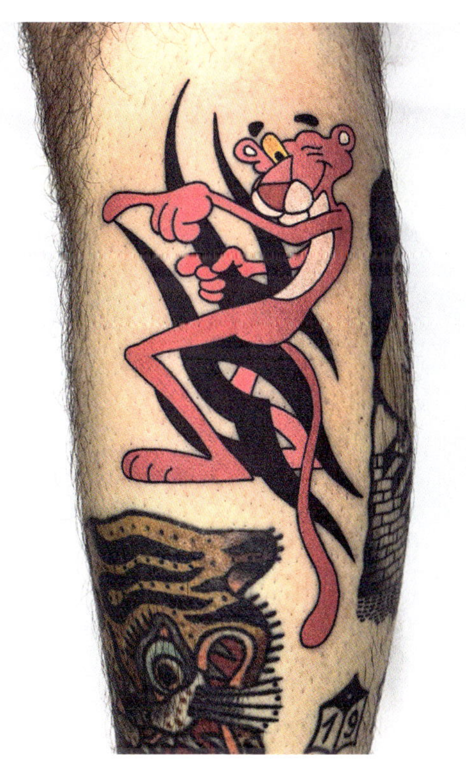

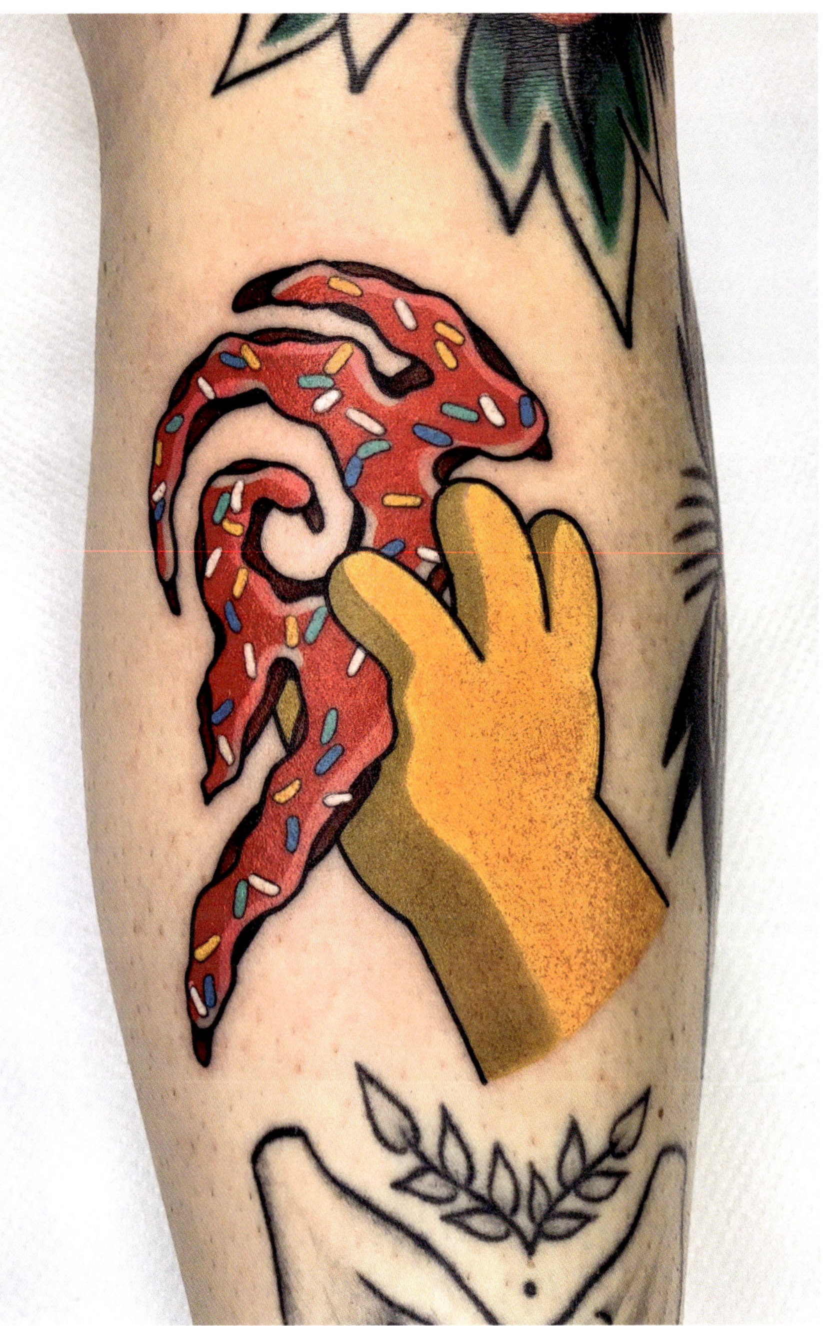

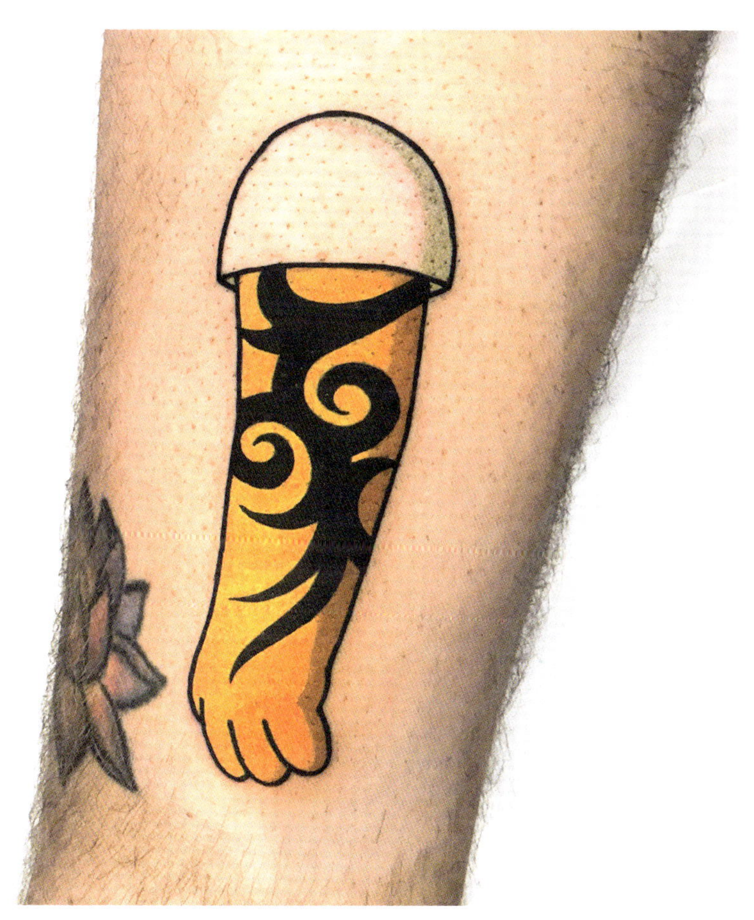

DIOR THE ARTIST

Nashville, USA

Dior the Artist is the alias of Dior Brown, a Nashville-based tattoo artist and self-proclaimed wizard, bringing a touch of magic to every piece she creates. Dior began her tattooing journey in 2023 and is now a resident artist at Dead Ahead Tattoo Co., renowned for her distinctive style that blends bold linework, vibrant primary colours and soft, rounded forms.

Her designs - often featuring wizards, goblins and other whimsical creatures - tell unique stories, with each character coming to life through its own name and personality. Inspired by graphic novels, cartoons and the playful energy of childhood, Dior infuses her work with warmth, charm and a deep sense of nostalgia.

Her artistry has taken her beyond Nashville, with guest spots in Los Angeles, Baltimore and Chicago, and she continues to expand her creative reach. Passionate about her craft and the connections it fosters, Dior is grateful for the opportunity to bring her clients' visions to life and looks forward to making magic, one tattoo at a time, for years to come.

07.

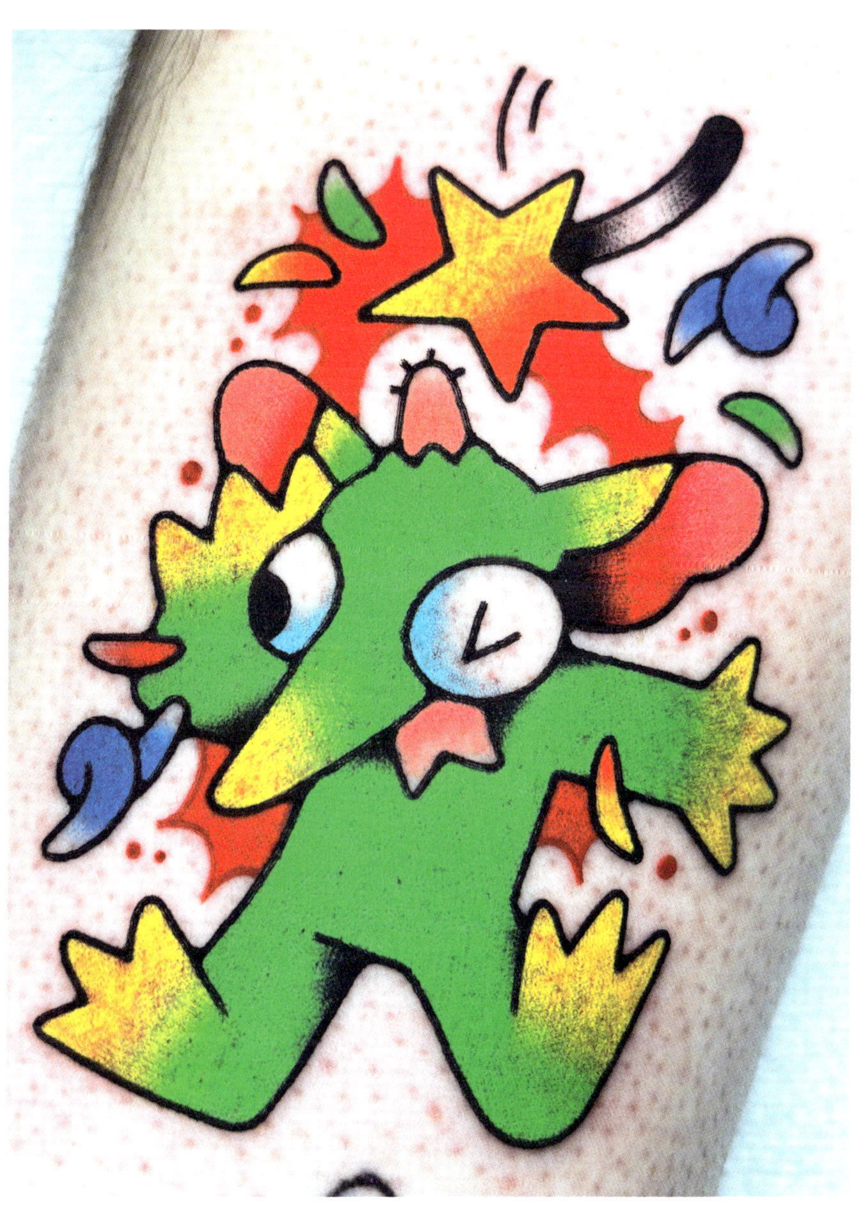

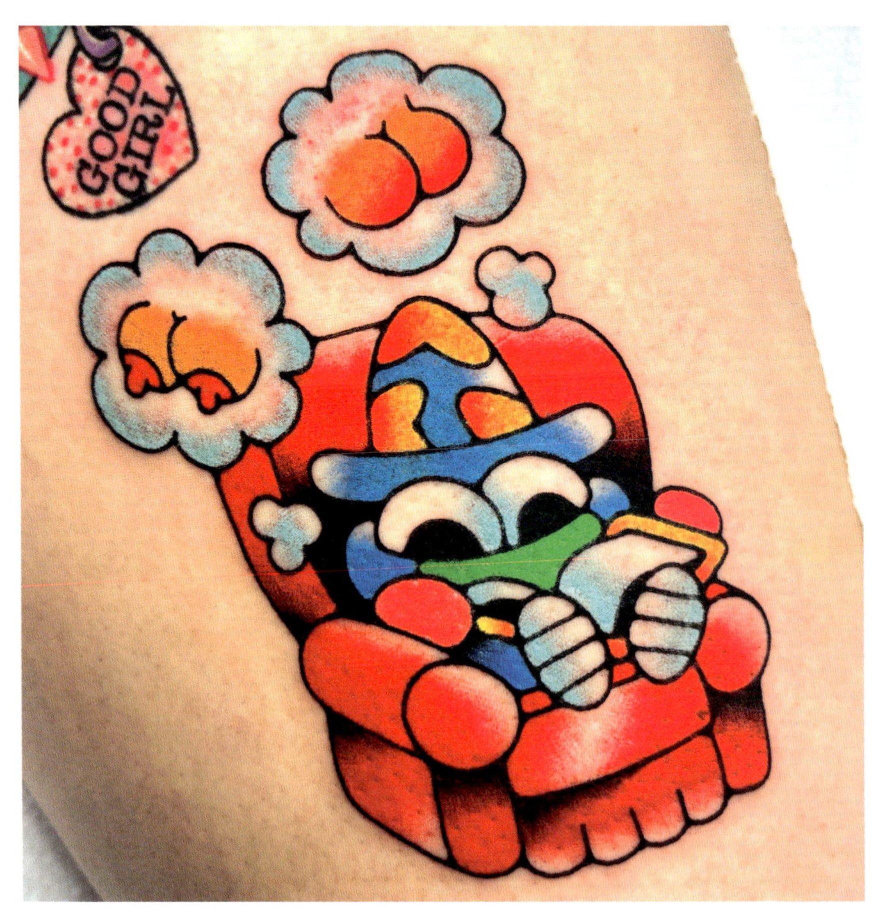
GOOD
GIRL

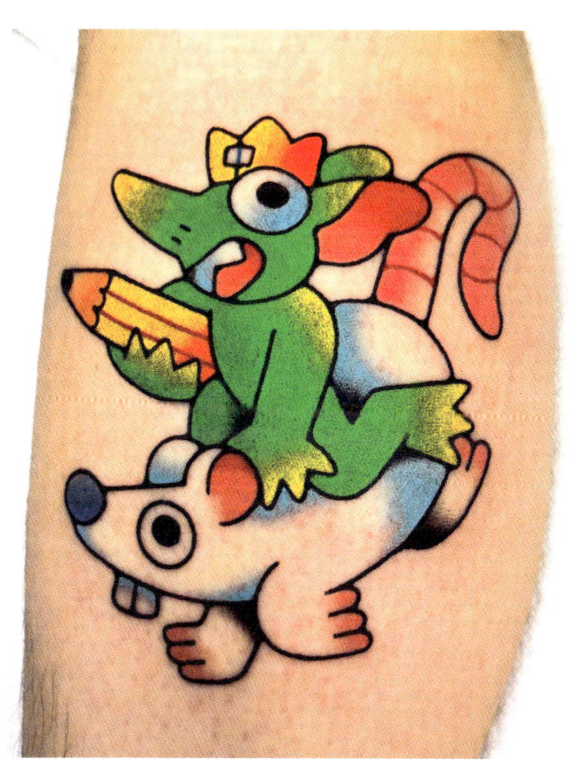

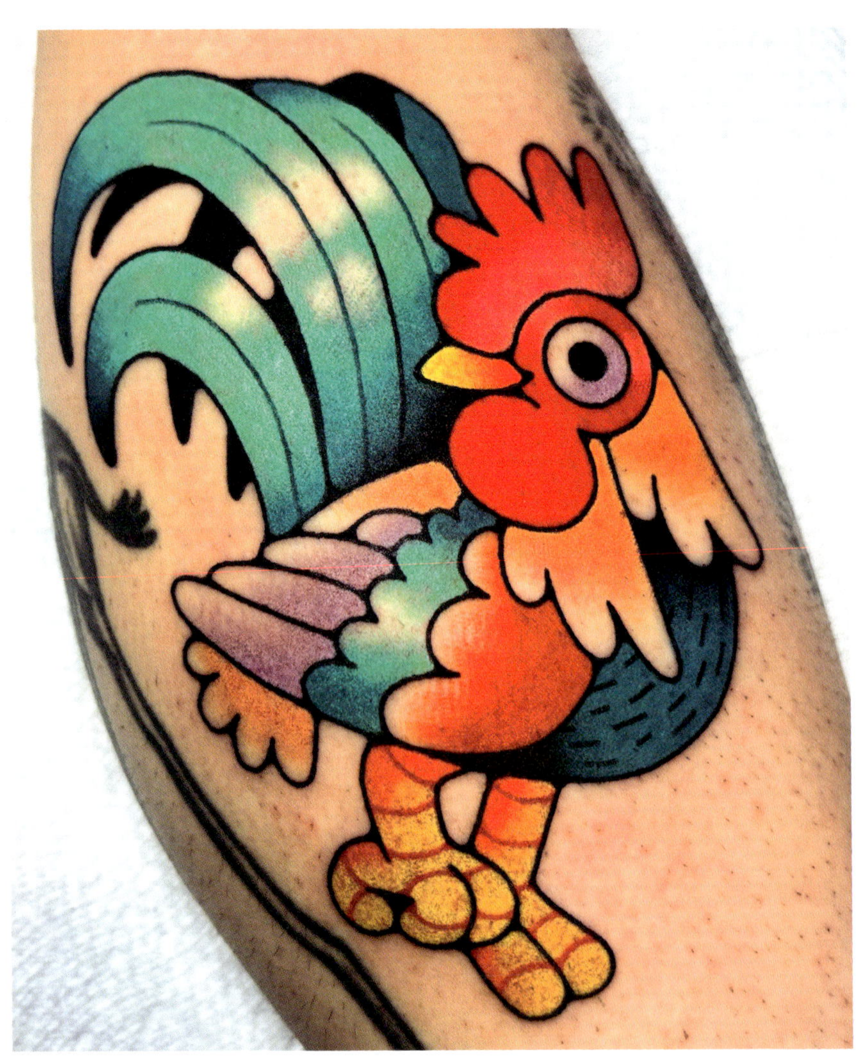

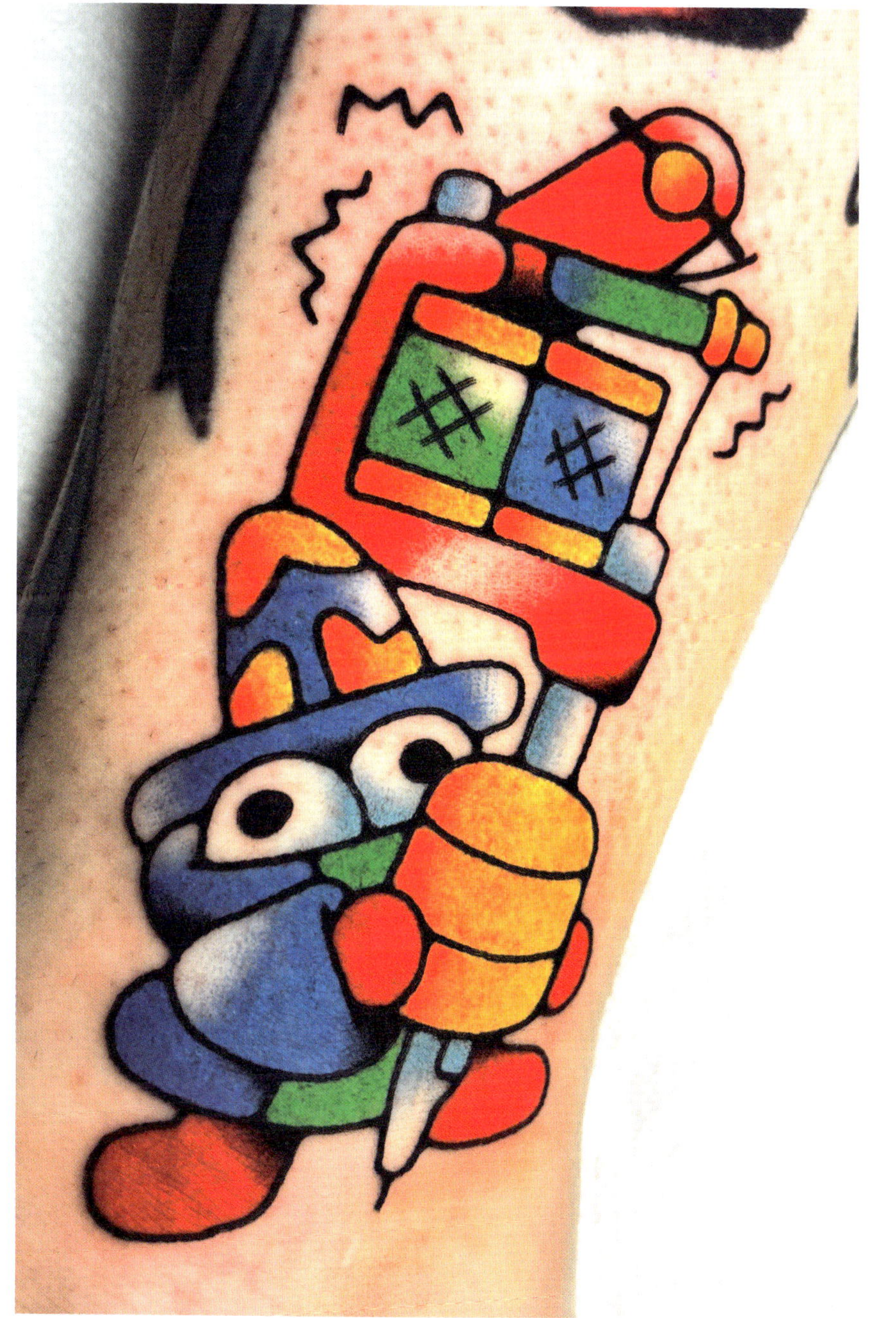

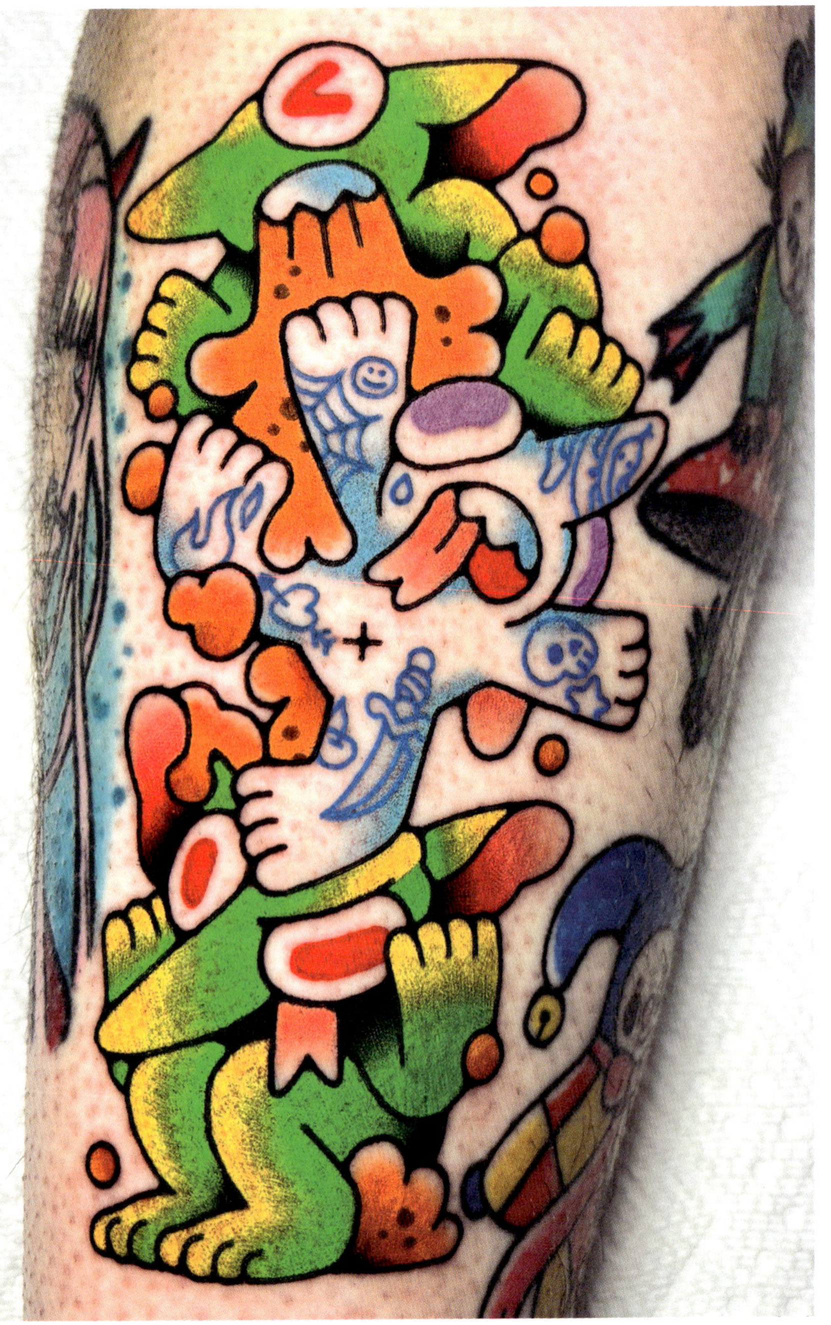

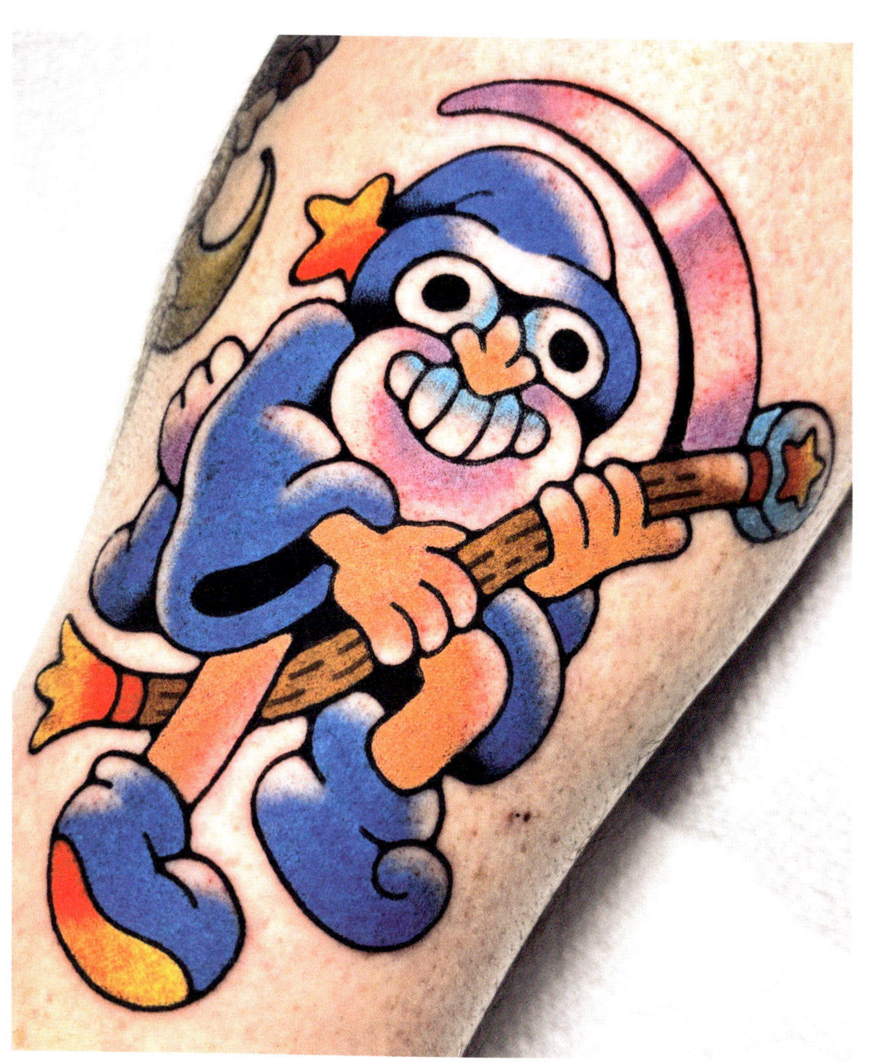

BEHIND THE TATTOO

'I take a lot of inspiration from my childhood and how I express that as an artist. The primary colours, round shapes, and silly characters all remind me of being a kid again. I grew up quiet, weird and was always daydreaming of worlds and characters made up in my head, which is what my art represents in the present day. Shows like Adventure Time and Bee & Puppycat really shaped my style into what it is now, and movies like Lord of the Rings gave me a great appreciation for the fantasy genre. I tend to focus on themes that are whimsical and happy, because I feel like that is being true to my inner child. My artwork allows me to keep daydreaming, making magic, and to help let people feel confident enough to express their inner kid as well!'

— DIOR THE ARTIST

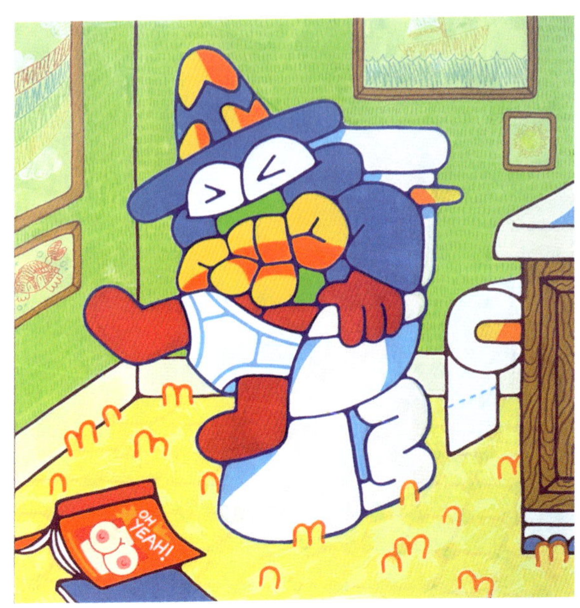

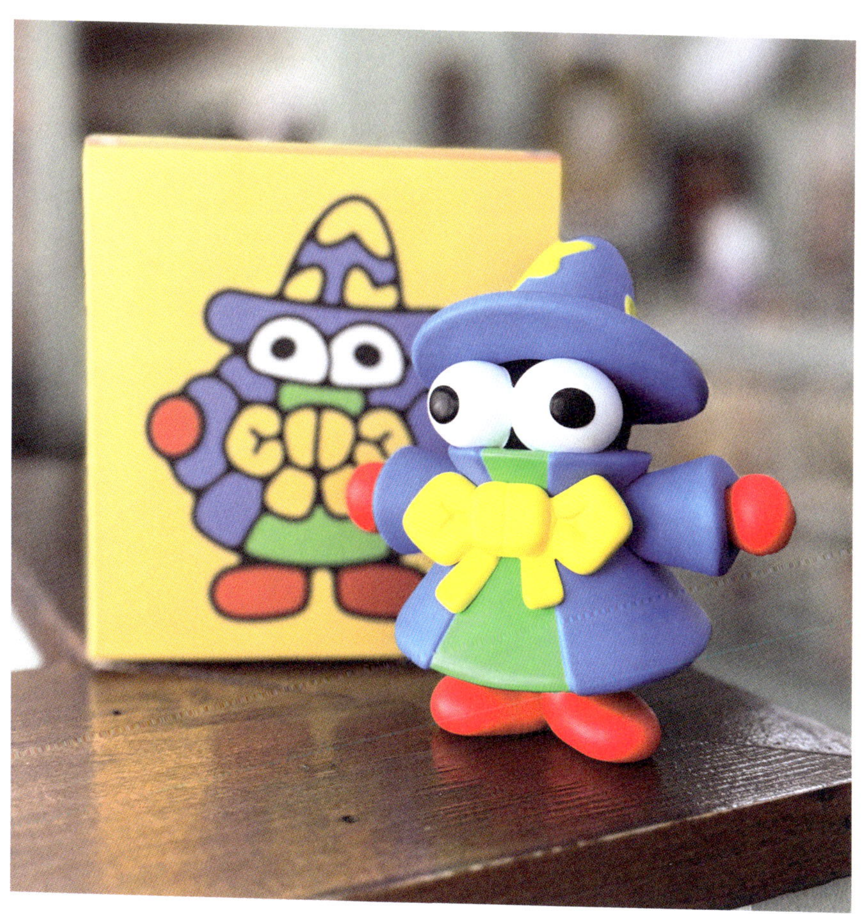

EDDY PRICKSTICK

Antwerp, Belgium

Born and raised in Antwerp, Belgium, Eddy Prickstick studied graphic design and illustration at the Royal Academy of Fine Arts in Antwerp, graduating in 2008. Before he started tattooing, Eddy worked as a courier for a medical laboratory.

Today, Eddy is renowned for his playful hand poke-tattoos and has been creating straightforward, happy designs since 2015 - art that embraces playfulness without any unnecessary complications. Drawing inspiration from everyday life, Eddy finds creativity in bizarre situations, strange conversations and folk art, which fuel his distinctive artistic approach.

Eddy brings his unique vision to Heart of Oak Tattoo in Antwerp, where clients can experience his fun, engaging and refreshingly unpretentious designs.

08.

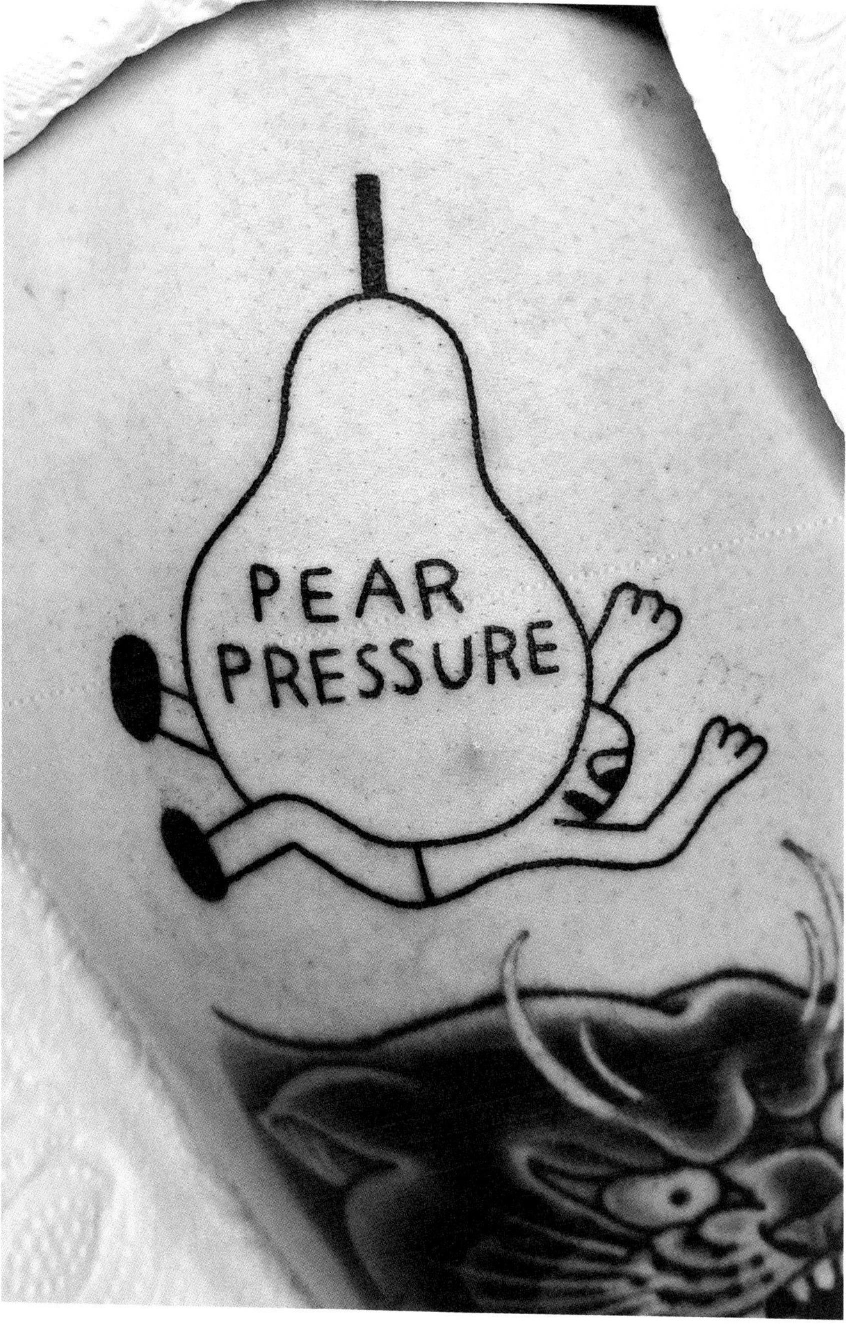
PEAR
PRESSURE

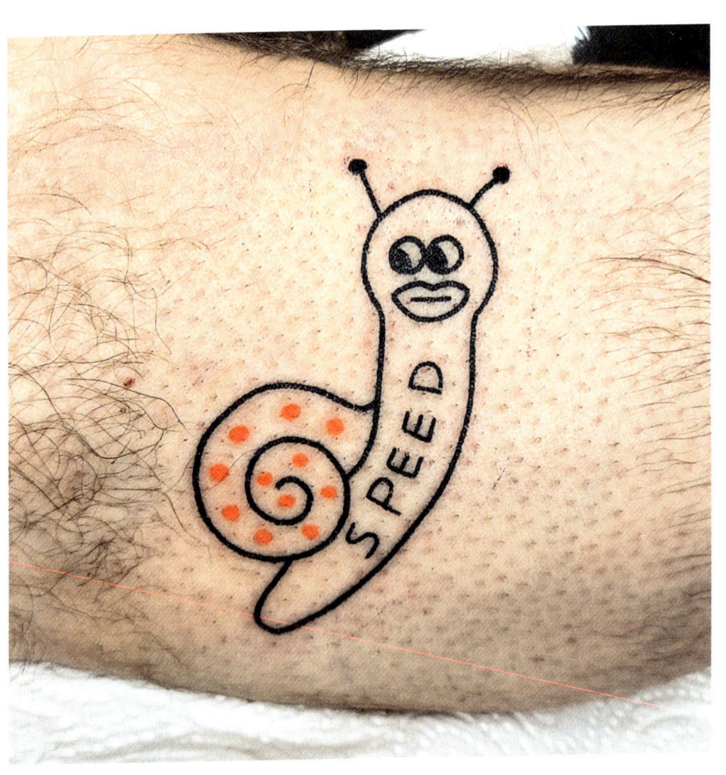
SPEED

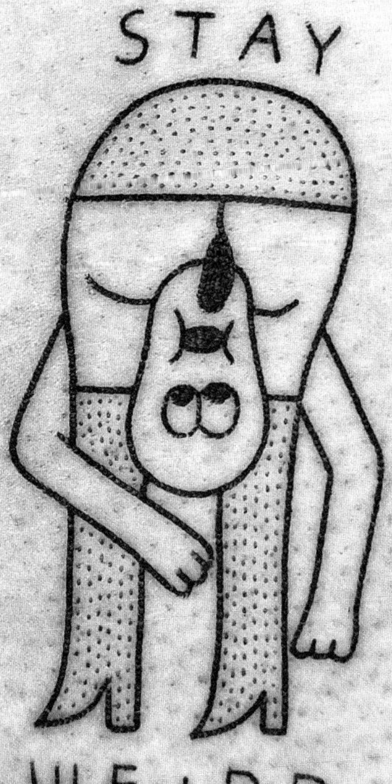
STAY
WEIRD

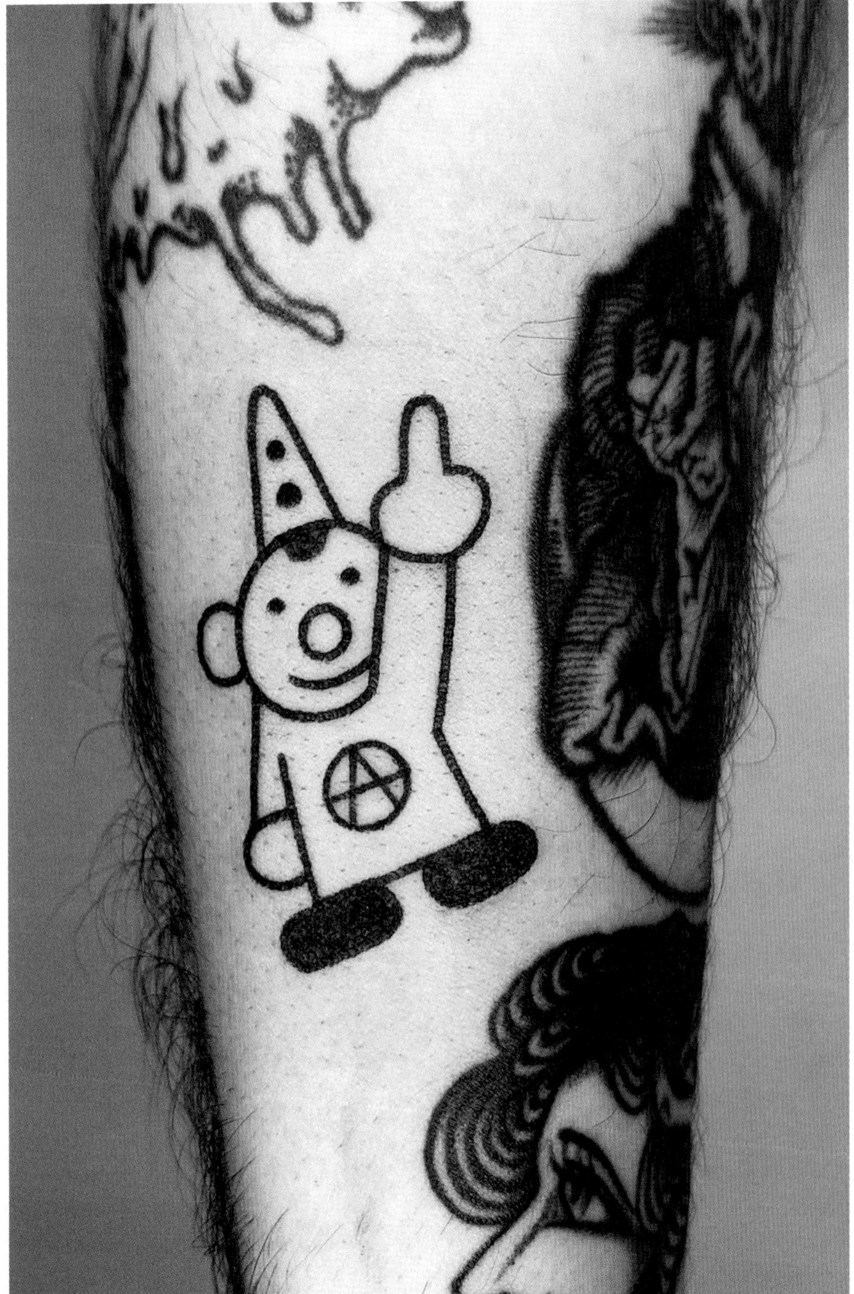

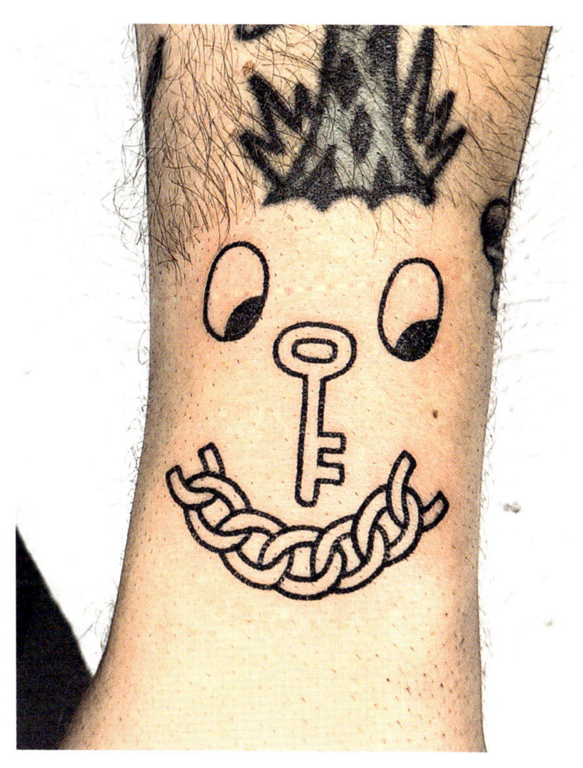

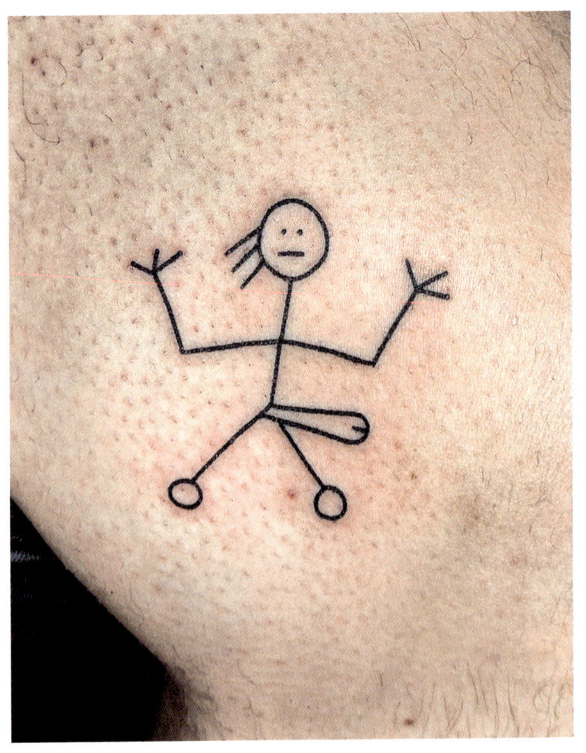

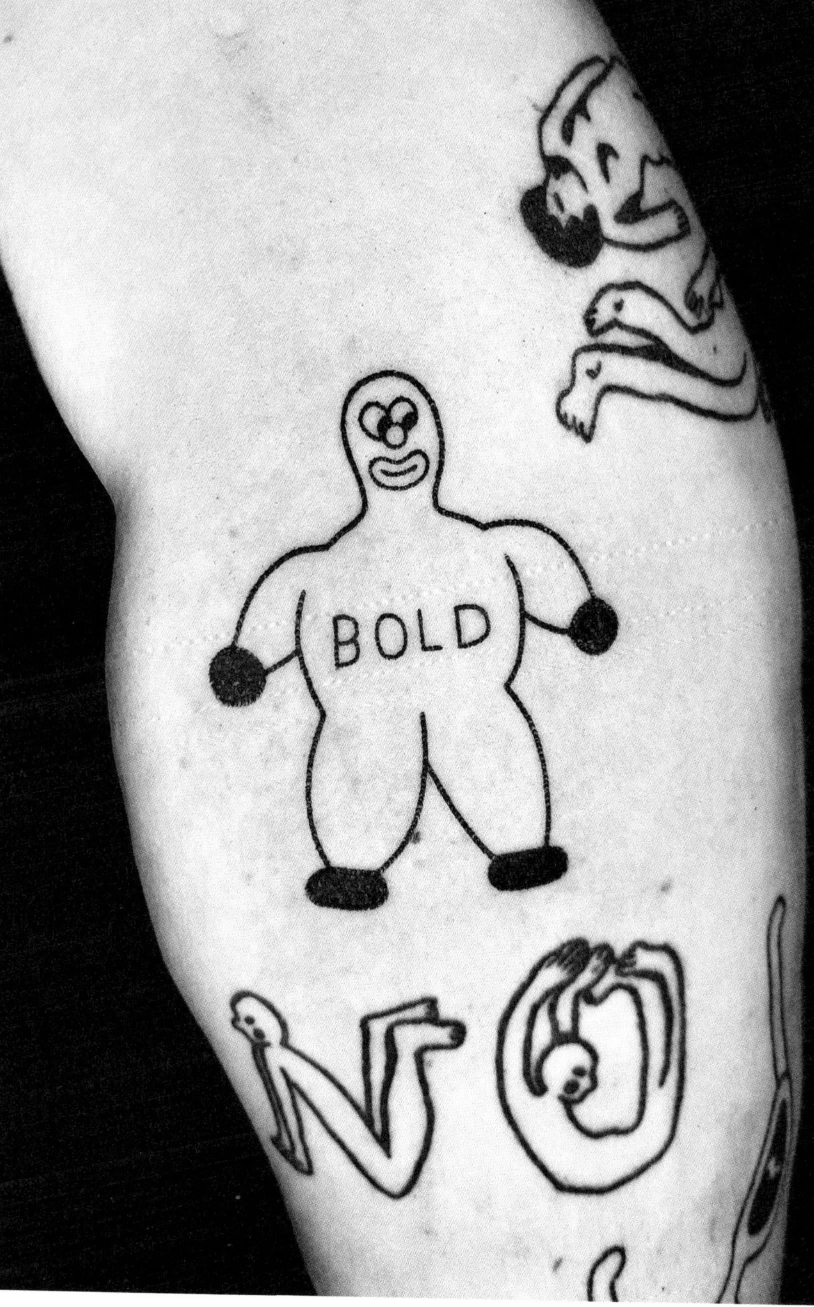
BOLD

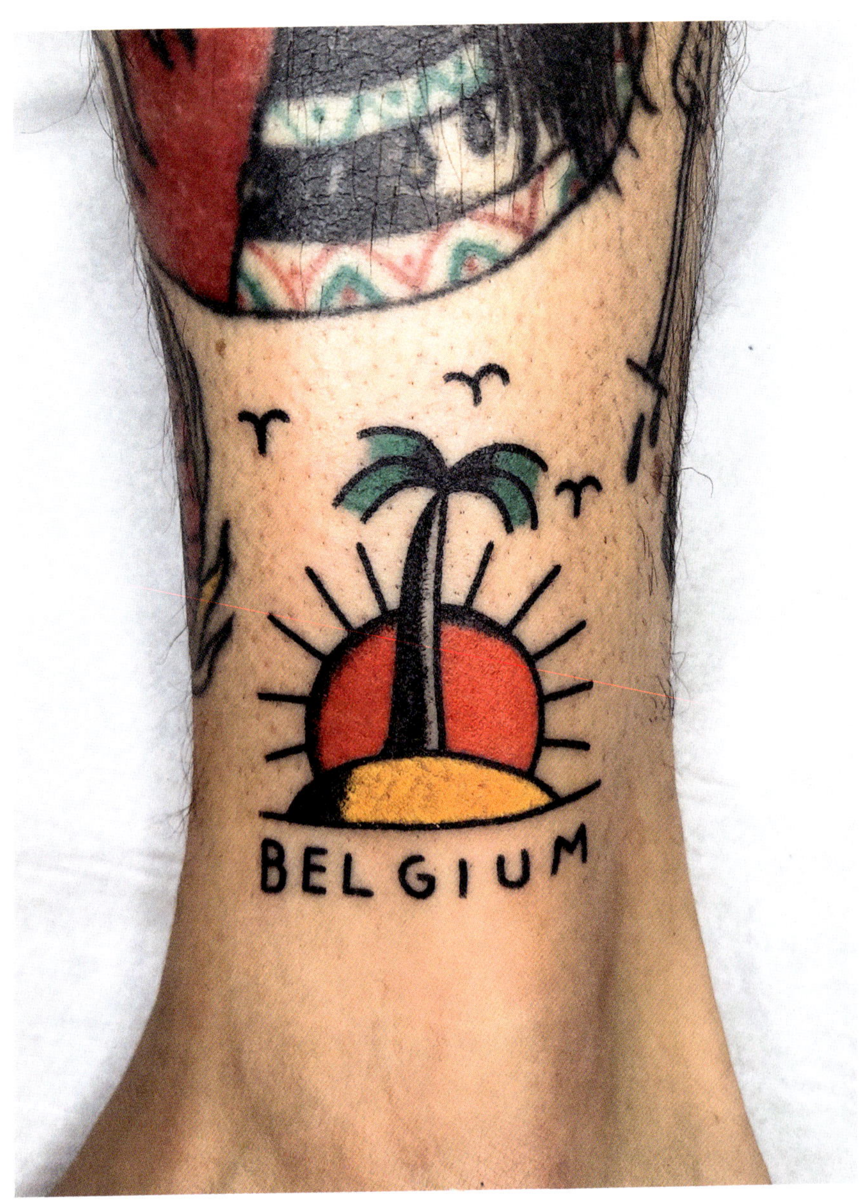
BELGIUM

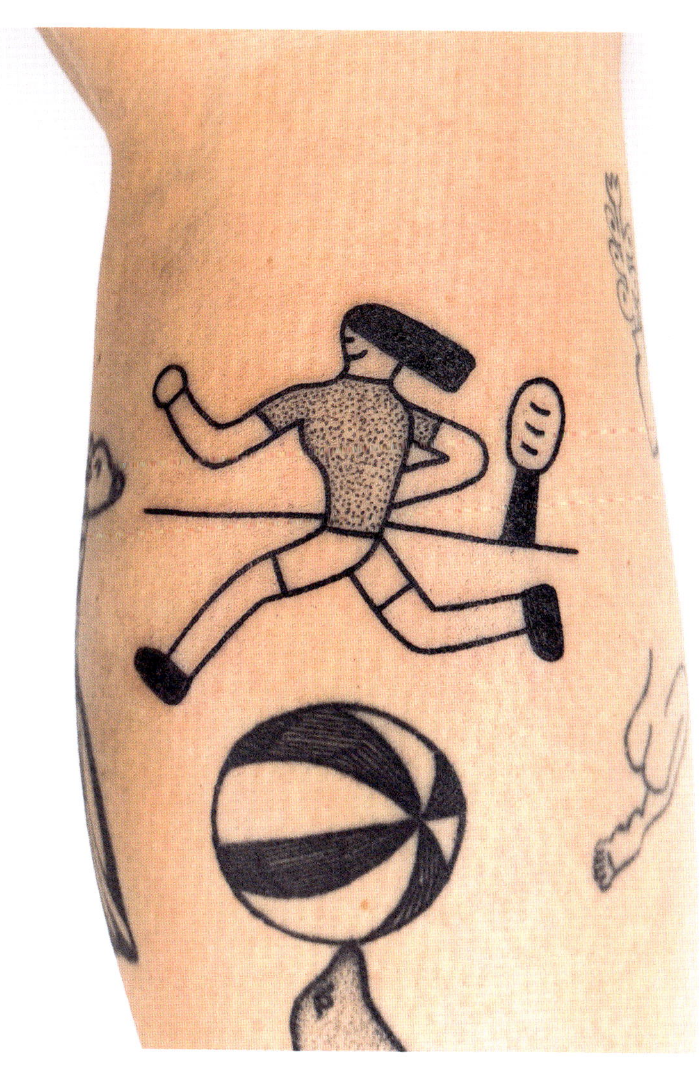

BEHIND THE TATTOO

'Creativity works like a muscle for me – the more I train it, the more creative I become. It's important for me to keep creating, to keep that muscle strong. That's why you'll often find me drawing on all kinds of surfaces – and yes, I even like to make art with my food. It's food for the brain!'

— EDDY PRICKSTICK

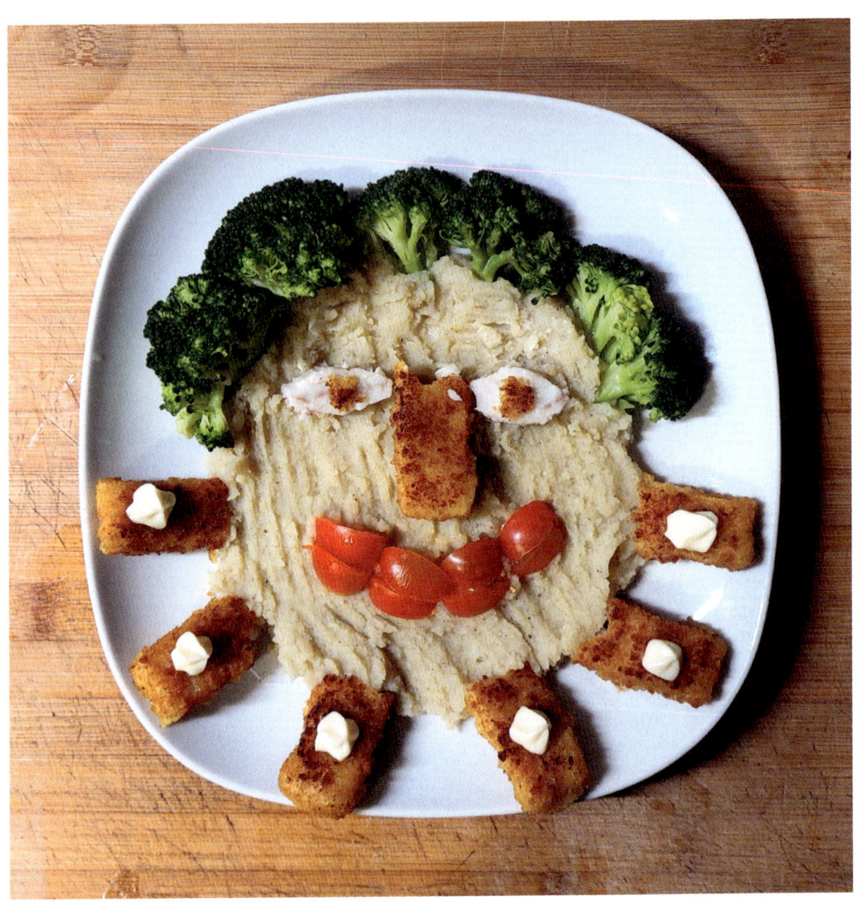

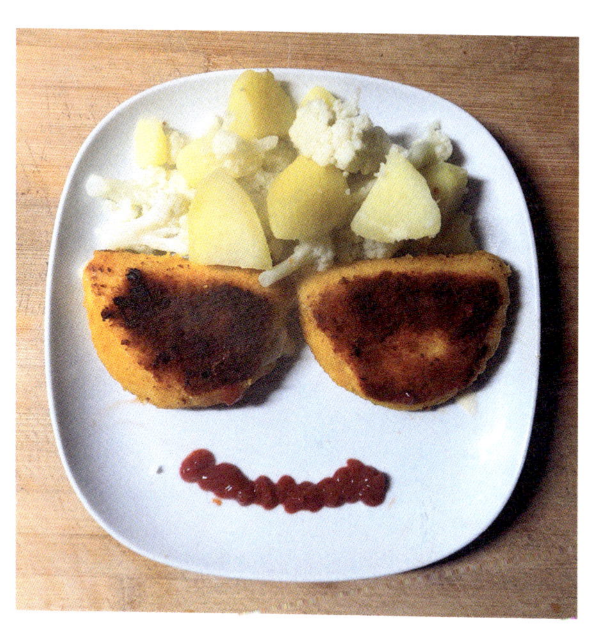

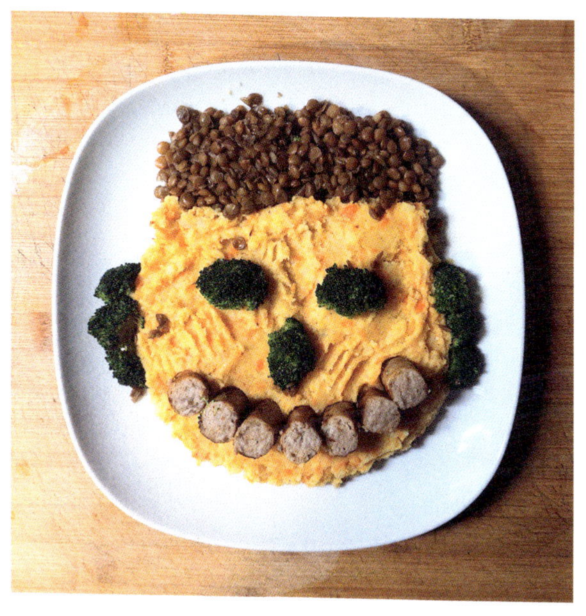

HAPPY-FISHHEAD

Portland, USA

Kat Audick, professionally known as Happyfishhead, is a distinguished tattoo and multimedia artist based in Portland, Oregon. Her work is characterised by playful, surreal imagery, often incorporating elements of food and whimsical characters. Beyond tattooing, she is known for curating interactive art exhibits and immersive events that explore similarly vibrant and unconventional themes.

As the owner of Fun Fun Tattoo, a dynamic and colourful studio in the heart of Portland, Kat has cultivated a welcoming space where artistry and self-expression thrive. Her personal philosophy, 'Just happy to be here', reflects her deep appreciation for the human experience and the privilege of making art for a living.

09.

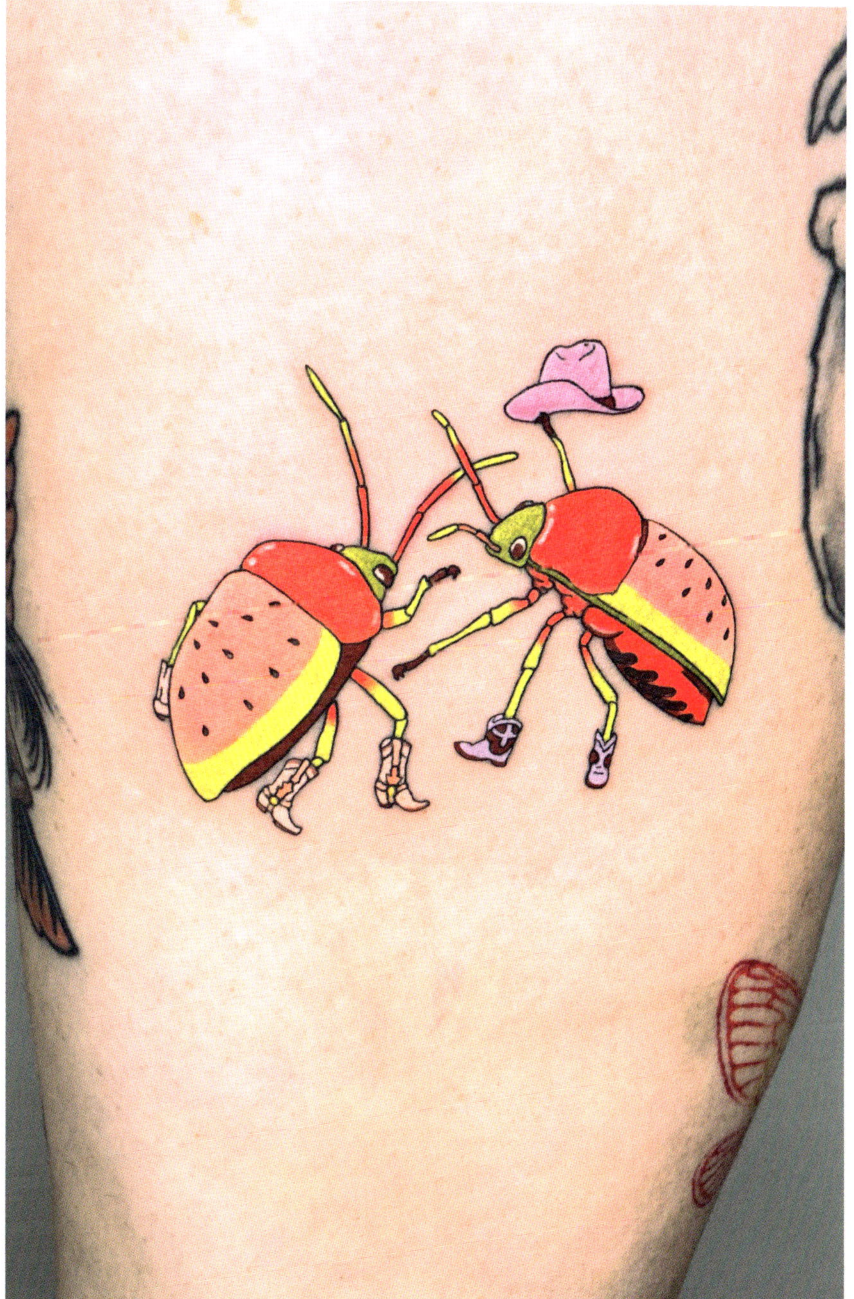

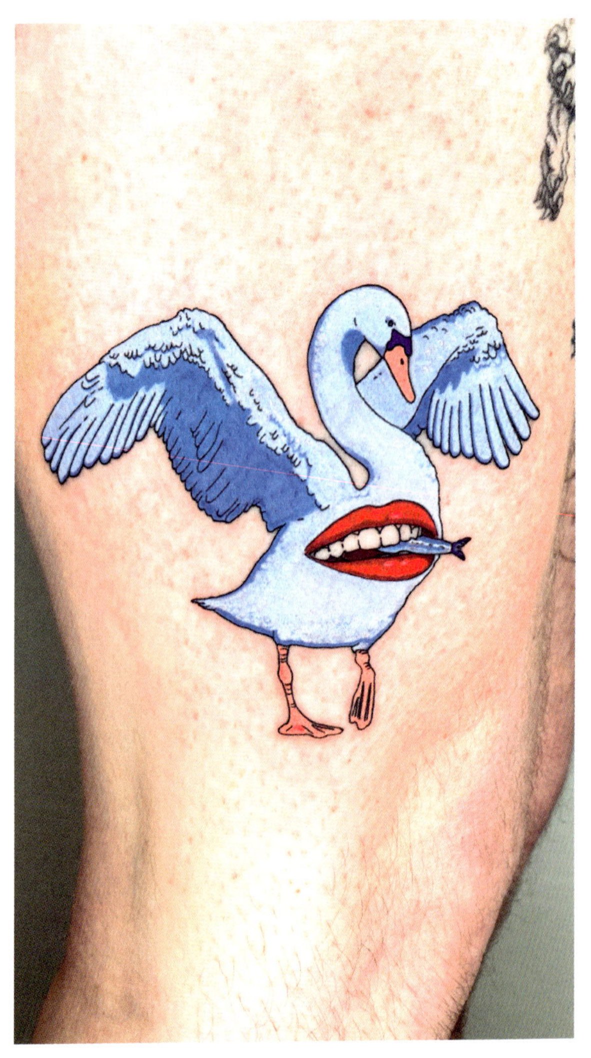

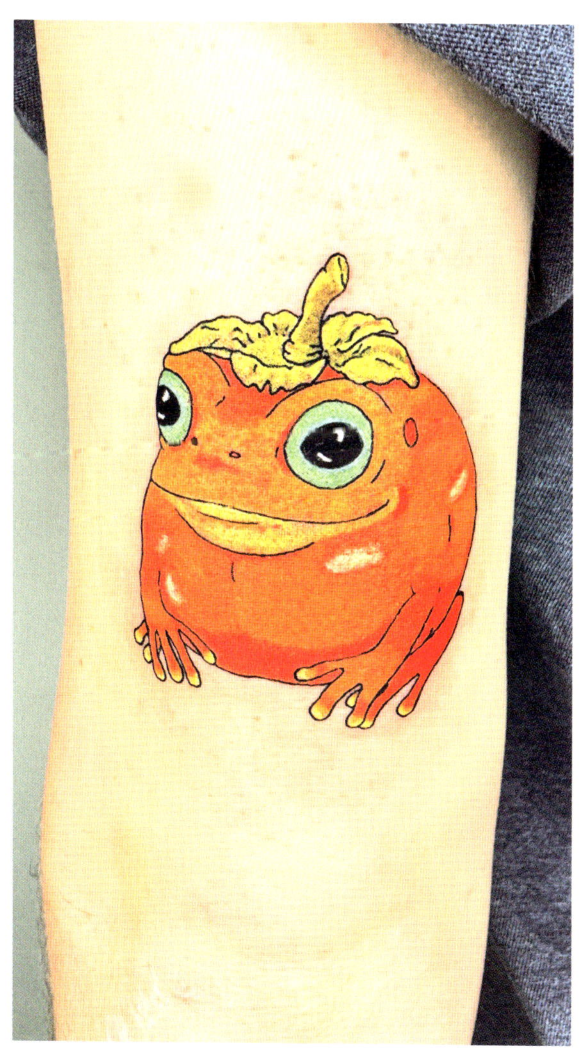

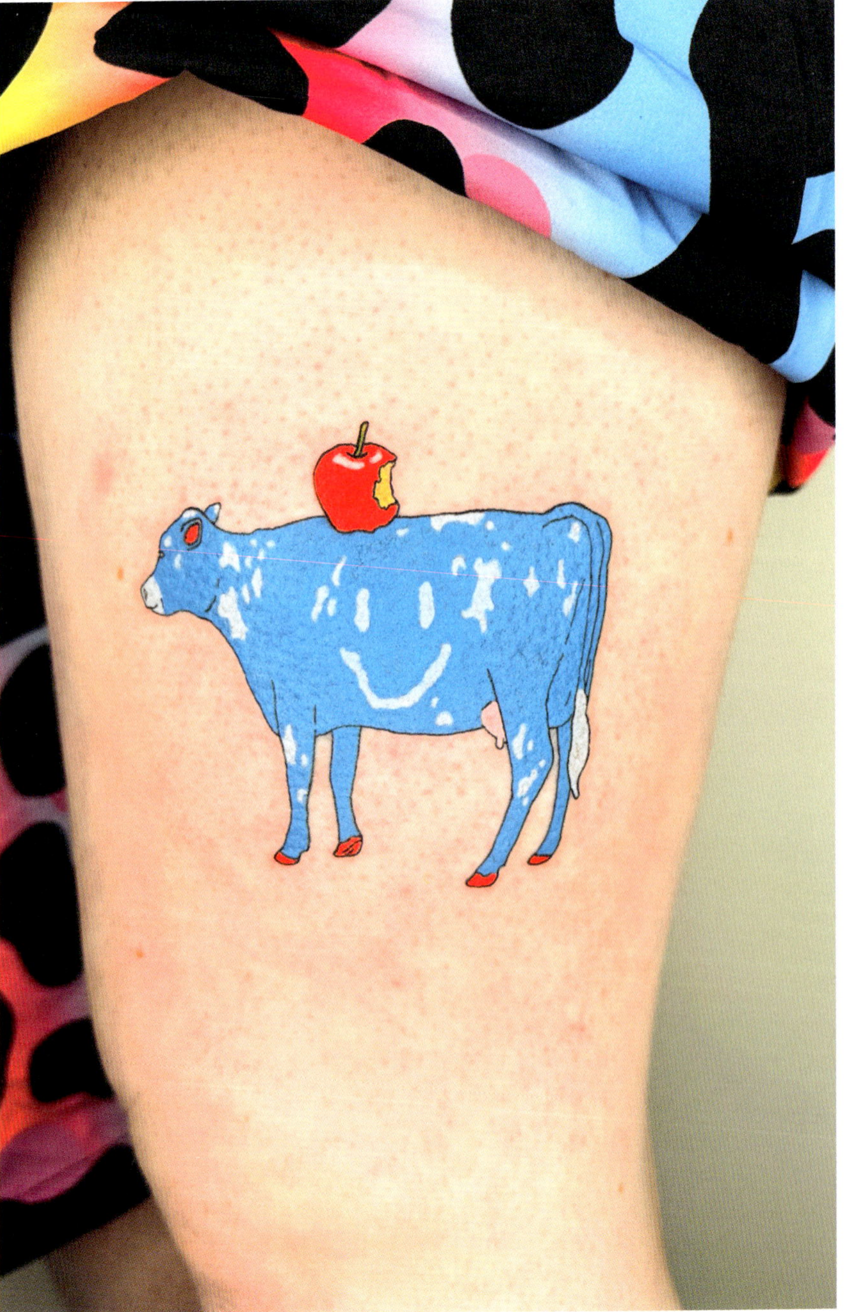

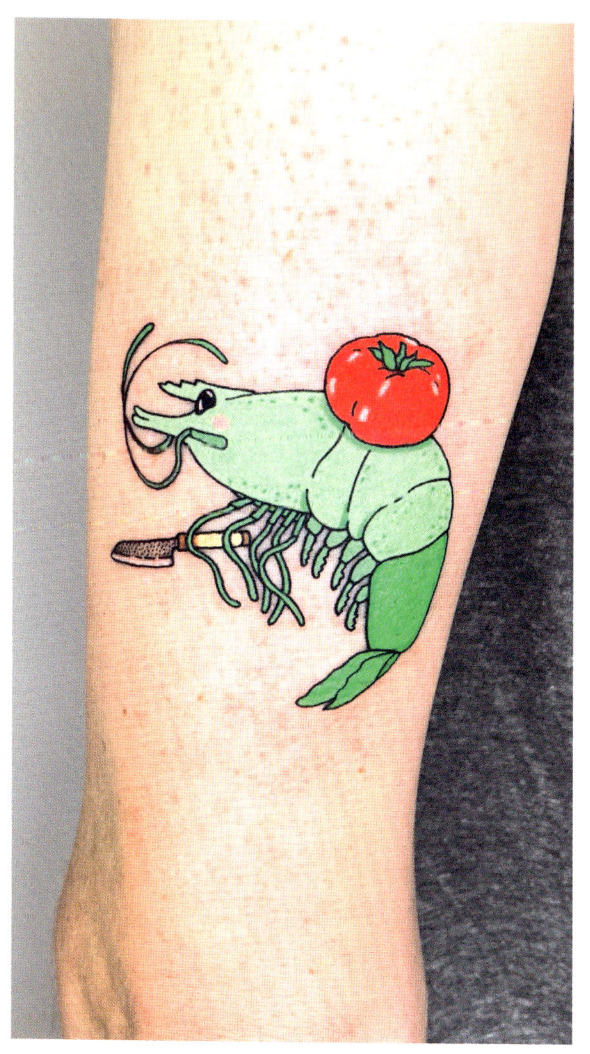

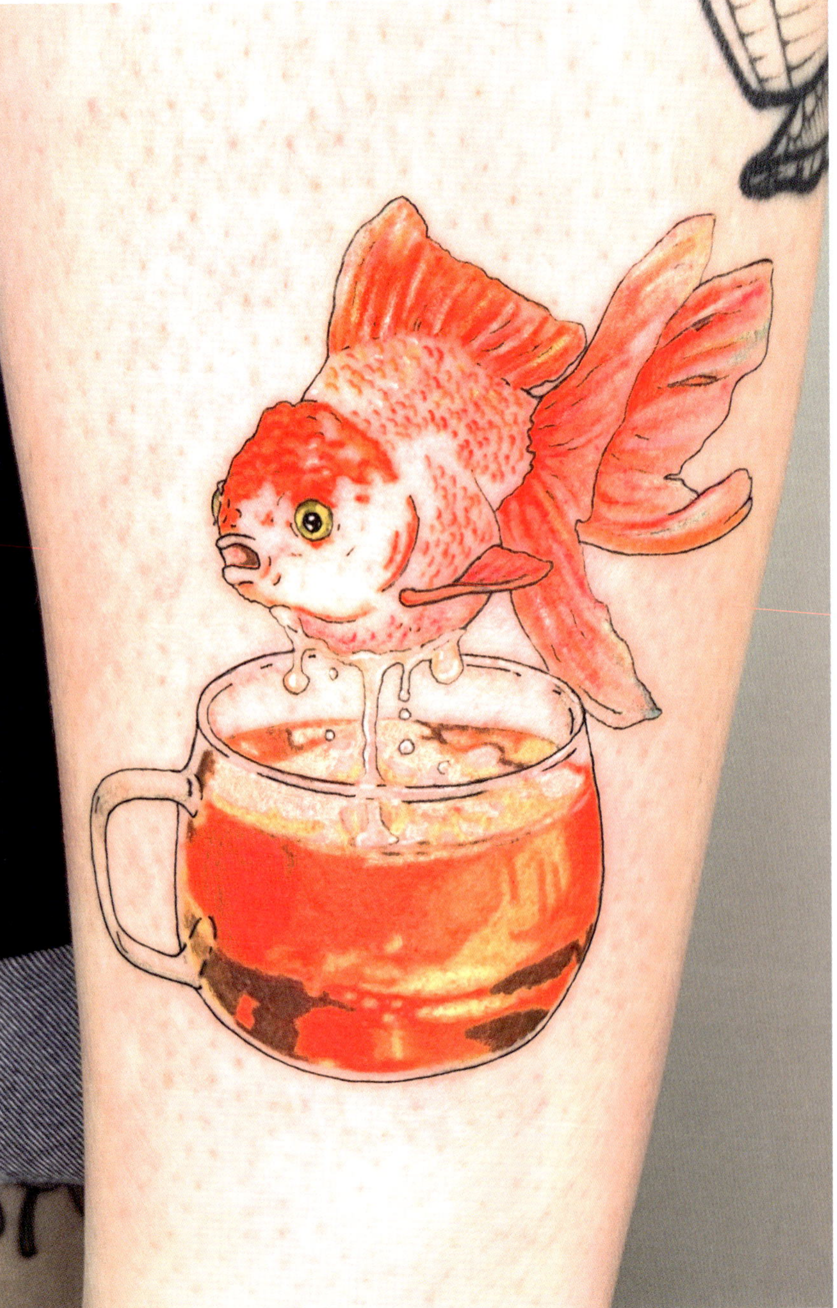

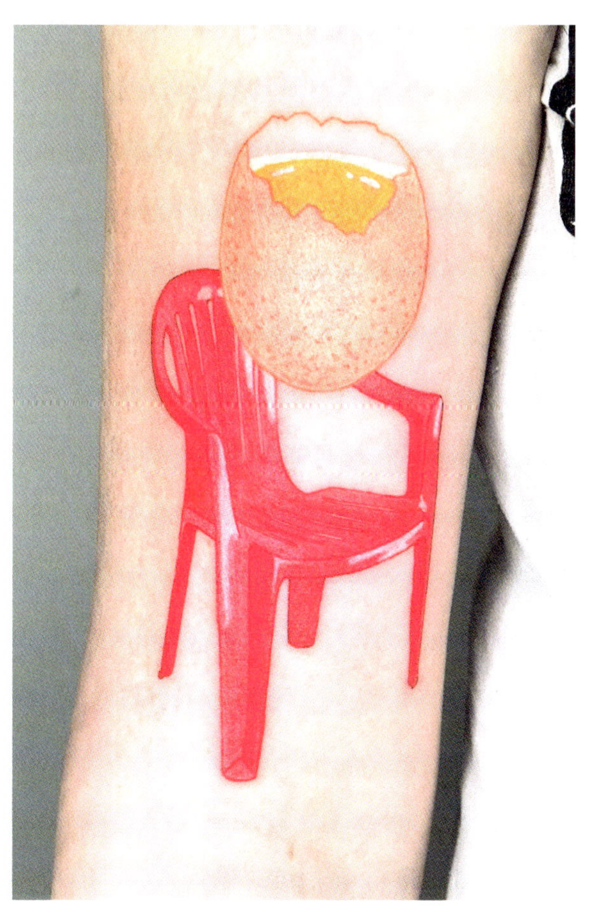

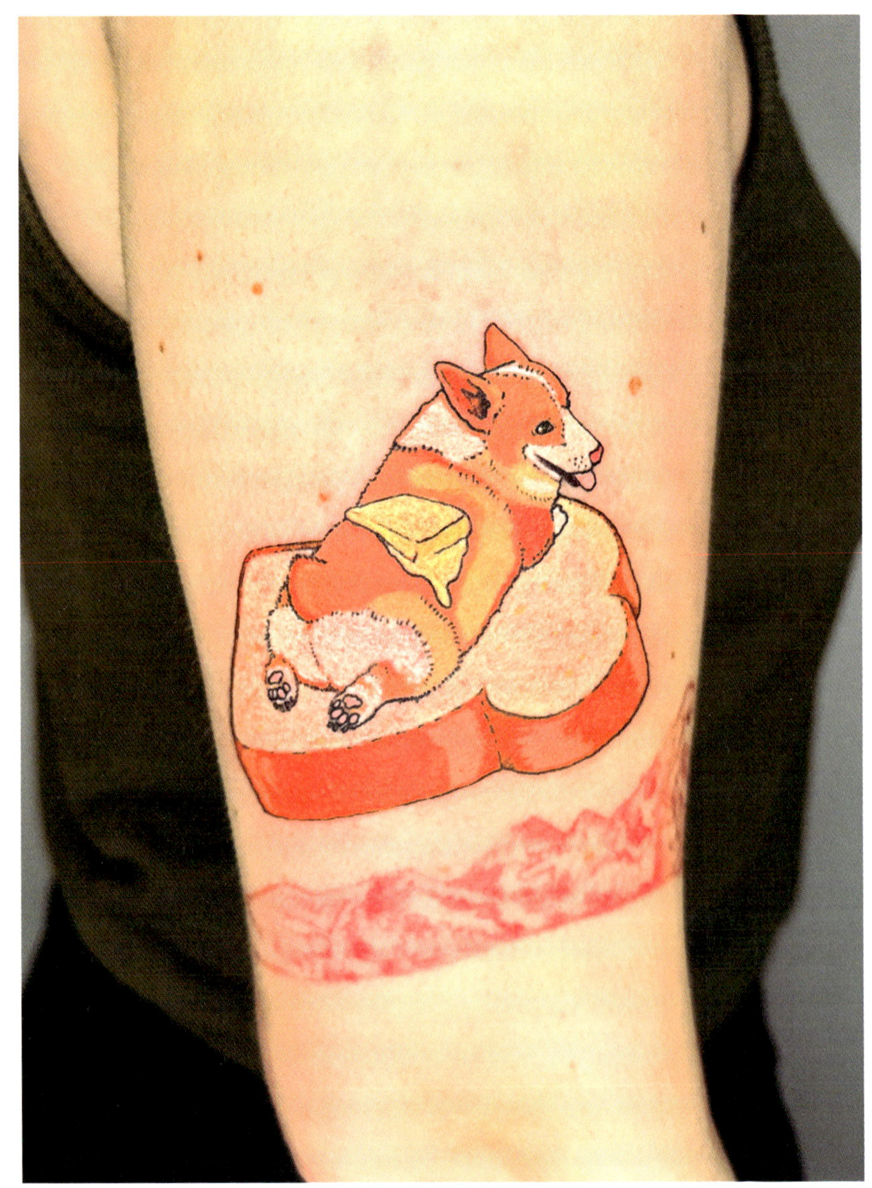

Where does the name Happyfishhead come from?
Happyfishhead is a playful name that really captures my spirit. I experienced some heavy things early on in life, including loss and grief, which gave me a deep appreciation for the present moment. That evolved into a kind of built-in optimism - even on the hard days, I find ways to centre myself in joy and gratitude.

The 'fishhead' part stems from my lifelong love of aquatic life. I'm fascinated by fish, and they've always been my go-to subject when I'm drawing for fun. It's 'fishhead' because I'm always thinking about fish - it just felt natural to combine those two parts of me into one name.

How did you first get involved in tattooing?
It started pretty organically. I had friends who had specific ideas for tattoos but struggled to explain them to artists. Since I was always drawing, I'd help bring their ideas to life on paper. At the time, I was working in the film industry and carried a sketchbook with me everywhere. Drawing during downtime became a kind of creative meditation.

Eventually, I realised that I wanted to make drawing my full-time job. I was already admiring tattoo artists from afar, and the more I learnt about the craft, the more curious I became. Once I tried it, I completely fell in love with it - the intimacy, the permanence, the artistry of it all.

In Oregon, where I'm based, we're the only US state that requires tattoo artists to graduate from an official tattoo school. It's a unique system: a blend between structured learning and self-guided experimentation. We were given basic guidance, but encouraged to explore different machines, styles and techniques to find our own approach. Since graduating, I've continued learning by connecting with and studying under artists I respect.

Do you remember your first tattoo?
Yes, I tattooed myself while in school. It was a little sardine wearing a human skeleton torso like a jacket. I didn't have the Happyfishhead name yet, but that design was already deeply 'me'. It felt like a rite of passage to tattoo myself, and I still love that piece. It's a personal reminder of where I started and why I do what I do.

What's the most unusual tattoo request you've received?
A client once asked me to tattoo a shrimp in place of his eyebrows after he'd shaved them off. As much as I appreciated the trust - and enjoyed the humour behind the idea - I had to say no. I adored the client, but I felt that particular joke might be best left as an inside joke rather than a lifelong commitment.

Has tattooing had a positive impact on your life?
Tattooing has given me total creative freedom. Every design I tattoo is something I genuinely want to make - I'm not just producing on demand. It's helped me build a lifestyle centred around my art and intuition.

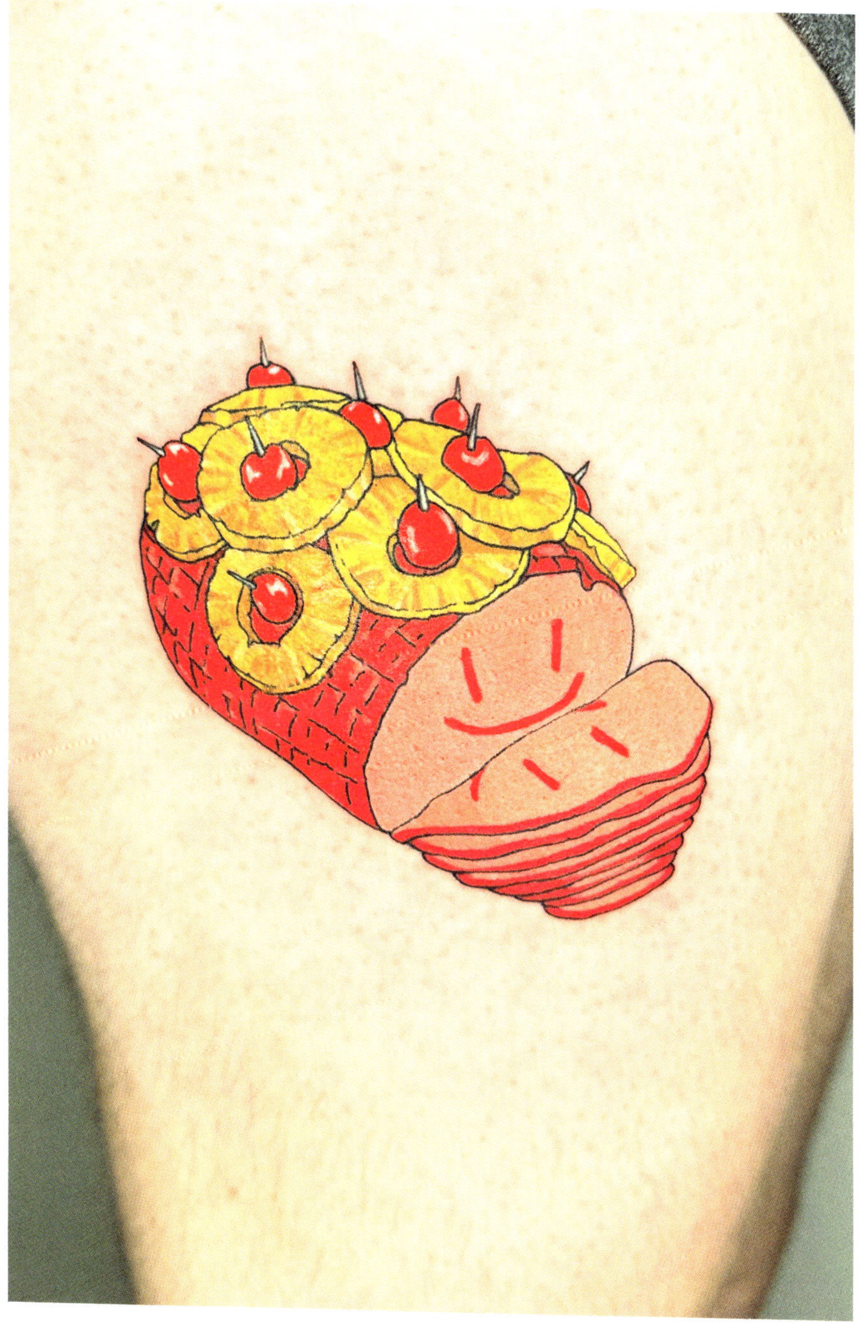

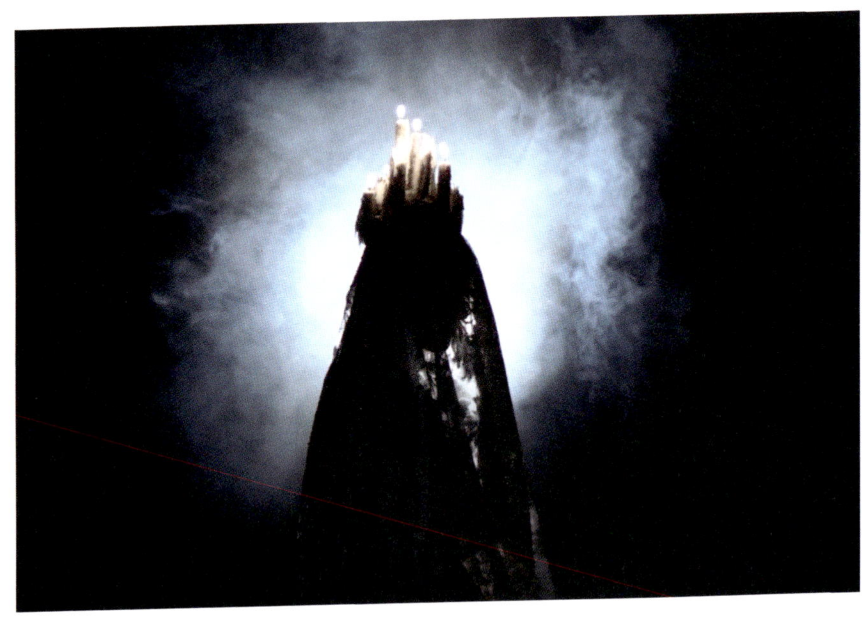

Mary the grave, music video by Kat Audick

It's also changed how I see the world. Everything becomes a potential source of inspiration. Even mundane experiences, like grocery shopping or overhearing snippets of conversation, can spark ideas.

My background in improv comedy plays a big role in my creative process. I constantly play word-association games in my head, combining animals, objects, emotions and phrases that normally wouldn't go together. I even mispronounce or morph common words to create new visual mash-ups. That playfulness translates into my tattoo designs and adds a layer of humour that many clients connect with.

Is there any part of tattooing that you find difficult?
The hardest part, honestly, is that it causes pain. Even though it's expected and temporary, I never enjoy hurting people, especially those who are nervous or new to the experience. It's part of the process, but it's something I approach with care and empathy every time.

What did your career look like before tattooing?
Before this, I worked in film and television as an art director and production designer for about a decade. I designed sets, built props, sewed costumes - basically, I brought creative worlds to life. The work was demanding with 12- to 16-hour days the norm, but the collaborative energy was unmatched. It often felt like a creative summer camp.

While tattooing is my main focus now, I still take on select film projects that align with my interests. I also continue creating outside the studio - painting, sculpting, working with ceramics. I love hosting immersive art experiences too, like themed dinners with costumes and playful food presentations. I've often been known to dress like a clown and make balloon animals. I love surprising people and giving them stories they'll tell for years to come.

How would you describe the tattoo culture in Portland, Oregon?
Portland has a really vibrant and eclectic tattoo scene. It's become a destination for tattoo tourism. I regularly meet clients who plan entire trips around getting tattooed by multiple local artists. What I love most is how supportive the community is. There's a spirit of collaboration here rather than competition. We share clients, celebrate each other's work, and genuinely want to see each other succeed.

What values guide how you work with your clients?
I'm incredibly grateful for everyone who chooses to wear my art. Many of my clients are repeat collectors, and I don't take their trust lightly. I want every session to be more than just a tattoo - I aim to create a memorable, positive experience they'll carry with them just as much as the artwork itself.

I make a point to connect with each person on a personal level. It's not just transactional - it's relational. Once someone has my work on their body, they become part of my walking art gallery, and that means a lot to me.

How do you approach designing your tattoos?
I work flash-only, which means I don't do custom designs based on client ideas. Instead, I create my own original artwork and tattoo each design just a handful of times - sometimes only once.

This approach keeps things exciting for me creatively, and it ensures my clients are getting something truly unique. It's less about mass production and more about offering a limited edition piece of wearable art.

Do you have any pre-tattoo rituals?
Definitely. I do little warm-up dances before sessions to get my energy moving and my blood flowing before it's time to sit very still for a few hours. It helps my body feel relaxed and focused. I sometimes share those moments online as a way to connect and let others see the behind-the-scenes process, even the silly parts. Over time, it's helped me feel more at home in my own skin and more open in how I show up for others.

What kind of atmosphere do you try to create for your clients?
I named my studio Fun Fun Tattoo because I want the whole experience to feel joyful - not just the artwork, but the environment too. We laugh a lot, swap stories, and make people feel at home.

When the studio is full of clients and artists, it feels like a gathering of friends. There's warmth and humour, and that's really intentional. I know getting a tattoo can feel intimidating, especially for first-timers, so creating a safe and inviting space is something I care deeply about.

What are your hopes for the next generation of tattoo artists?
I hope they continue to push boundaries - stylistically, technically and creatively. I love seeing tattooing evolve into an art form that rivals painting, fabric and sculpture. There's so much innovation happening right now, and I can't wait to see what future artists dream up next.

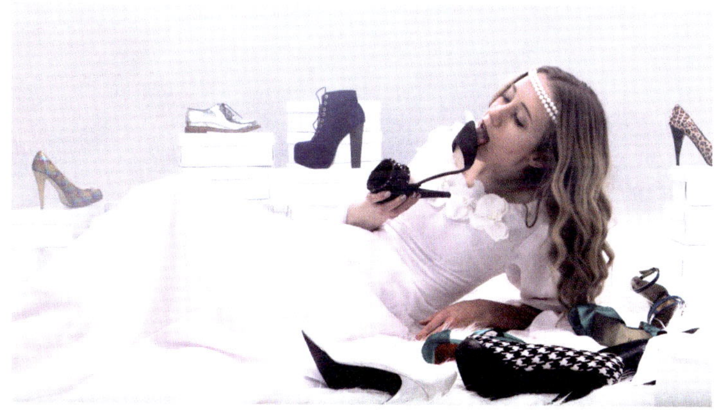

Girls love shoes, music video by Kat Audick

HELLO NUMI

Barcelona, Spain

Numi is a Spanish multidisciplinary artist who works from her own private studio in Barcelona. Splitting her time between the city and the countryside near Girona, she explores tattooing, ceramics and painting, creating a diverse and vibrant body of work.

Numi studied graphic design at Elisava in Barcelona before moving to Seoul, where she spent four years and discovered her passion for tattooing. Her artistic style is characterised by a colourful, playful and naive aesthetic, featuring simple forms and bold colours. Influenced by the world of kawaii, Asian cartoons and nostalgic visual culture, her work evokes a sense of joy and whimsy.

She draws inspiration from packaging design, advertisements and everyday visual elements, seamlessly integrating them into her creative practice. Whether on skin, ceramics or canvas, her art reflects a unique blend of bold creativity and childlike wonder.

10.

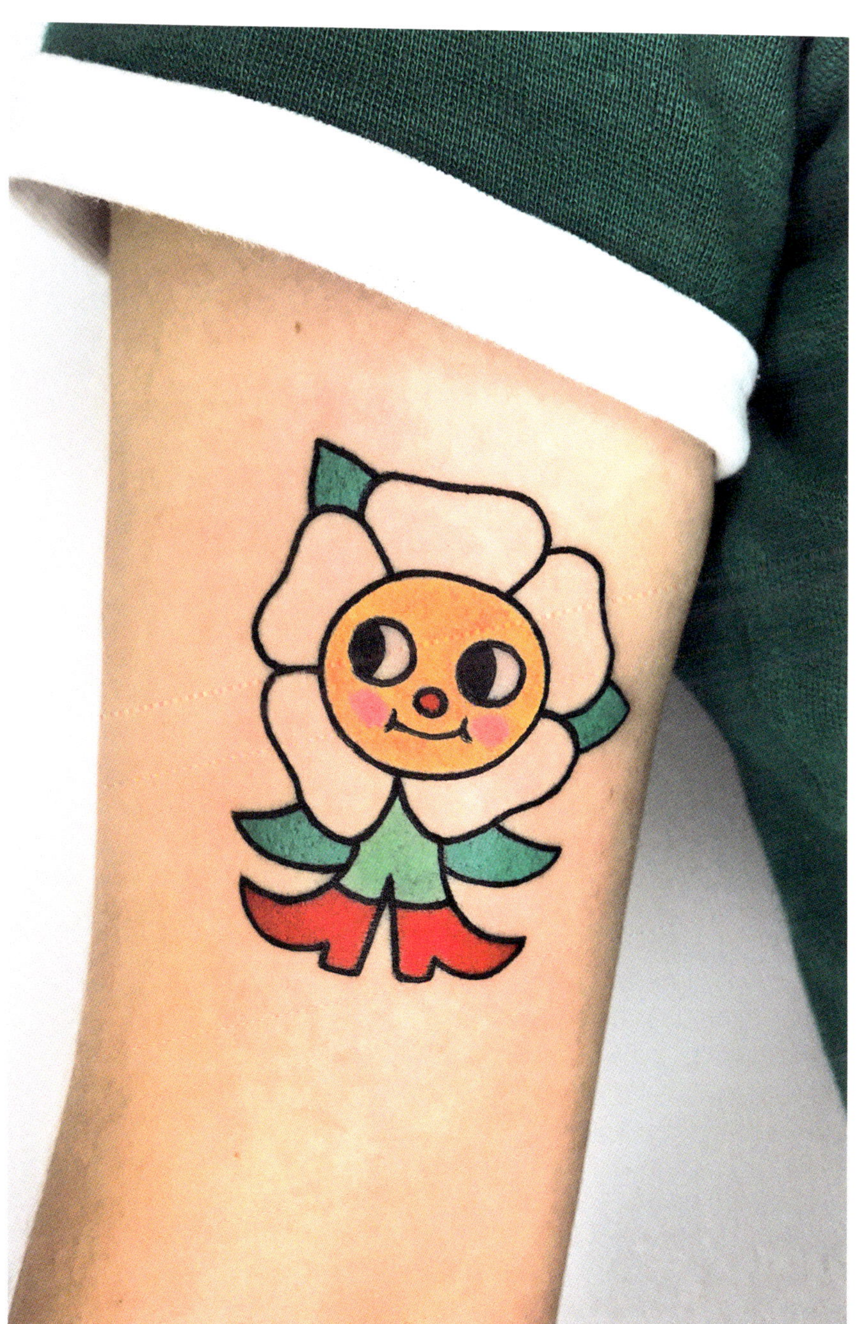

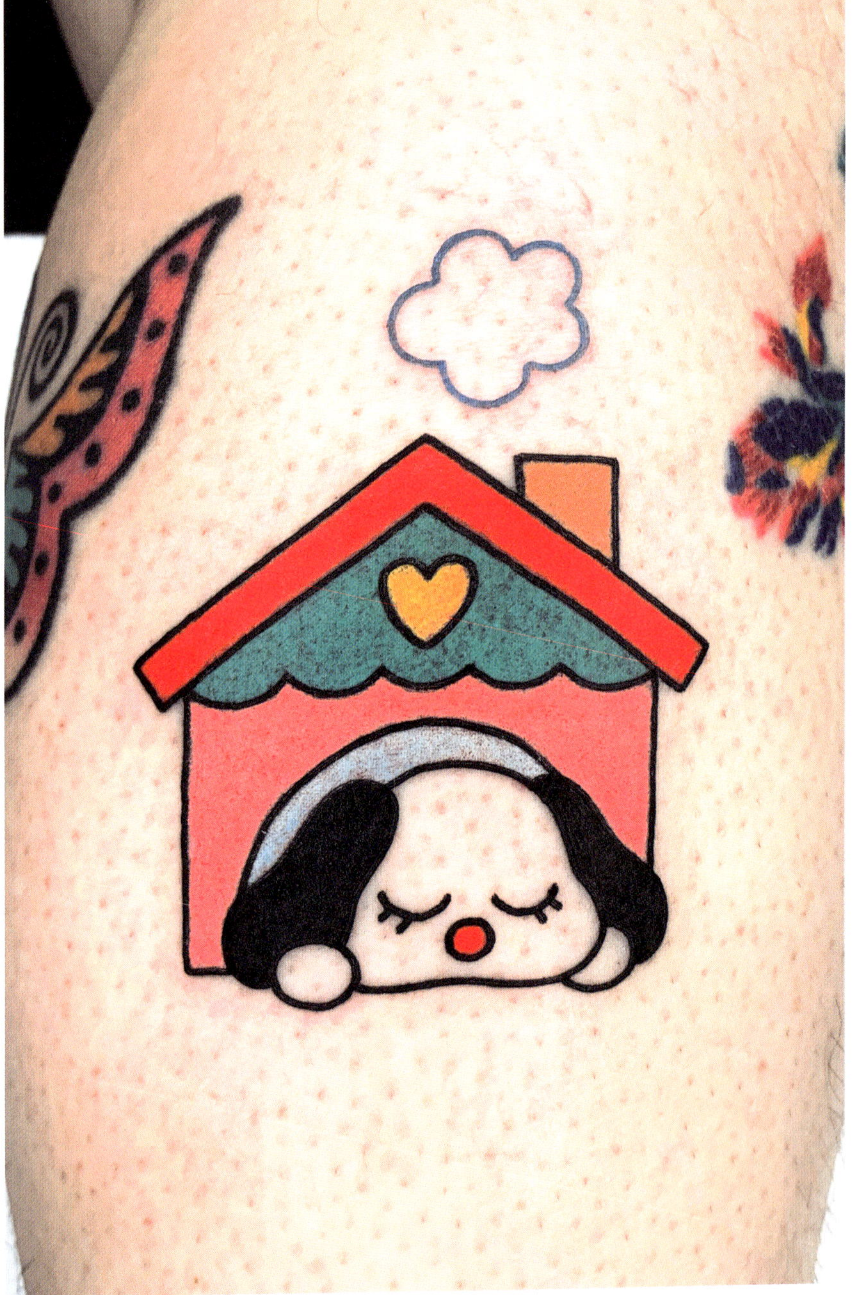

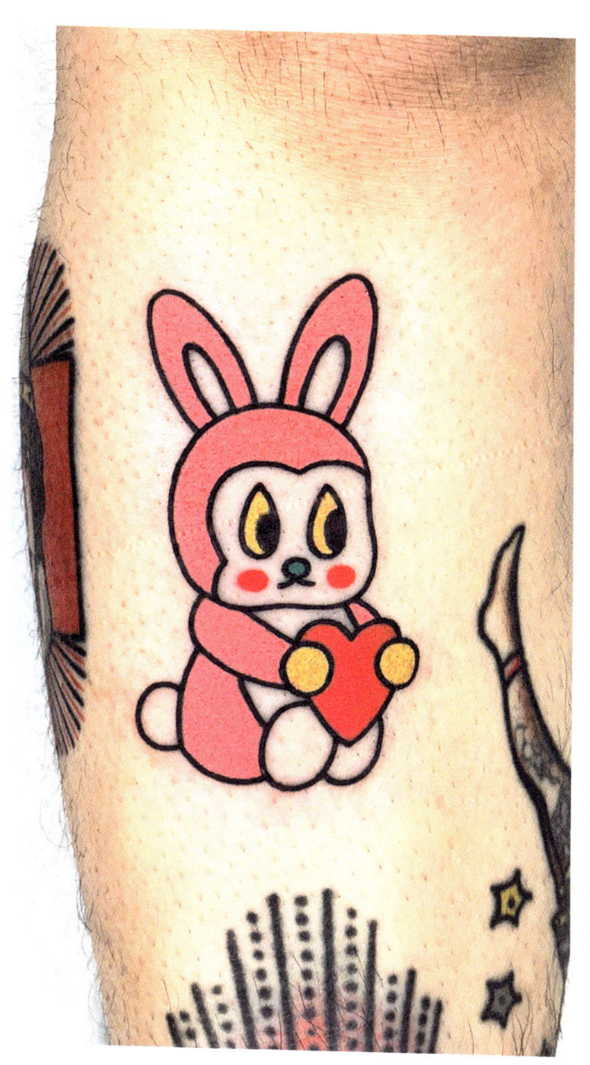

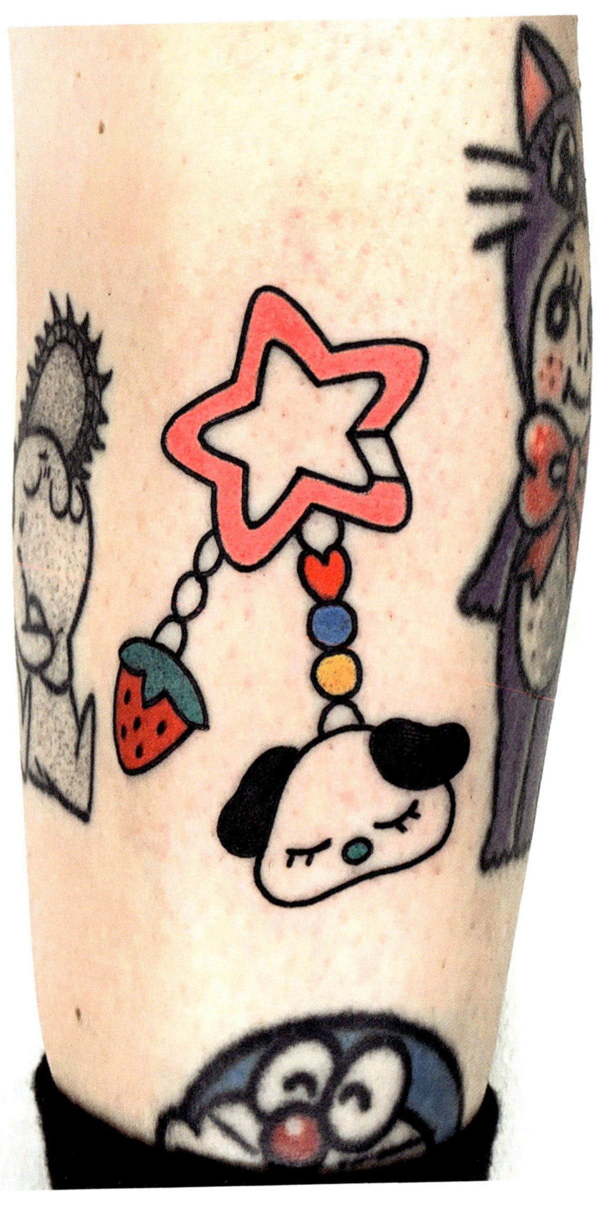

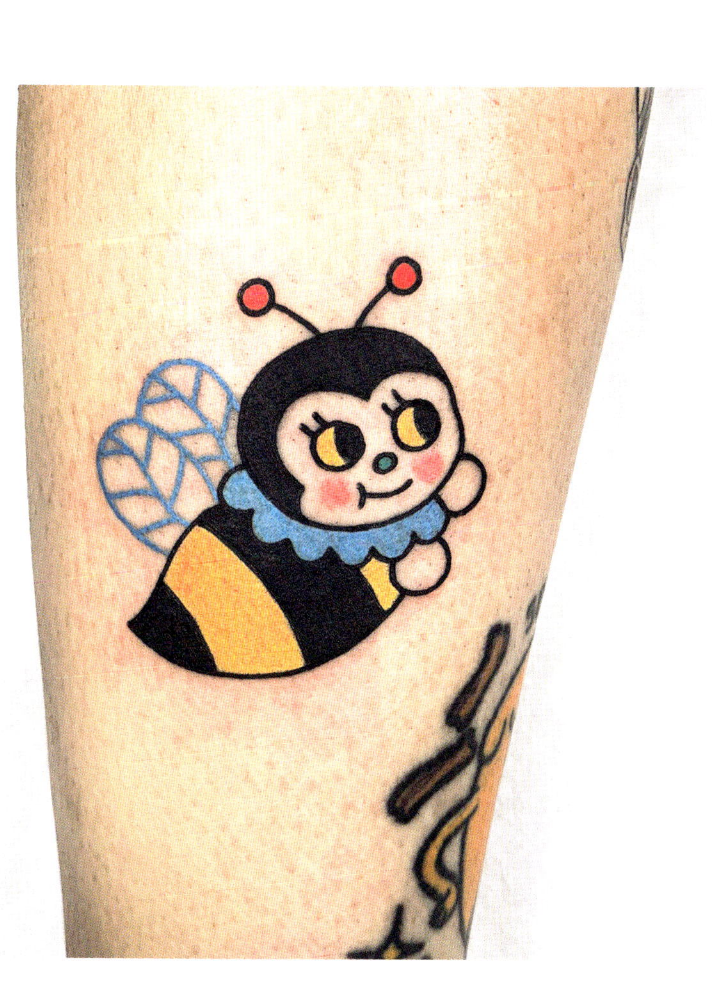

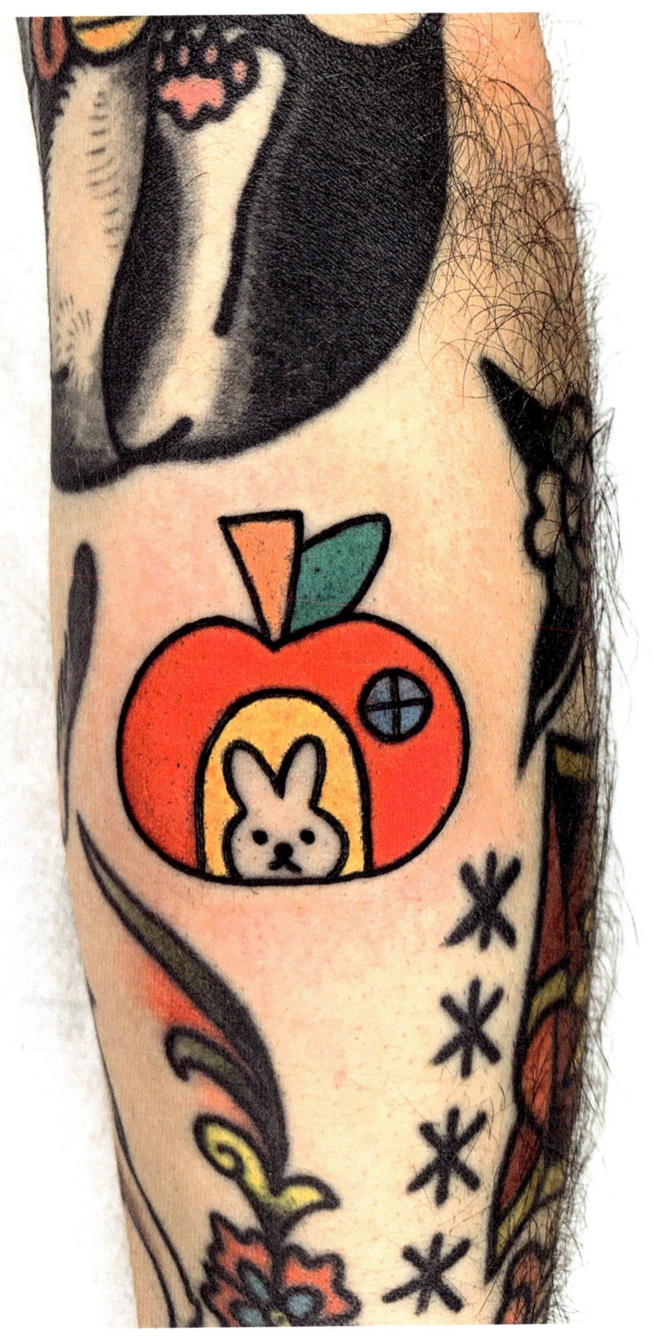

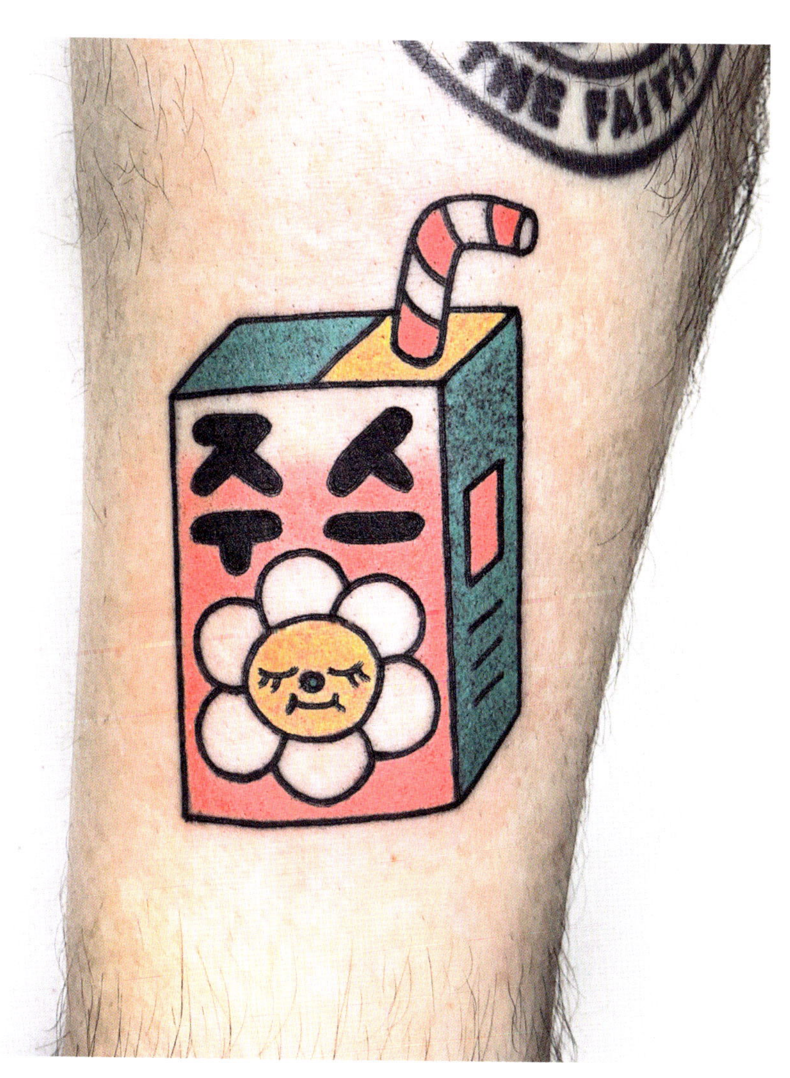
THE FAITH

BEHIND THE TATTOO

‘My ceramics are influenced by the visual language I developed through tattooing. I’ve always been drawn to bold, graphic imagery, and working with clay—particularly through hand-building—provided a new avenue to bring those ideas into the physical world. Unlike tattooing, where each mark is permanent and precision is critical, ceramics offers a more experimental and forgiving process. It allows room for mistakes, spontaneity, and discovery. That freedom encouraged me to explore new creative directions, enabling my designs to take on volume, texture, and a more playful, tactile form of expression.’

— HELLO NUMI

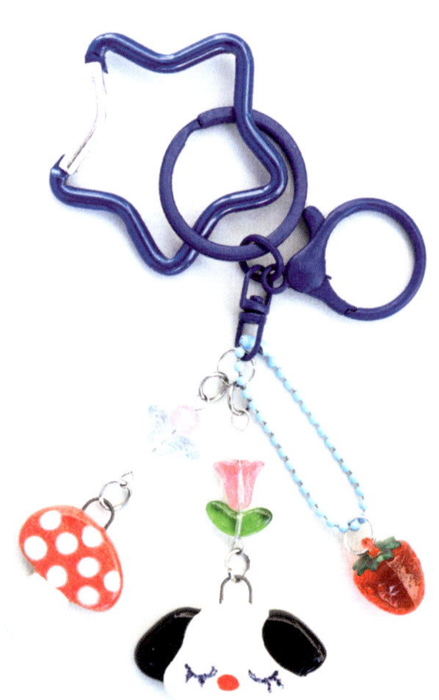

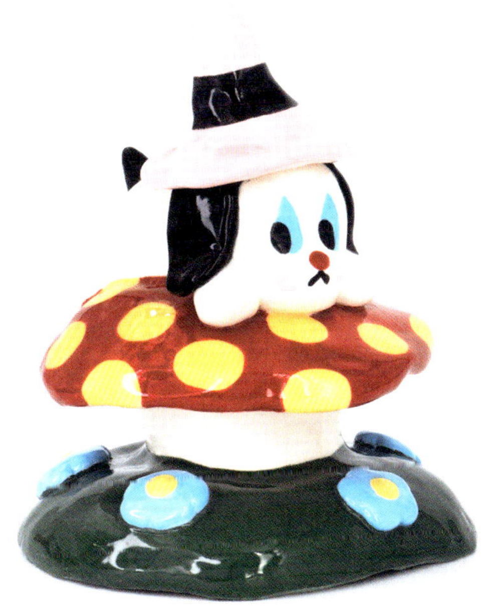

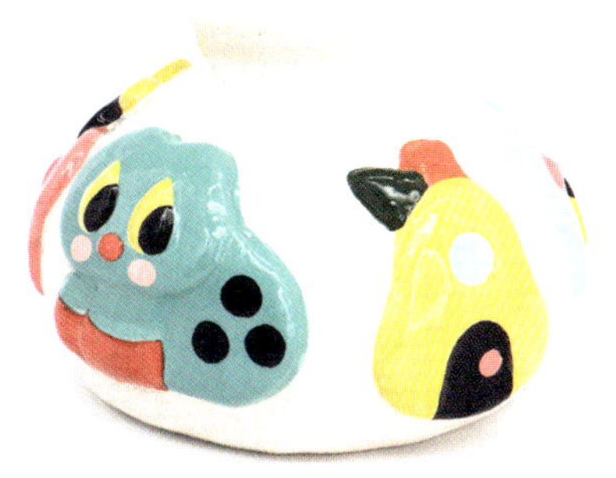

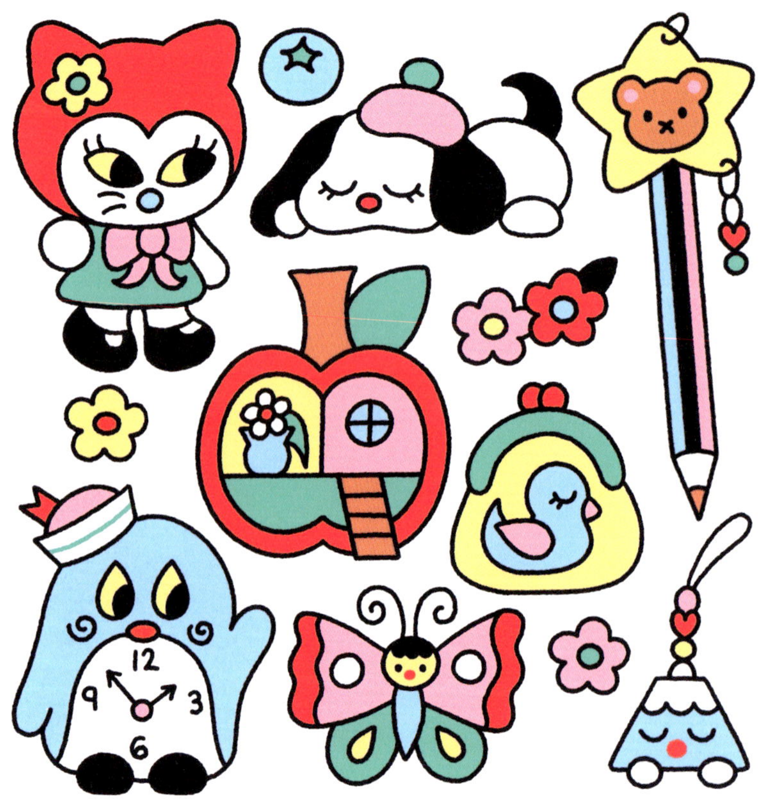
12
9
3
6

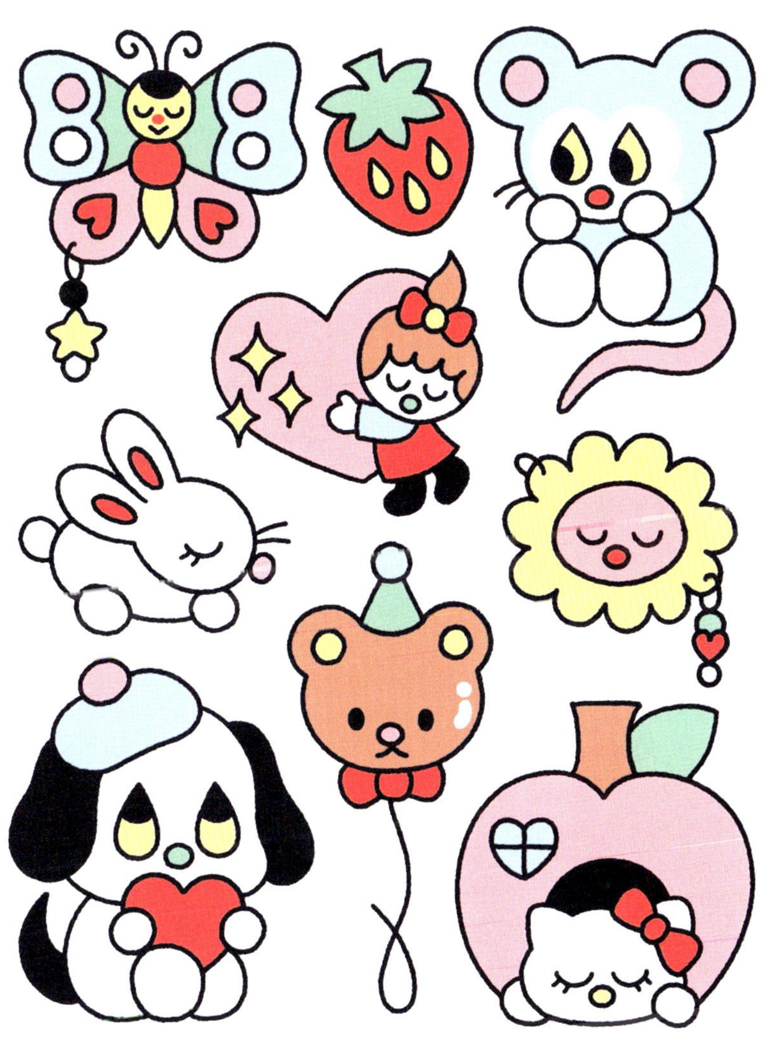

HORIMITSU

Tokyo, Japan

Horimitsu is an internationally acclaimed Japanese artist with nearly 32 years of experience. Based in Ikebukuro, Tokyo, he operates his own private studio, where he brings his bold artistic style to life.

Before pursuing a career in tattooing, Horimitsu worked corporate jobs, but soon realised his true passion lay in artistic expression.

Inspired by nature, space and old books, his work embodies a refined balance of simplicity and storytelling. Recognised for his distinctive cute and fun designs, he strives to create lasting and meaningful memories with each of his clients.

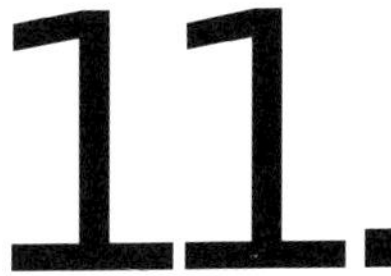

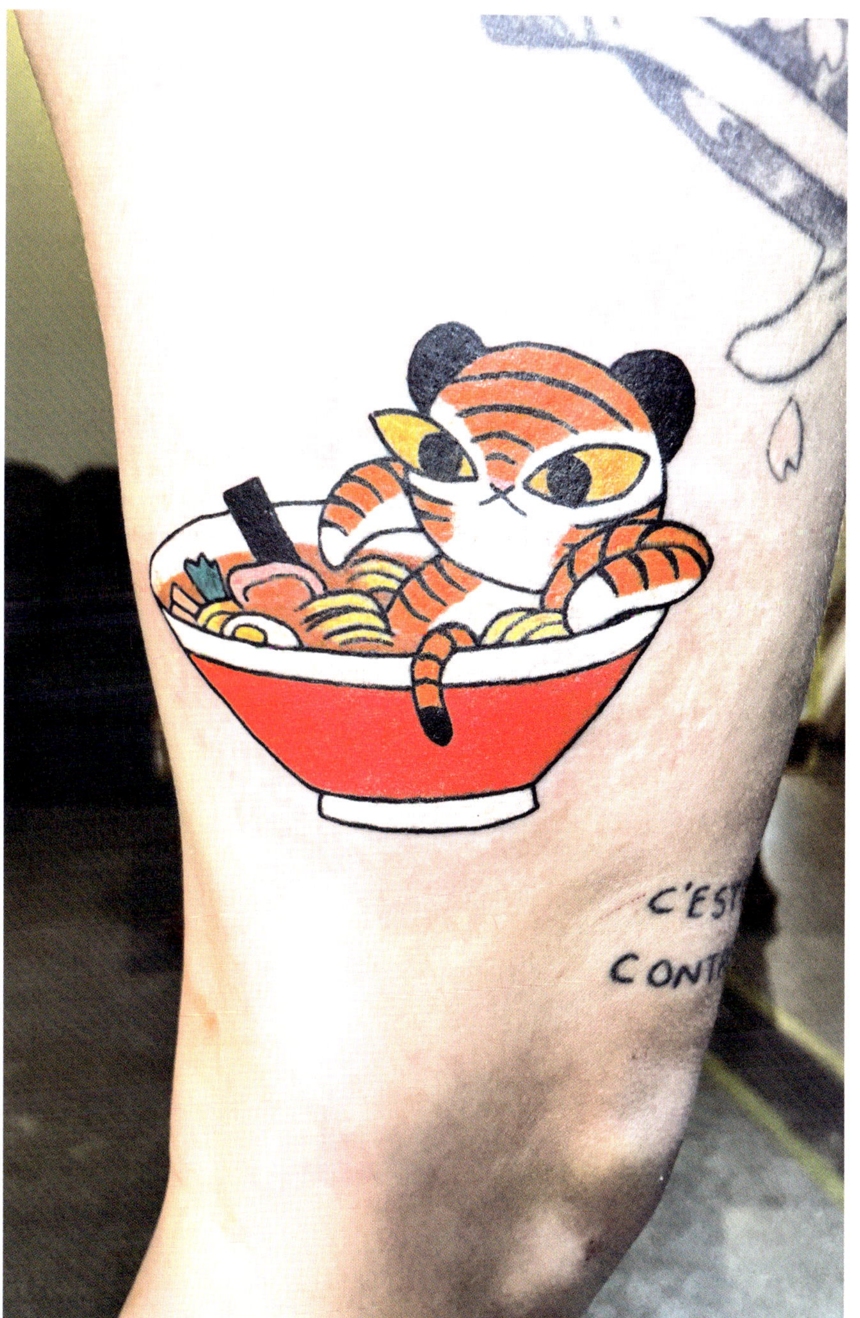

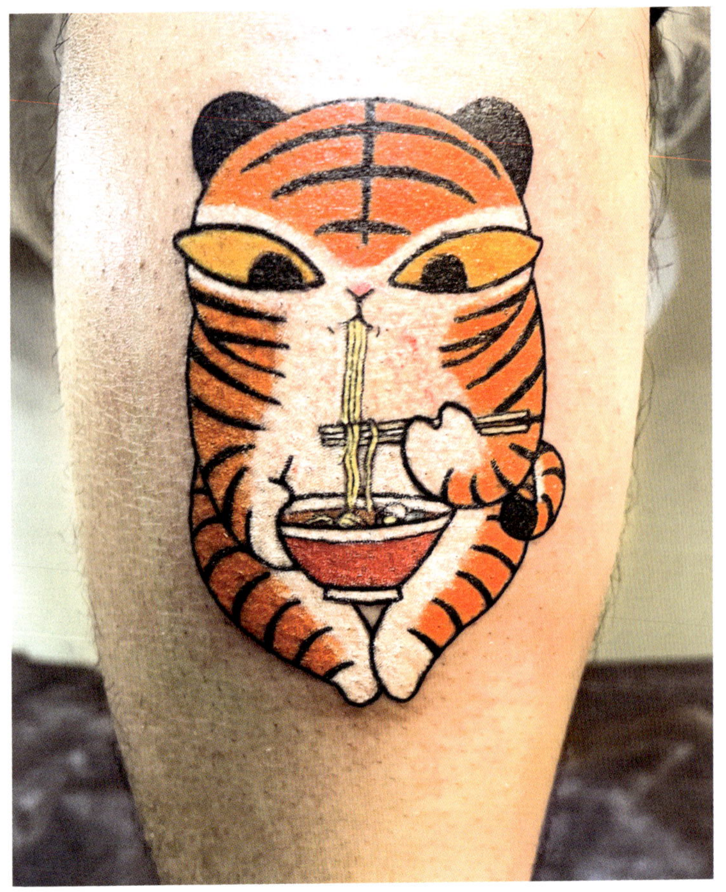

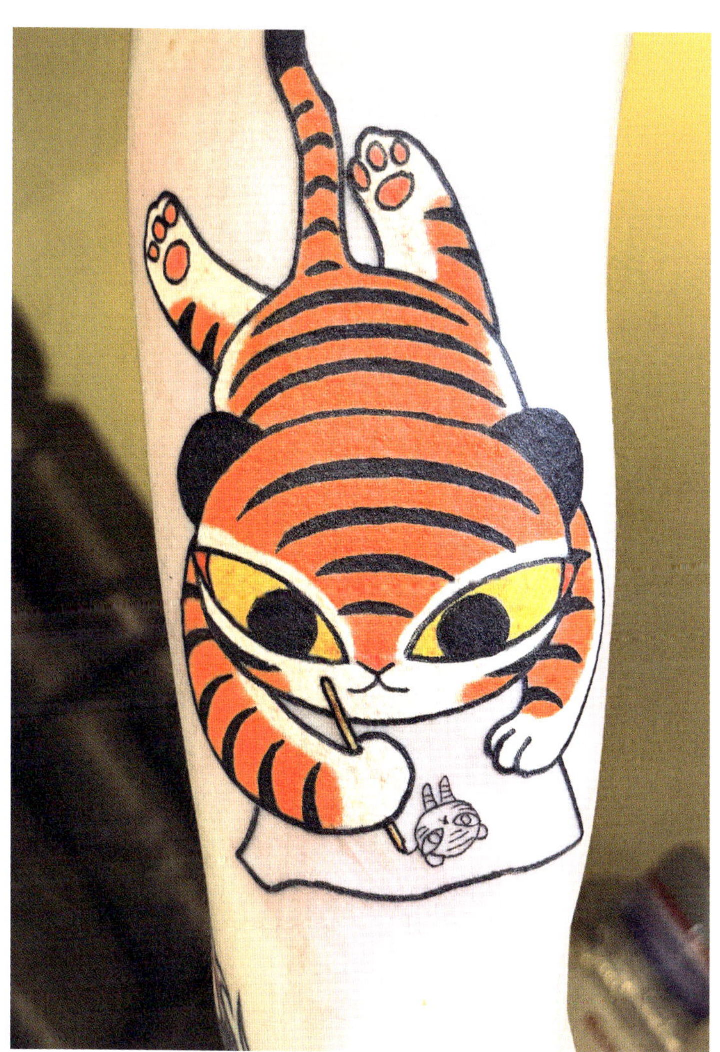

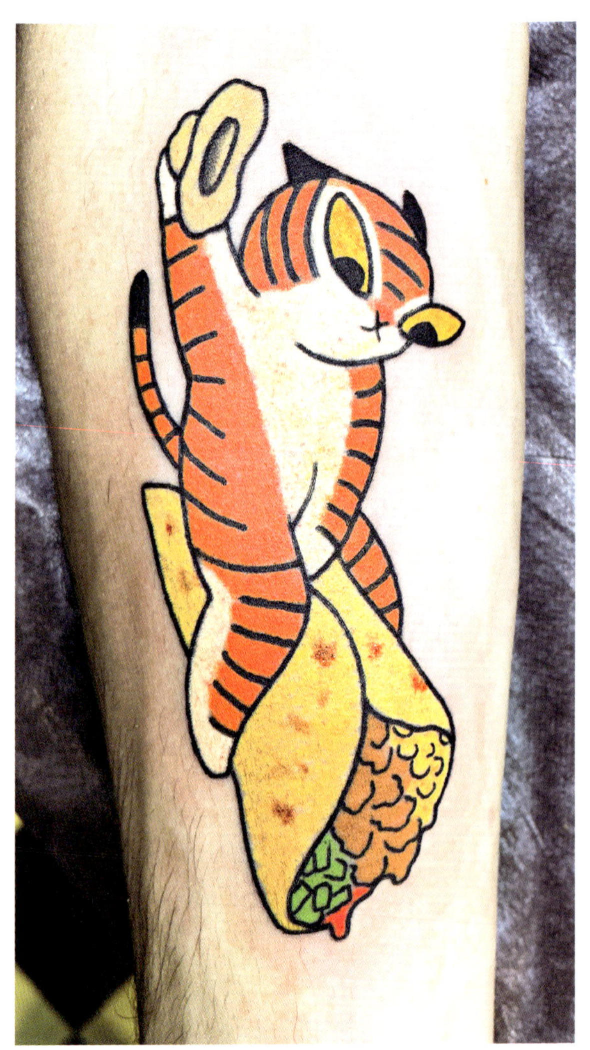

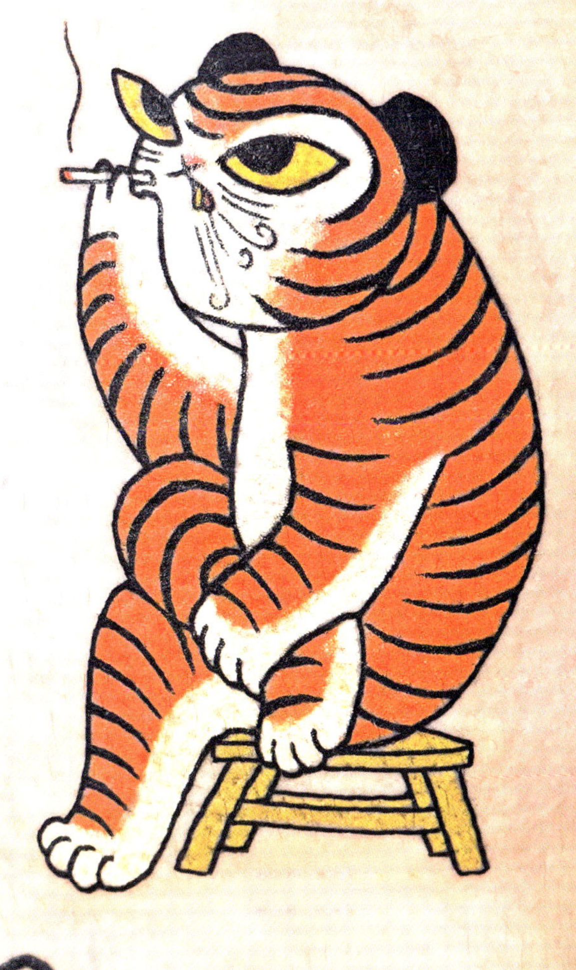

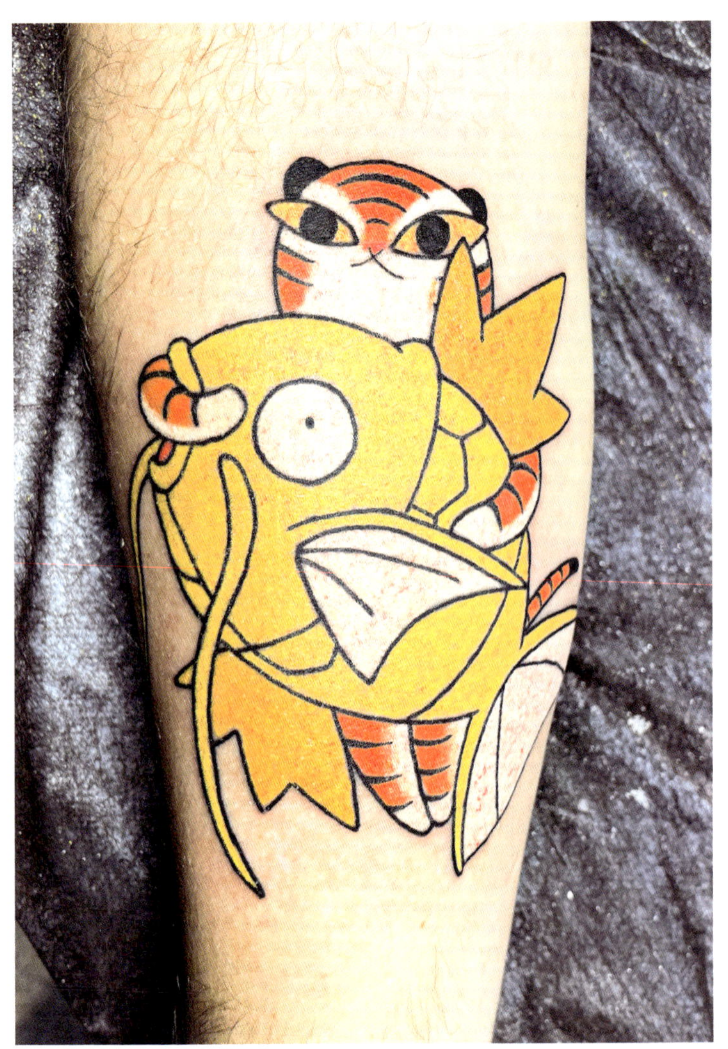

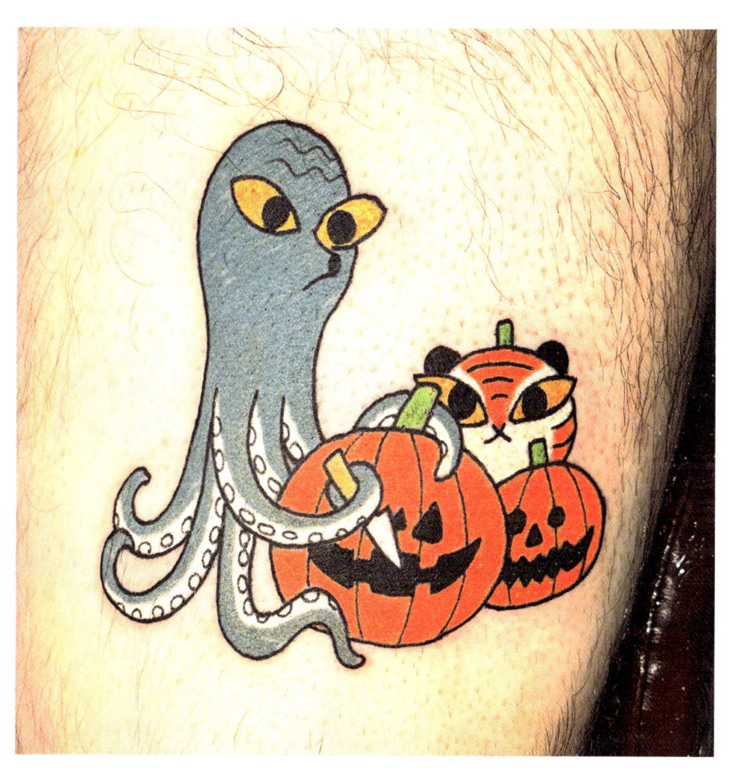

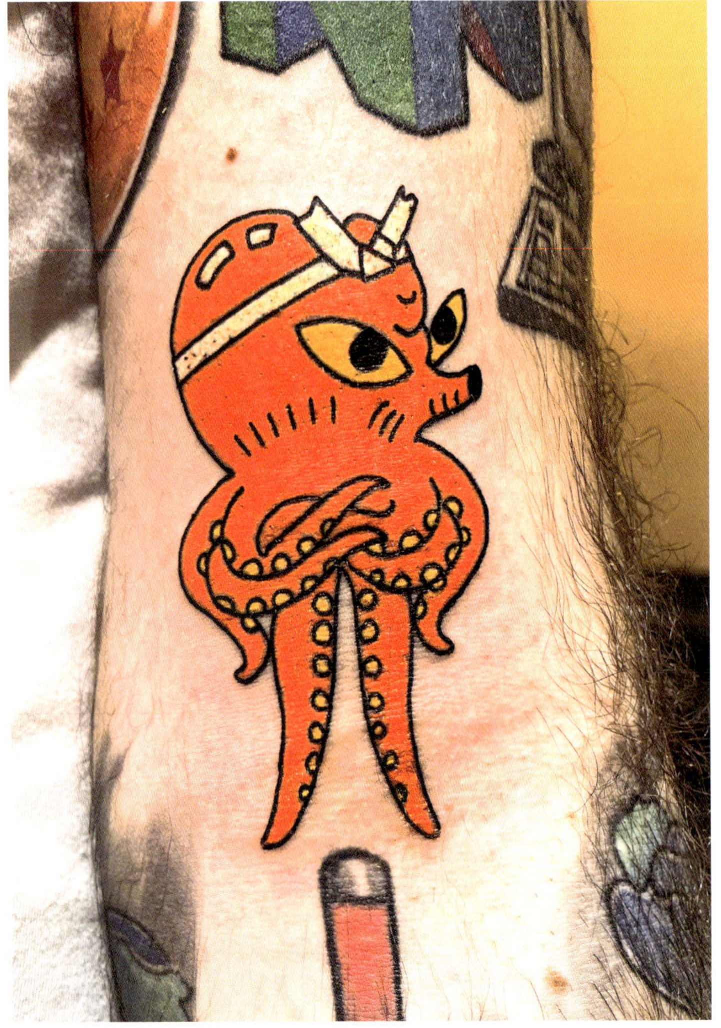

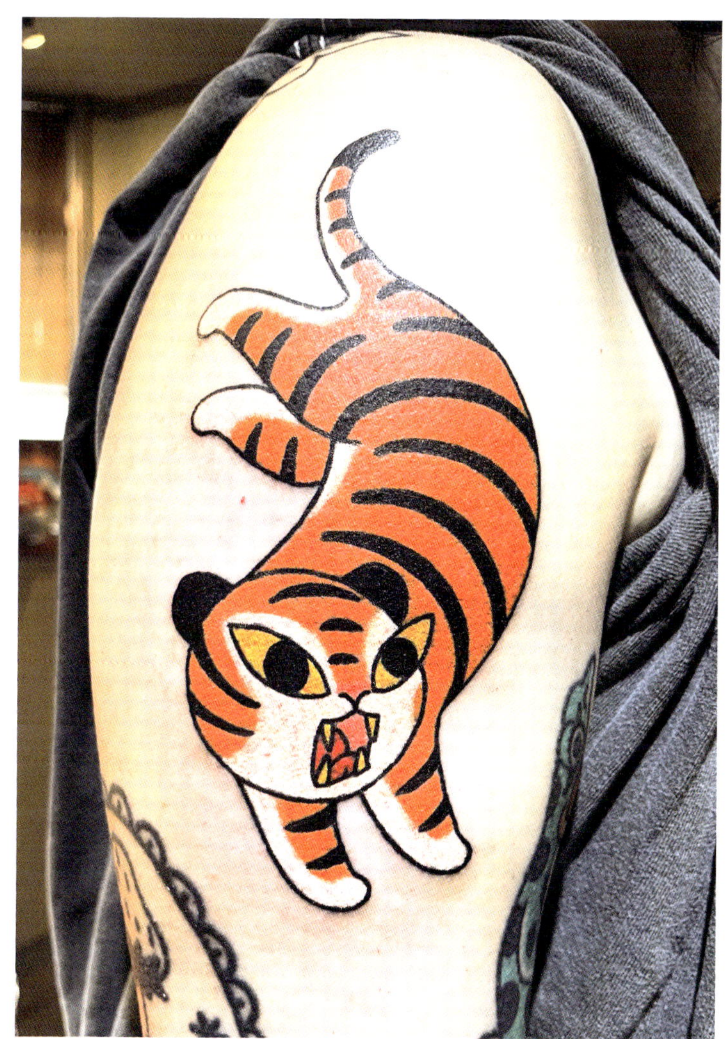

KIWIS N' TREES

Ohio, USA

Kellie Burch, professionally known as Kiwis n' Trees, is a tattoo artist and illustrator based in Ohio, USA. Her career path began in an unexpected place - a traditional office environment - where she thrived in a stable career. Although she had long dismissed her imaginative sketches as not fitting the conventional definitions of 'art', her inner world told a different story. Inspired by whimsical daydreams of moss, fruit with faces and everyday objects wearing socks, Kellie eventually embraced these ideas as meaningful expressions of her identity.

Her introduction to tattooing came through an unexpected opportunity: an invitation from a close friend to become her apprentice. Accepting that offer marked a turning point in her life and career. Today, Kellie is deeply grateful to have found a profession that allows her to connect with others through creativity and storytelling. Through tattooing, she shares artwork that reflects a deep sense of joy, peace and belonging - emotions she hopes to pass on to each person who carries her work.

12.

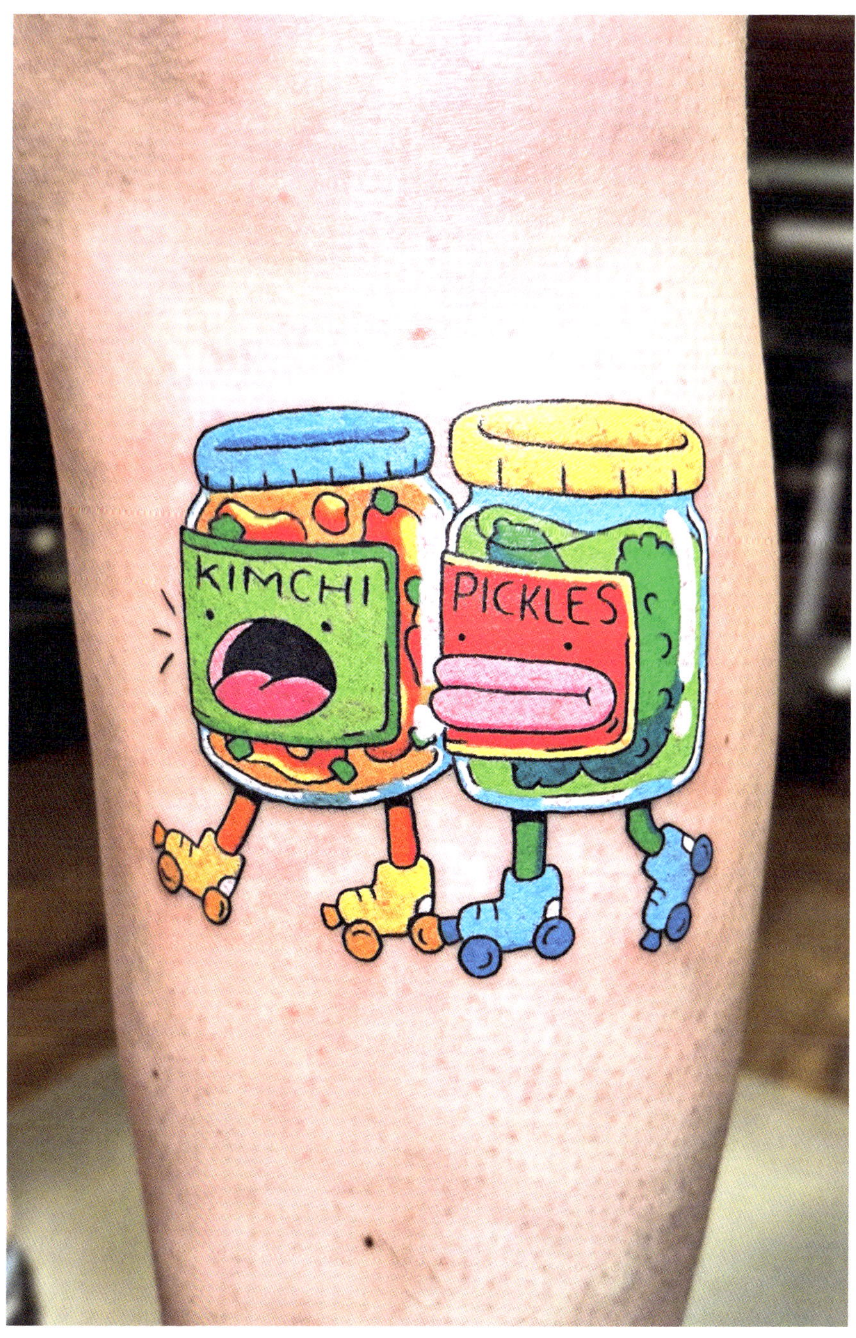
KIMCHI
PICKLES

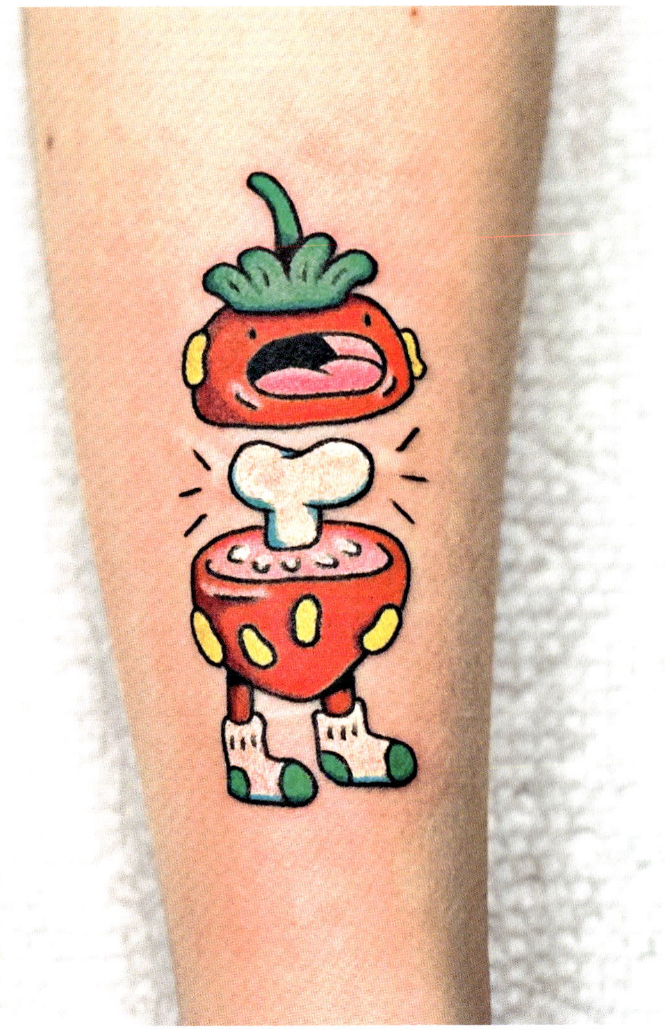

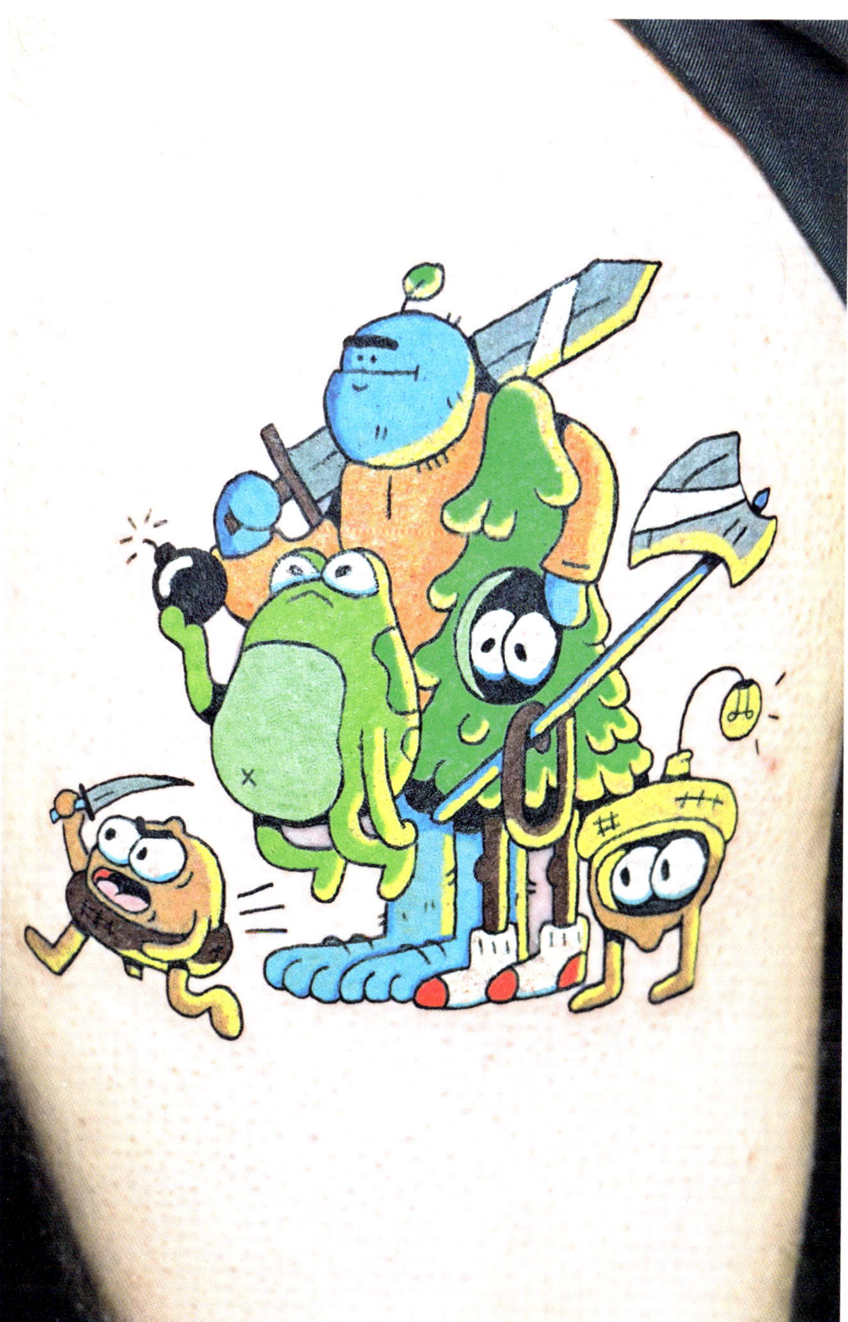

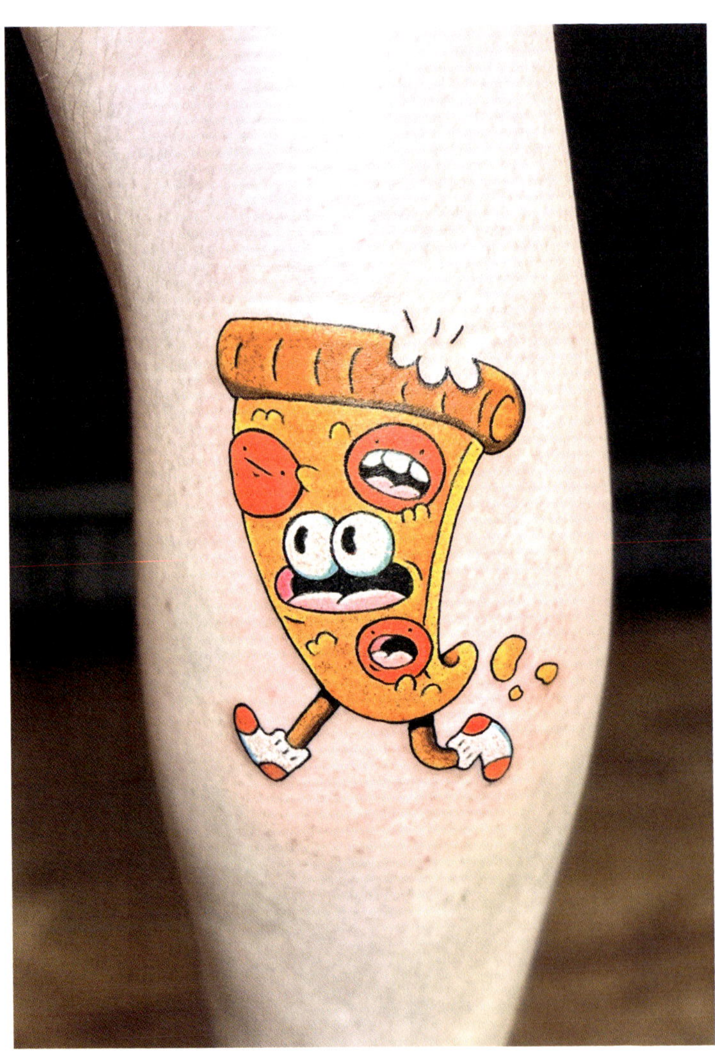

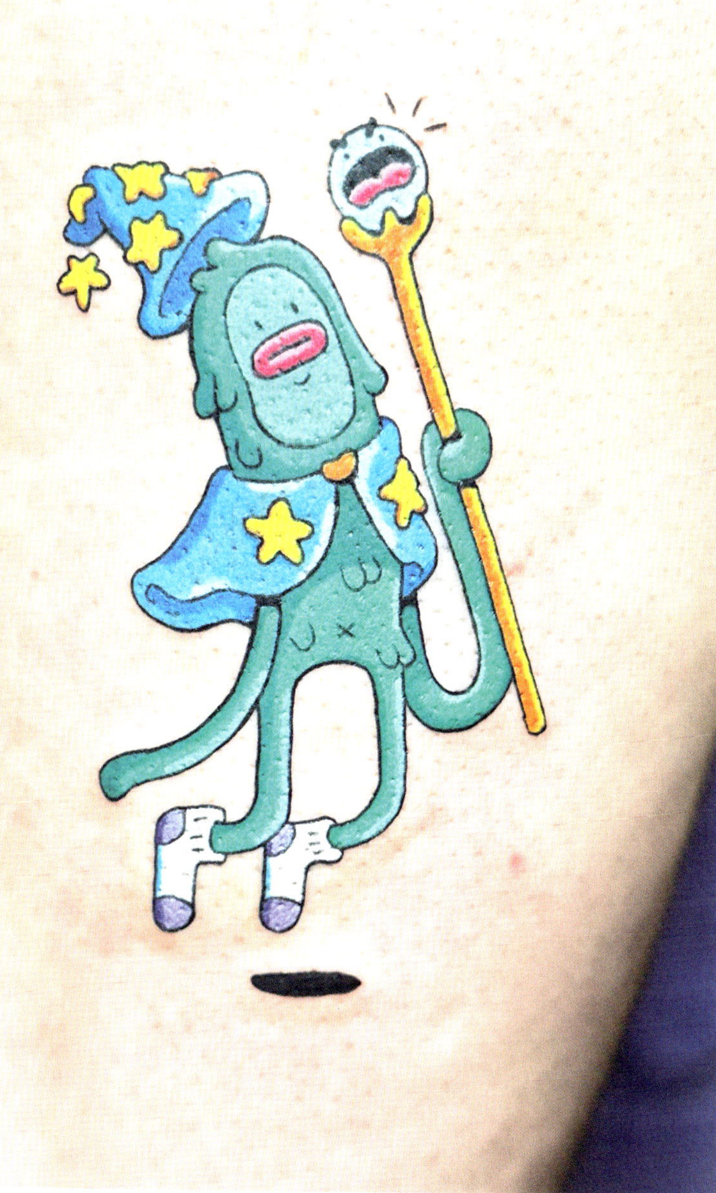

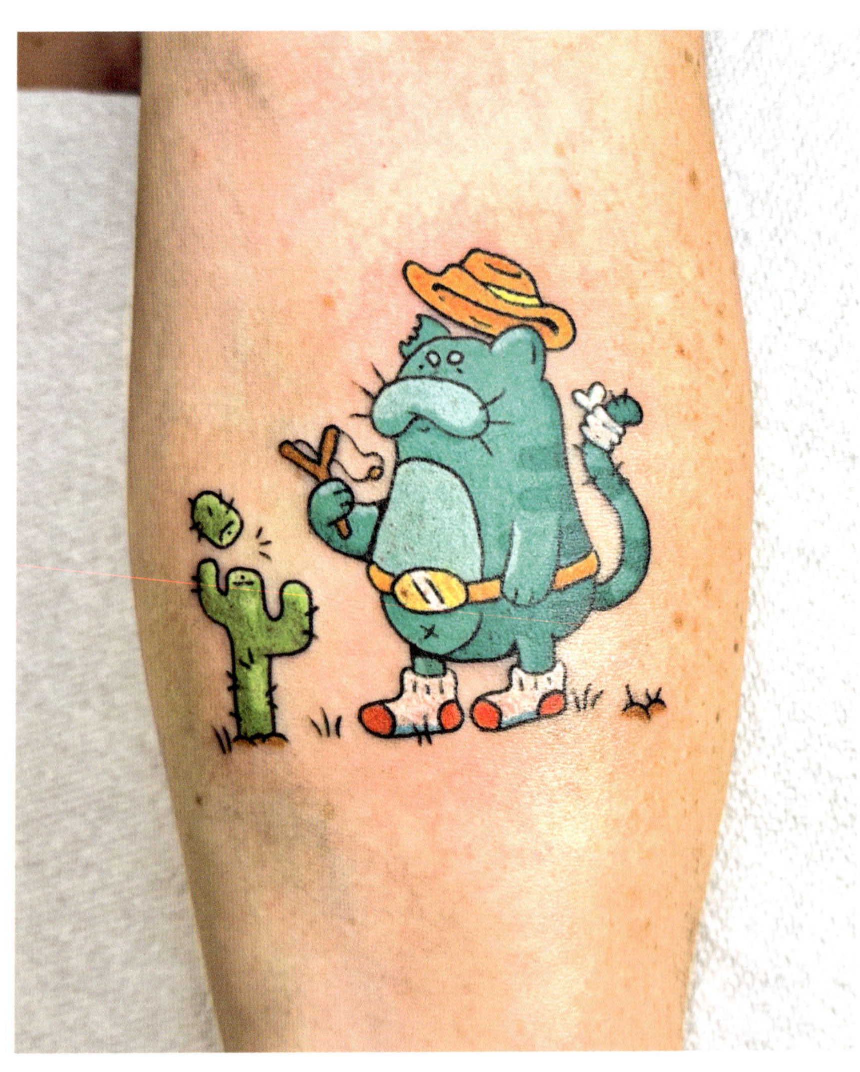

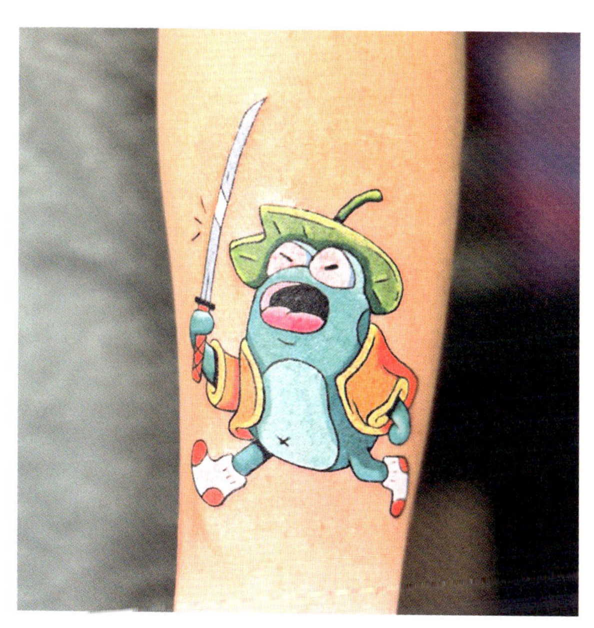

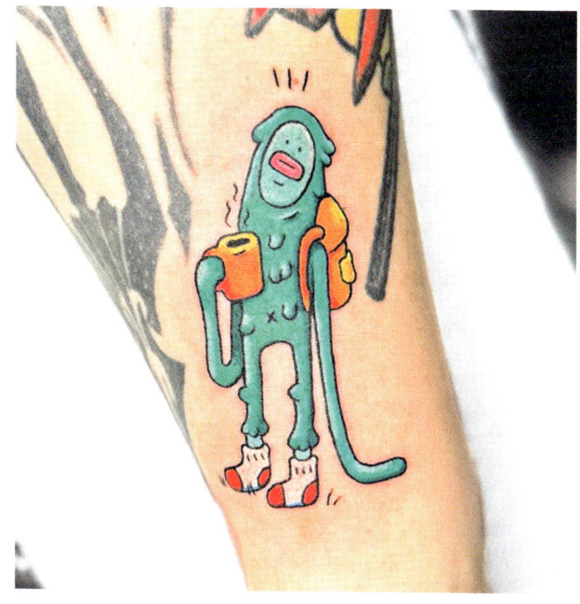

KOBLIN

Seoul, South Korea

Koblin, the alias of Young Kwang Kim, is a tattoo artist based in Seoul, South Korea, working alongside friends at Jangsu Malbeol. His artistic journey began when he took a break from art school and worked part-time at a PC bang and a Korean BBQ restaurant, ultimately realising that corporate life wasn't for him.

In 2019, he committed to his craft and began his tattooing career. Initially drawing inspiration from media and books, he now likes to observe everyday life on the streets, finding creativity in the small details of his surroundings.

Known for his playful, childlike and linocut-inspired aesthetic, Koblin's work captures a sense of nostalgia and fun, making each tattoo a unique and memorable piece. Lately, he has taken a particular interest in gnomes, embracing whimsical ideas that add charm to his art. Always grateful for the opportunity to share his work, he continues to explore new creative directions while staying true to his style.

13.

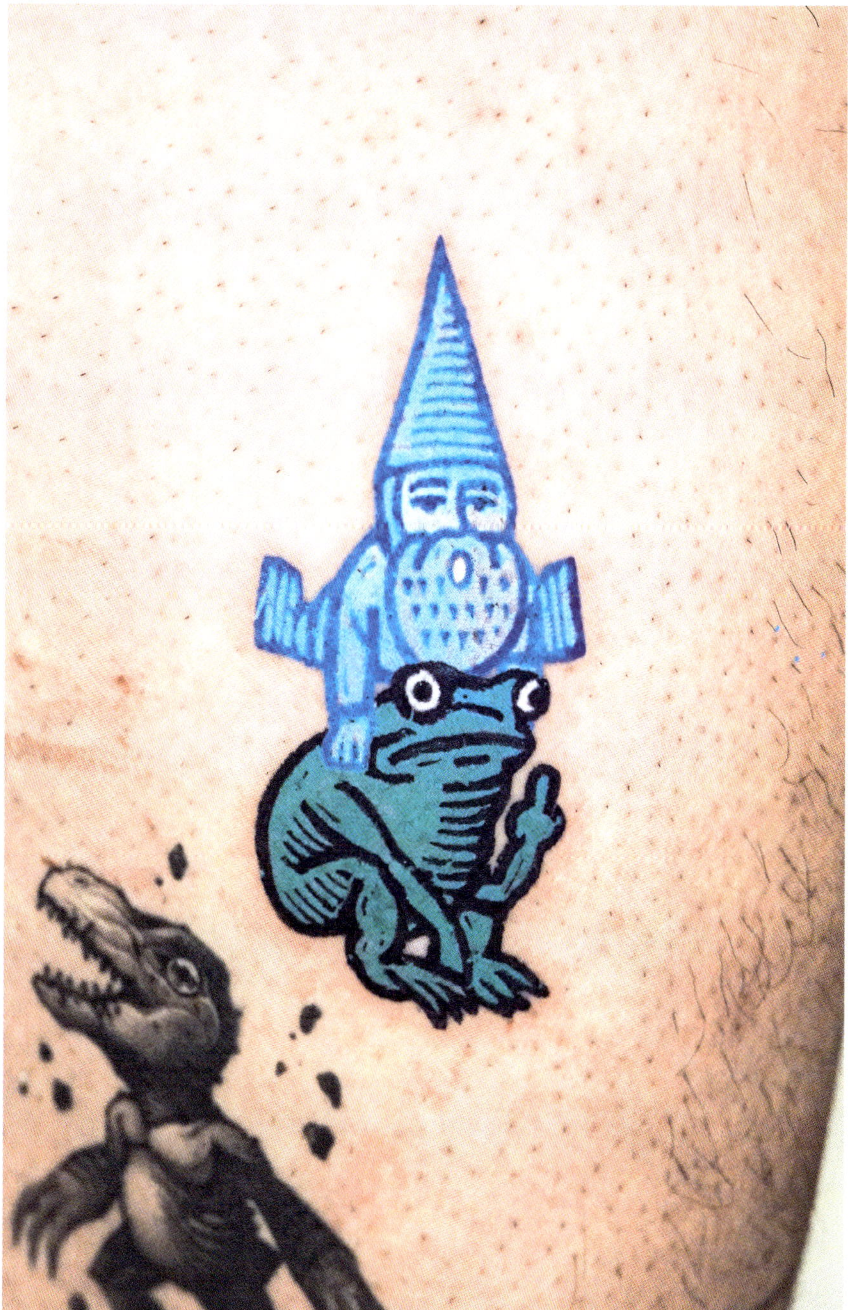

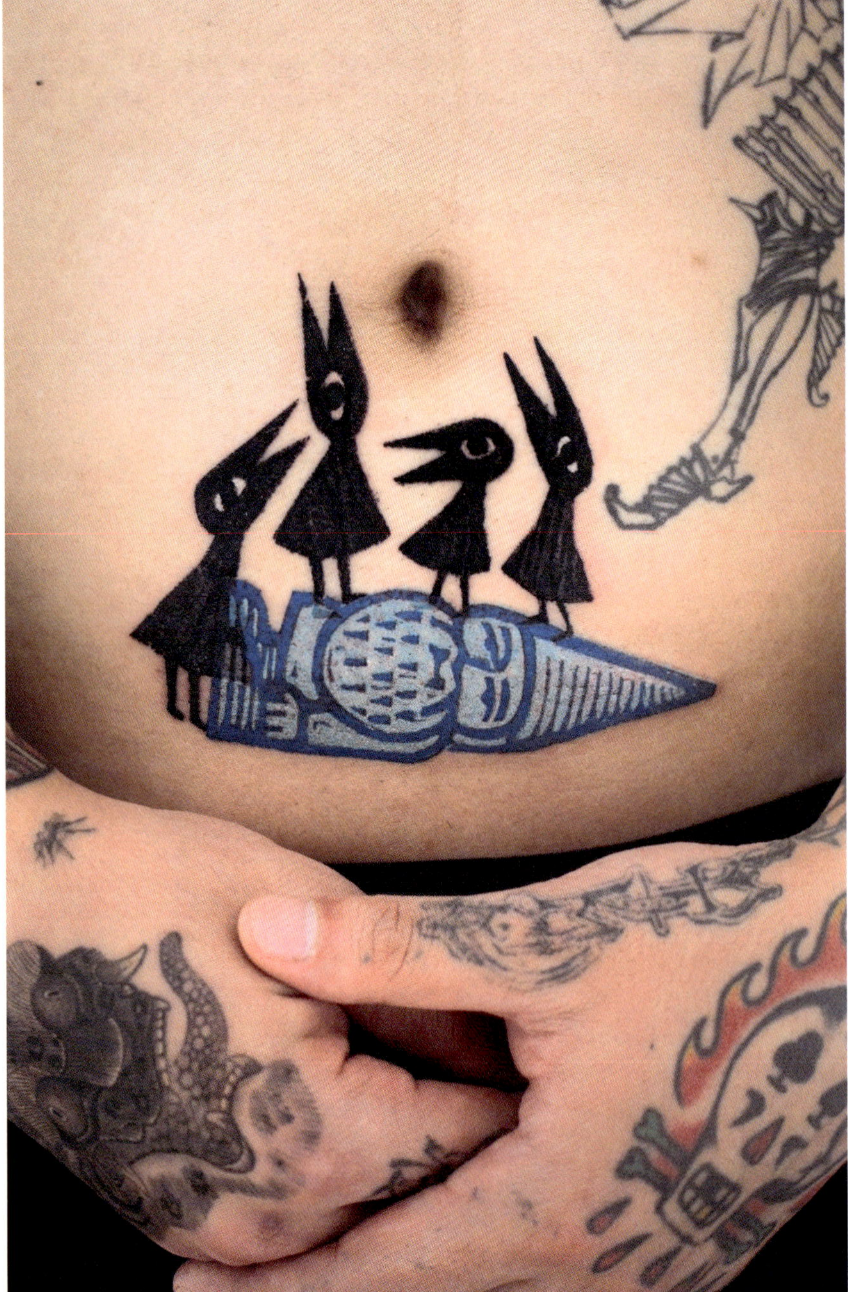

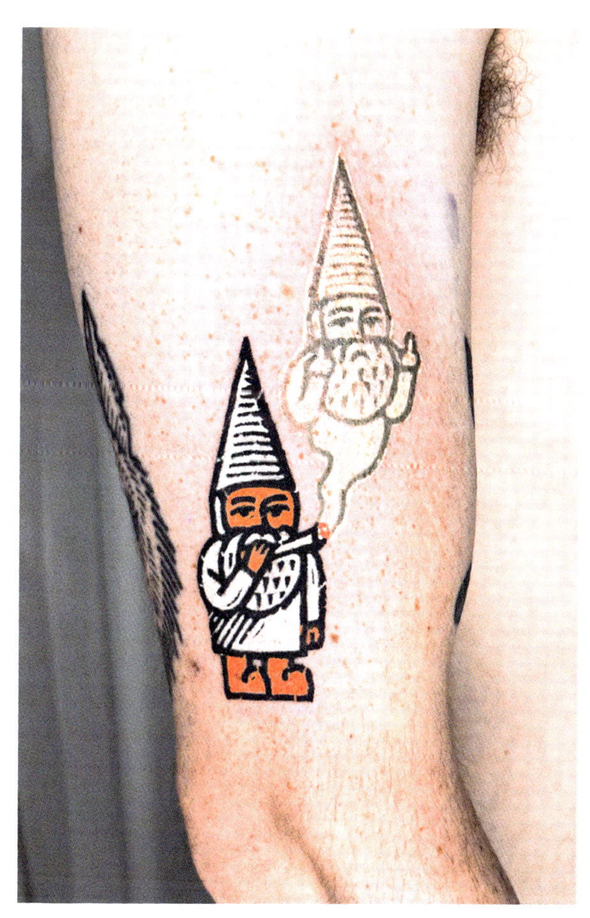

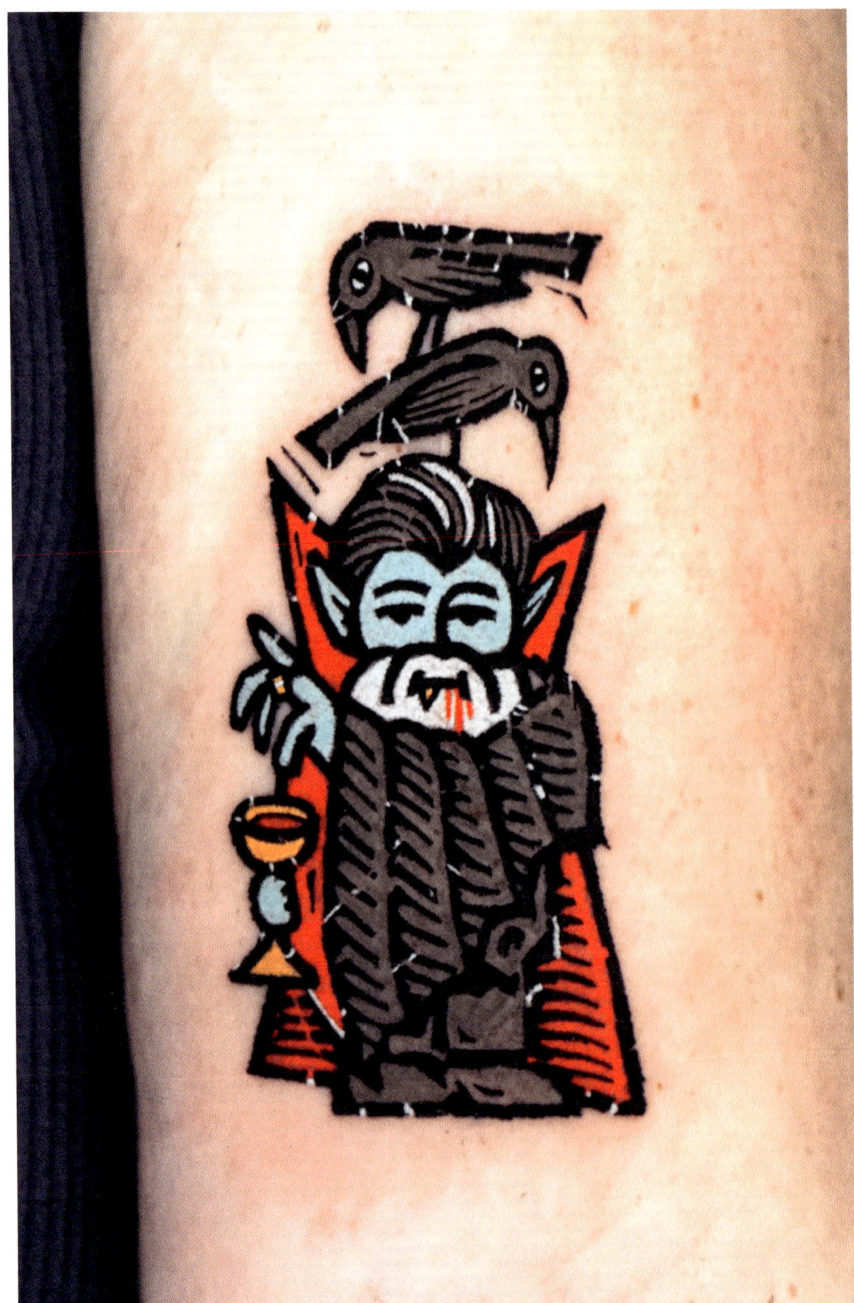

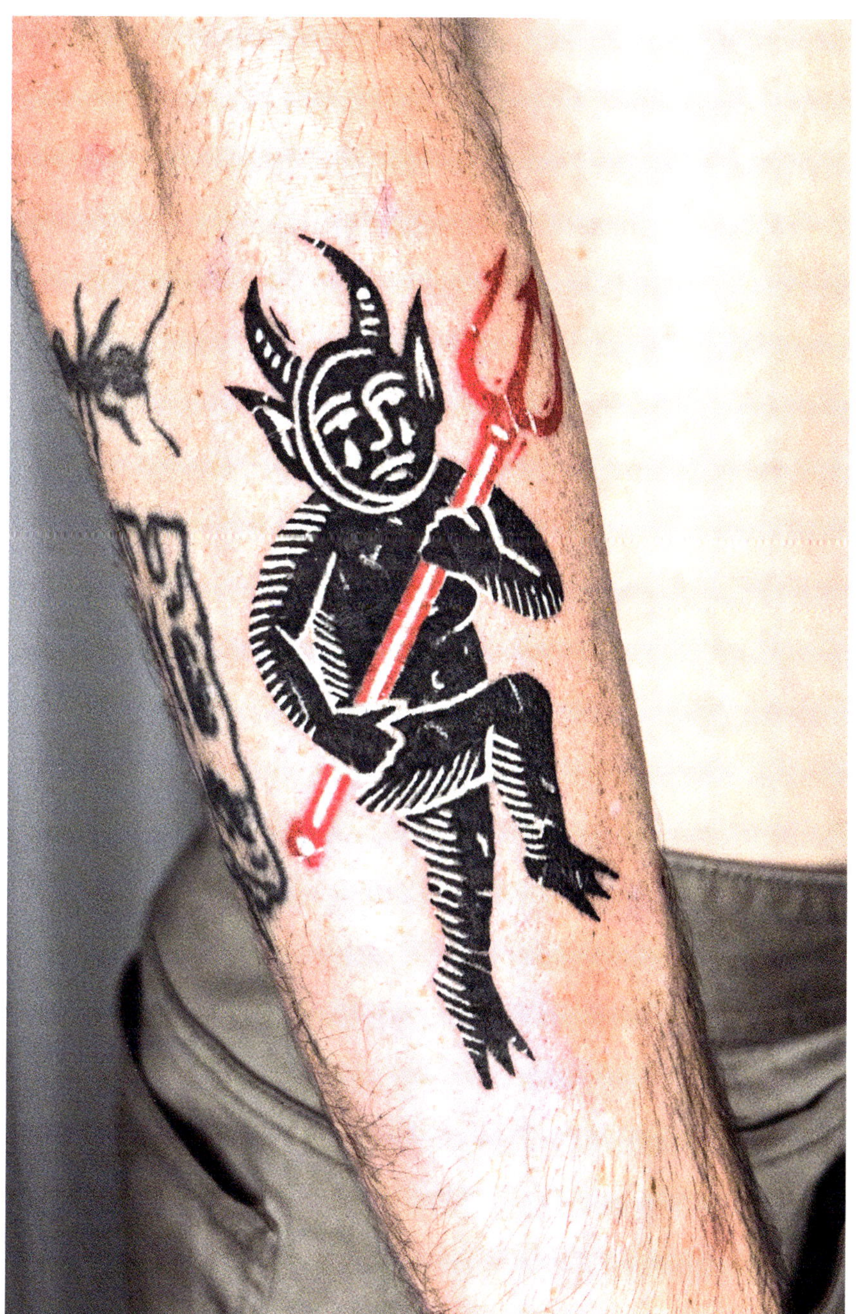

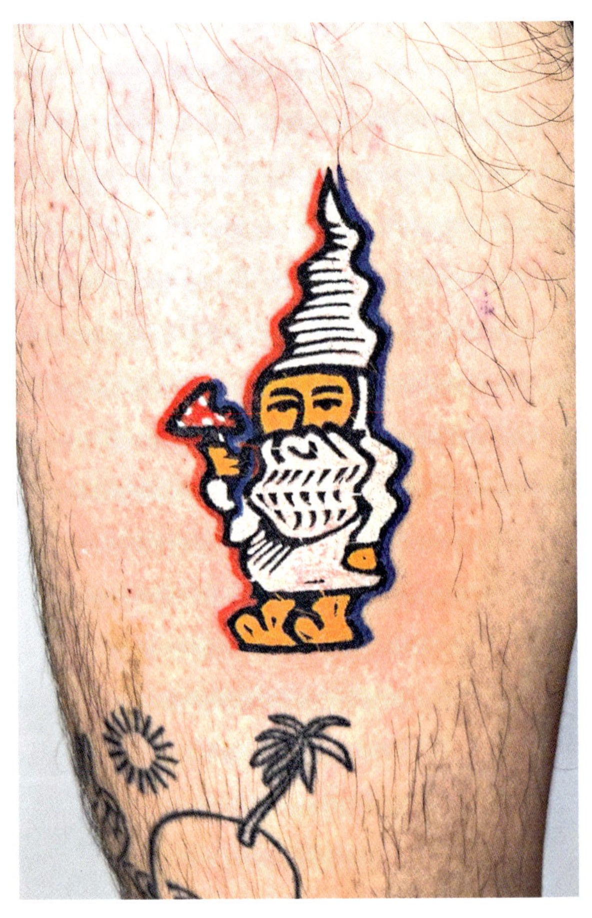

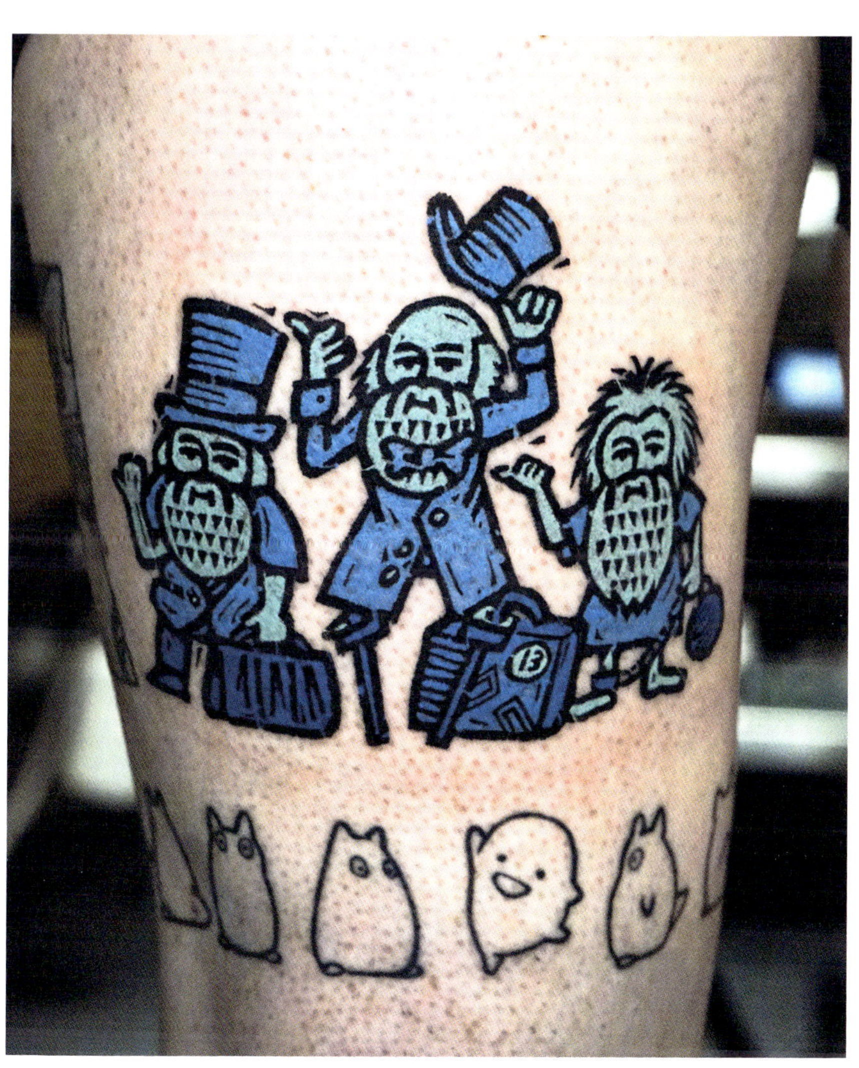
13

LINDA FLOWERS

Rome, Italy

Linda Rocchi, professionally known as Linda Flowers, is a tattoo artist and illustrator based in Rome, Italy, currently working at Area Industriale. Her work is distinguished by a unique fusion of dark humour, emotional depth and surrealism, often depicting creatures that personify inner struggles in both tender and ironic ways. Through her art, Linda seeks to craft a world that is more captivating and thought-provoking than reality itself.

Beyond tattooing, she is deeply passionate about film and continuously explores new artistic techniques, pushing the boundaries of her creative expression. When she's not immersed in her work, Linda enjoys cooking, discovering new flavours and spending time with her two black cats, Mulder and Scully, who provide both companionship and inspiration.

14.

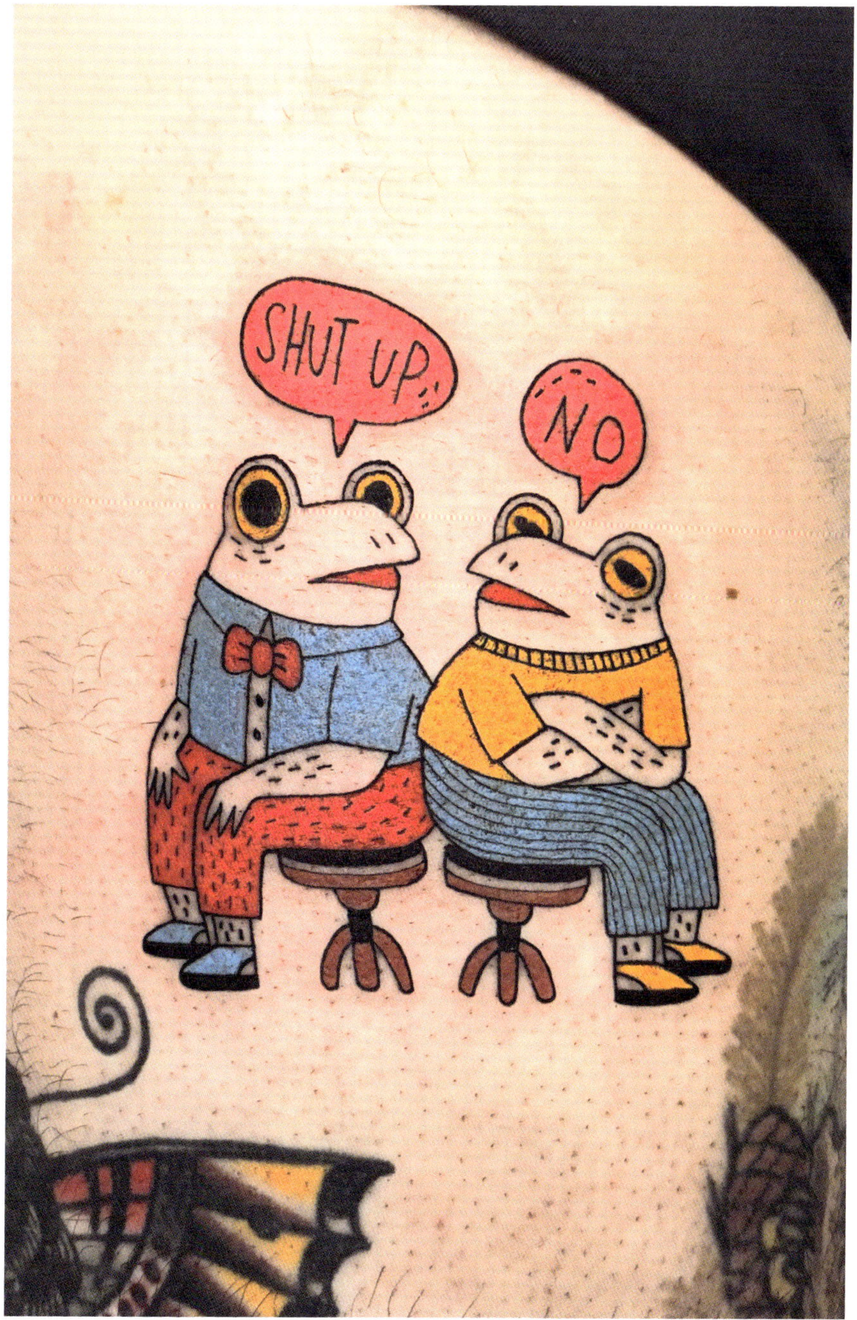
SHUT UP
NO

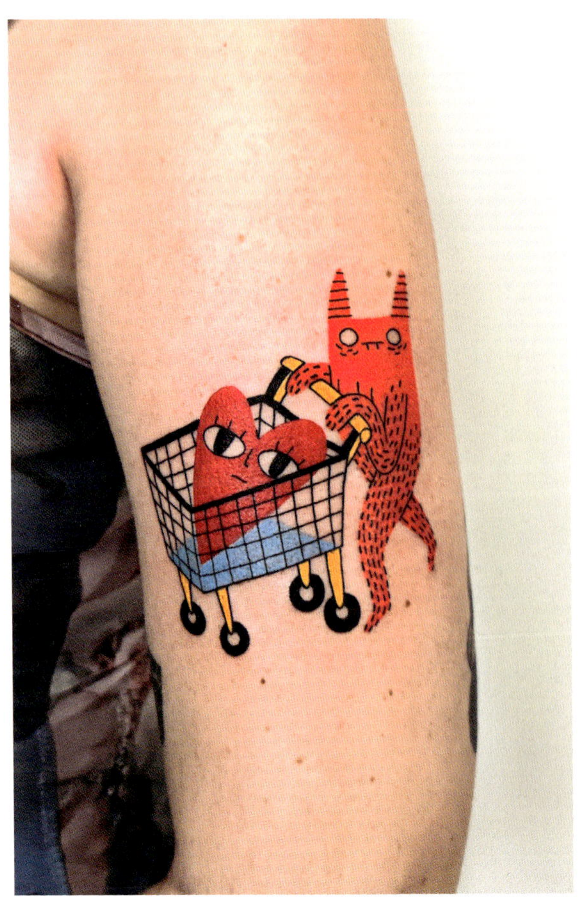

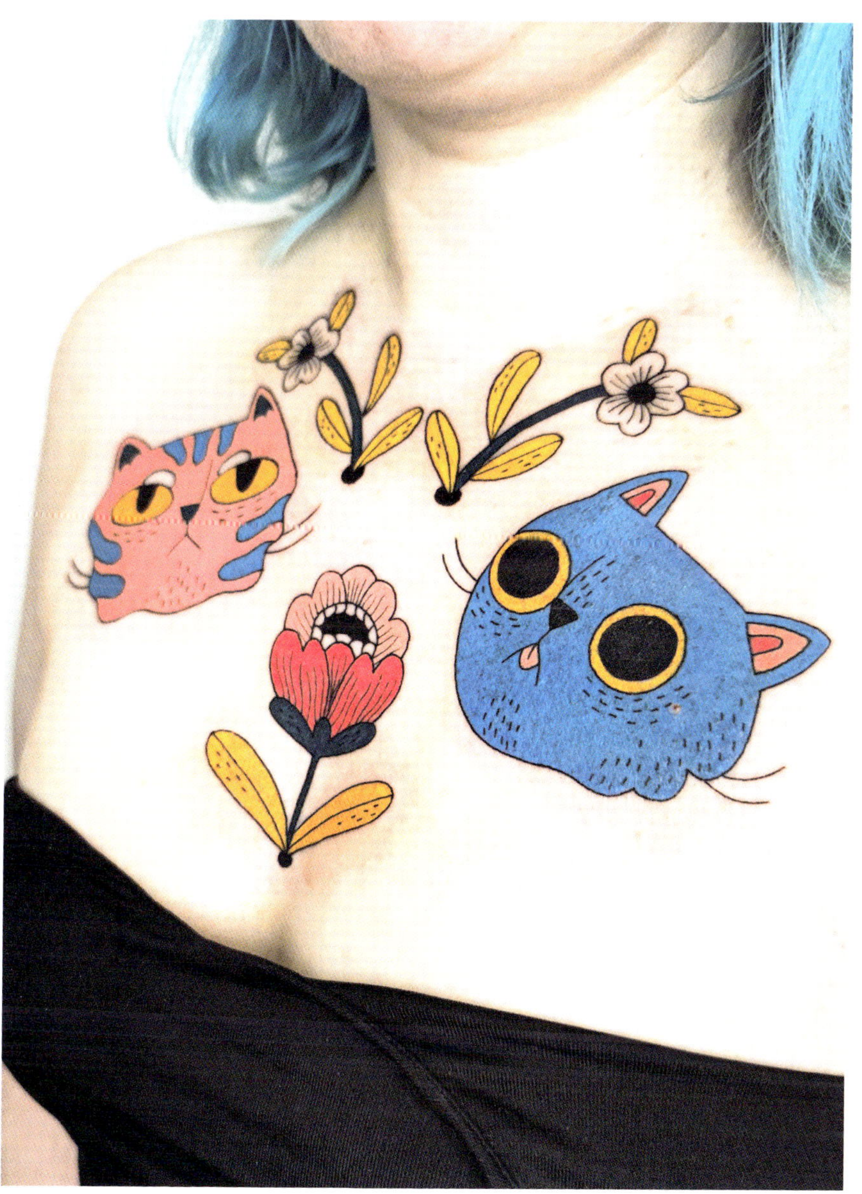

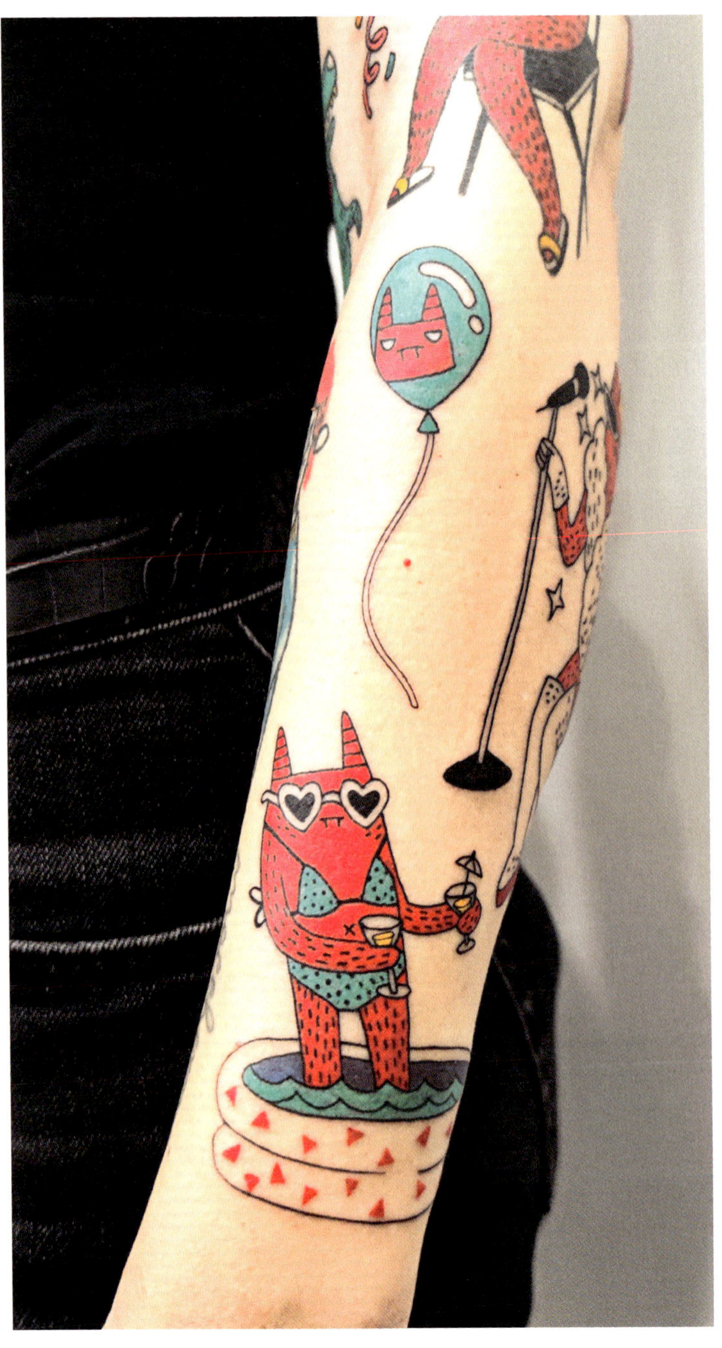

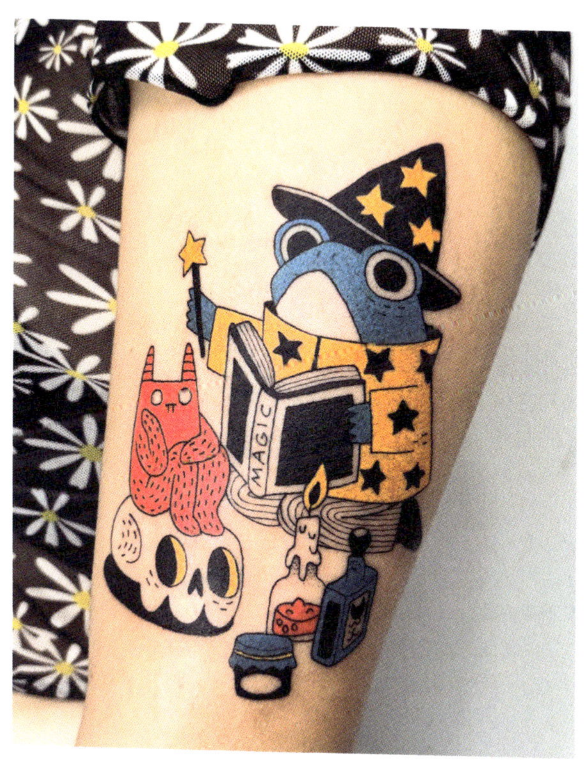
MAGIC

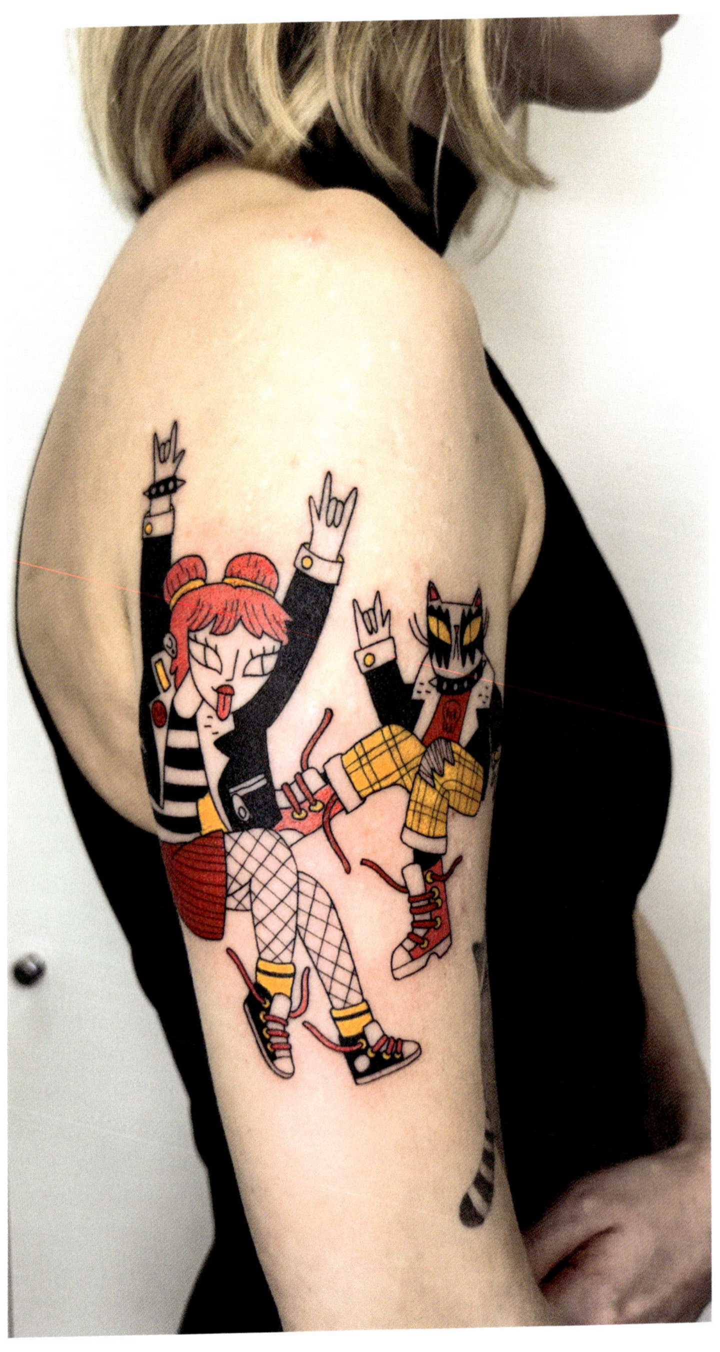

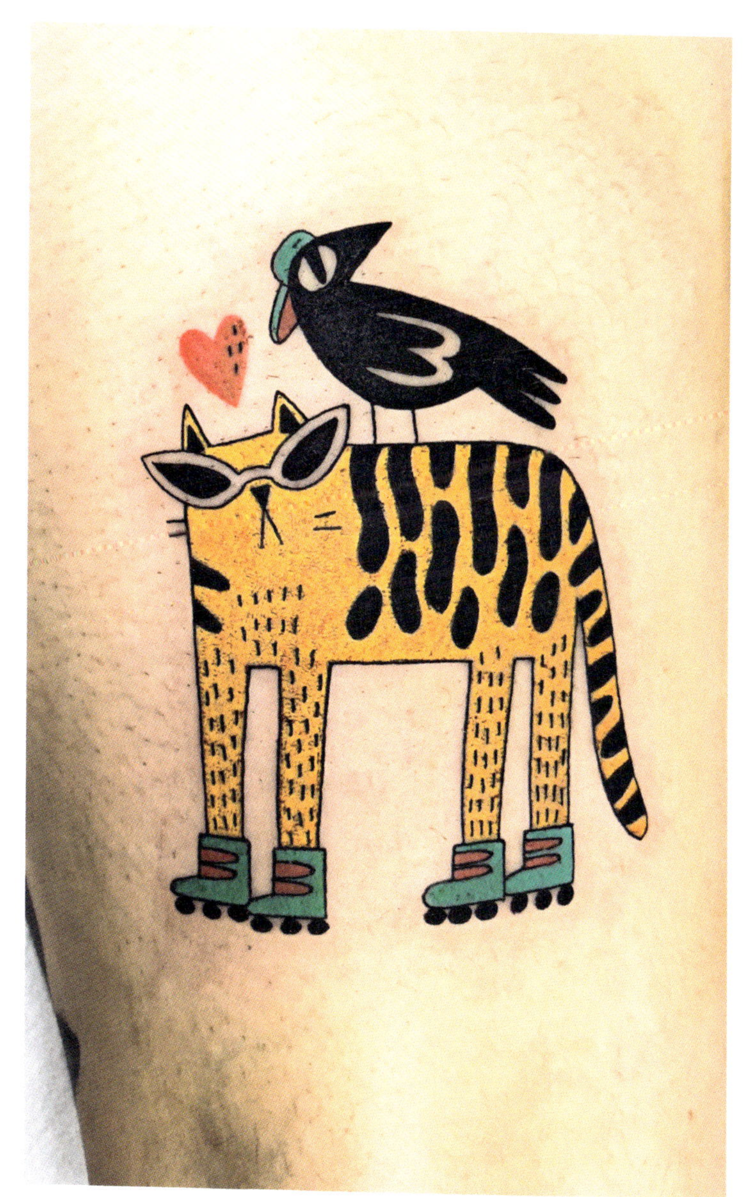

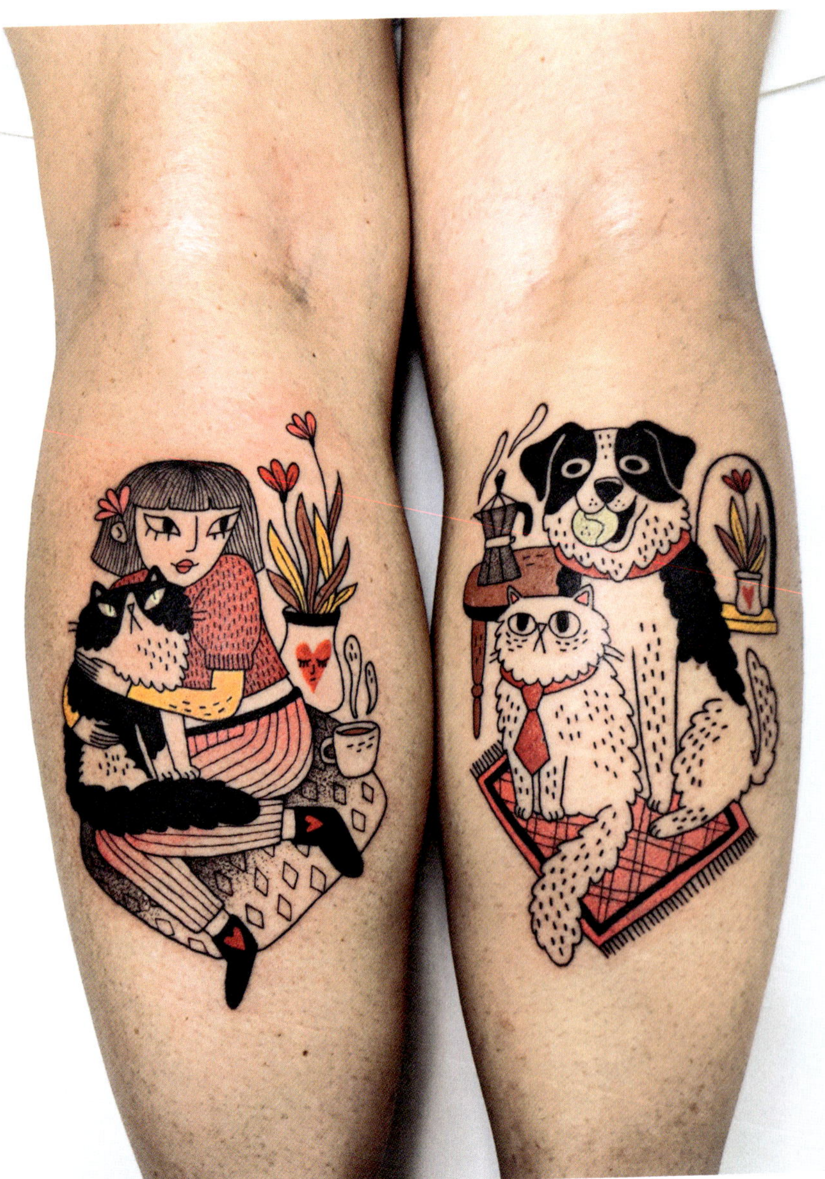

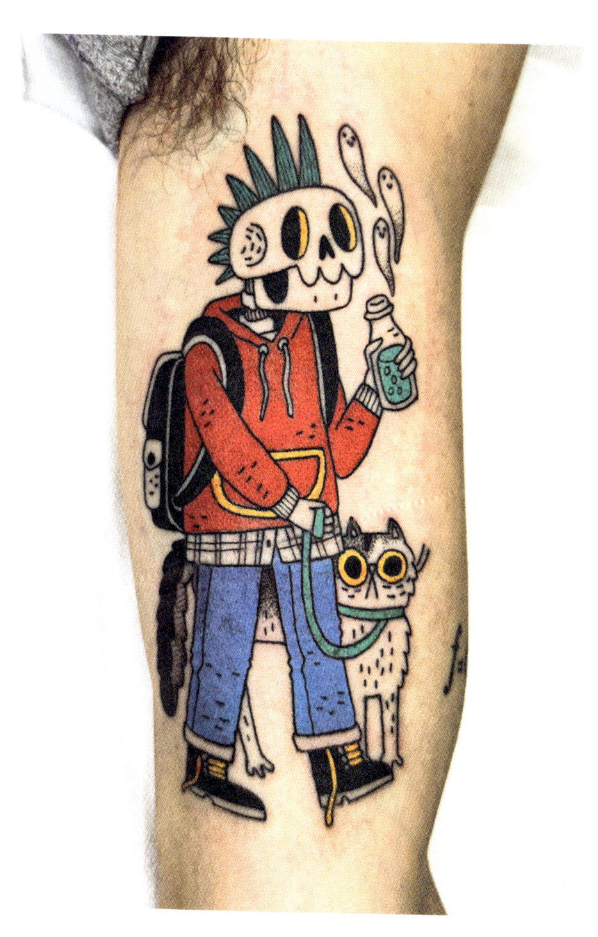

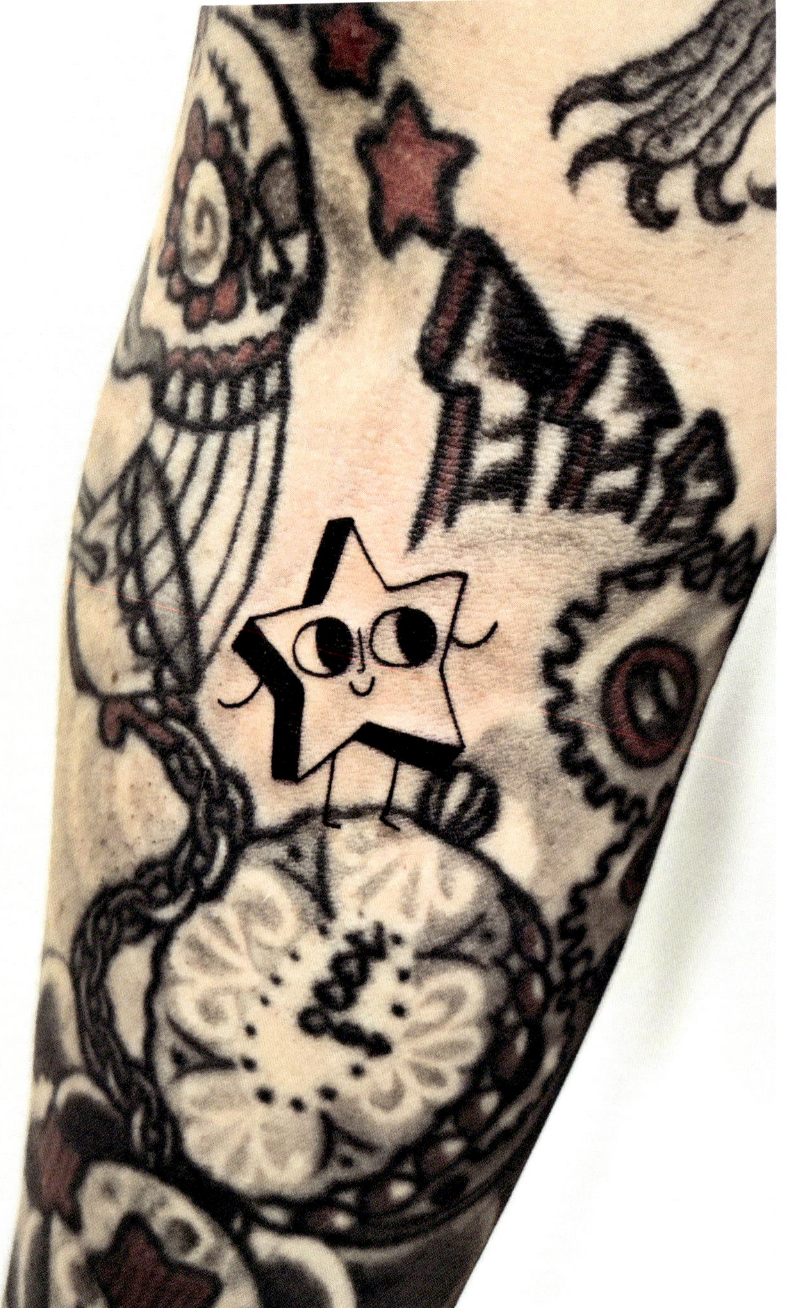

Hi Linda, how did you come up with your artist's name?
My full name is Linda Rocchi, but on social media I go by Linda Flowers. I originally chose it because I didn't want to use my real name on Facebook, but I kept it for so long that it eventually became my artist's name without me even realising it! It comes from Ramona Flowers, a character from the comic *Scott Pilgrim*. Back when I picked the name, I was a huge fan of the series (and still am!).

How did you get into tattooing?
It all started because I wanted to move abroad, but I also wanted to have a job I loved before making such a big change. Encouraged mainly by a friend, I started studying to become a tattoo artist – and in the end, I never moved! I've been tattooing professionally for seven years now, but I studied for five years before making it my actual job. I also did a traditional apprenticeship for about a year, where my role was to assist the tattoo artist who was mentoring me, watch them work and help with cleaning the studio.

What was the first tattoo you ever did?
The first tattoo I ever did was a small Frank from *Donnie Darko* on my ankle. I only had enough money to buy the machine, so I tattooed myself. It was super exciting – and also one of the worst spots to find out what it feels like!

Do you remember your very first customer?
Oh, I remember this one! It was a ridiculously long script tattoo on the ribs, with a lipstick kiss at the end. I was sweating so much!

Do you remember a specific customer or story that stands out?

I remember this guy who came all the way from Los Angeles to get tattooed by me. He asked for three custom designs, and one of them was a portrait of his mum holding their dog. Everything was going great until I suddenly realised I had just given the dog a fifth leg! I panicked and was completely mortified. But he reacted in the sweetest way possible, calmed me down, and gave me time to think of a solution. In the end, I managed to fix it, and he liked it even more than the original design. We laughed about it afterwards, but I'll never forget the terror I felt in that moment!

What makes your tattoos special?

I would say my designs are positive, tragic, surreal and magical. They almost always bring a smile to someone's face, even on a bad day. I've been told this several times, and I really like it as a description.

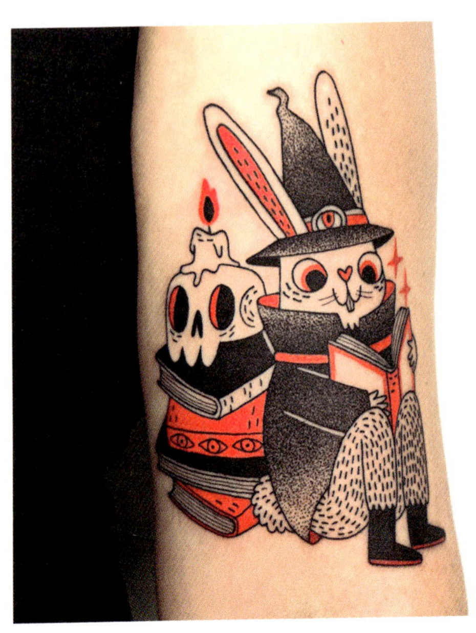

What is your main inspiration?
Life itself. I try to fill it with cats and other animals, witches, demons and magic - placing them in a modern setting with an ironic twist. I follow many illustrators who inspire me technically, but I also draw inspiration from everything around me - my feelings, my cats, movies, comics, video games and people.

Why did you choose the technique you work with today?
I don't think I ever consciously chose the technique I use for tattooing. It was the result of research and figuring out what I like best in terms of outcome. The learning process never really stops, so every now and then, I try to add something new and refine the rest.

How do you approach the design process with your clients?
I always start by listening to the client's ideas. I allow as much space as possible for their vision, try to understand how to bring it to life, and then discuss it again with them once I've set everything up. I always give them the chance to modify anything - even completely change it - as long as we both like the final design.

Has the tattoo landscape changed a lot since you first started?
I like it better now. There are always opportunities to discover new tattoo artists, techniques and perspectives. Since I started, everything has changed a lot, from tattoo machines to social media. The approach and challenges are different. Before, it was hard to get noticed and to learn how to tattoo with coil machines. Now, the challenge is to stay consistent and stand out in the crowd of tattoo artists.

Do you think social media has affected tattooing?
It's a double-edged sword. It gives exposure and opportunities, but it also pressures artists to be influencers, which I find exhausting.

Has tattooing had a positive impact on your life?
Yes! Now I have a job that I love, and sometimes, when I think about the fact that I can make a living doing what I enjoy, it feels like a dream. One of the biggest benefits has been on a personal level – I'm naturally quite introverted, and working in environments with other people, travelling, and being in such close contact with clients has helped me grow so much as a person.

Were your parents or family happy about your career choice?
My parents have always supported me. They've been a huge help, and my mum even got her first tattoo from me when I was just starting out. My dad doesn't really see the point of tattoos, but he supports me anyway. If I could tell all of this to my younger self, she'd be shocked!

How do you think society's perception of tattoos has evolved over time?
I live in a big city with tons of tattoo studios, but only in recent years have I noticed that people pay less attention to who has tattoos and who doesn't. Of course, there will always be people who judge you just because you have tattoos, but times are changing. My mum, for example, is proof of that – she was born in the 1950s, but to her credit she has no prejudice against tattoos.

Do you think tattoos can make the world a happier place?

I don't think tattoos can save the world, but they can make it better - just like any other form of art. Even though tattoos are often seen as just a trend or a temporary act of rebellion, they have the power to create positive change in society.

Do you ever think about getting older as a tattoo artist?

Yeah, and I always picture myself with wrist pain in some weird, twisted position like a shrimp. But seriously, sometimes I like to think I'll pass on my tattooing work to someone else, but I'll still be doing something in the art world.

Besides tattooing, what other creative fields make you happy?

I love trying out every artistic technique. I wish I could live in an art supplies shop, so I'd have all the materials available to me and could experiment with everything. I also love cooking, creating digital illustrations and animating in 2D.

What three things are you passionate about beyond tattooing?

I love having breakfast, making animations, and I really like grocery shopping in supermarkets abroad.

What do you wish for the future generation of tattoo artists?

I hope they make the best use of AI without losing their creativity, that they have as much fun as possible, and that they come up with a method to make tattooing less painful for those who love tattoos but suffer a lot (I also wish this for future clients). I also hope they no longer have to be influencers just to be able to do their job.

LIPNE TATTOO

Kraków, Poland

Szymon Lipowski, known professionally as Lipne Tattoo, is a Polish tattoo artist based in Kraków, specialising in the 'ignorant' style of tattoos. His artistic journey began in 2019 as a form of therapeutic self-expression, following a personal struggle with mental health and substance use. Inspired by his tattoo-covered therapist, he began to dream of creating art on people, hoping to inspire others through his work.

A graduate of the Academy of Fine Arts in Katowice, Lipowski is deeply interested in psychology and travel, frequently working in studios around the world. His work continues to evolve as he connects with diverse artistic communities, using tattooing as a medium for both self-reflection and shared experience.

At the heart of Lipowski's artistry is his original character, George, a figure that explores themes of existential anxiety, depression and emotional confusion. With a heavily ironic tone and strong ties to internet culture, George embodies feelings of solitude, sadness and being lost in reality, all while evoking joy and resilience.

15.

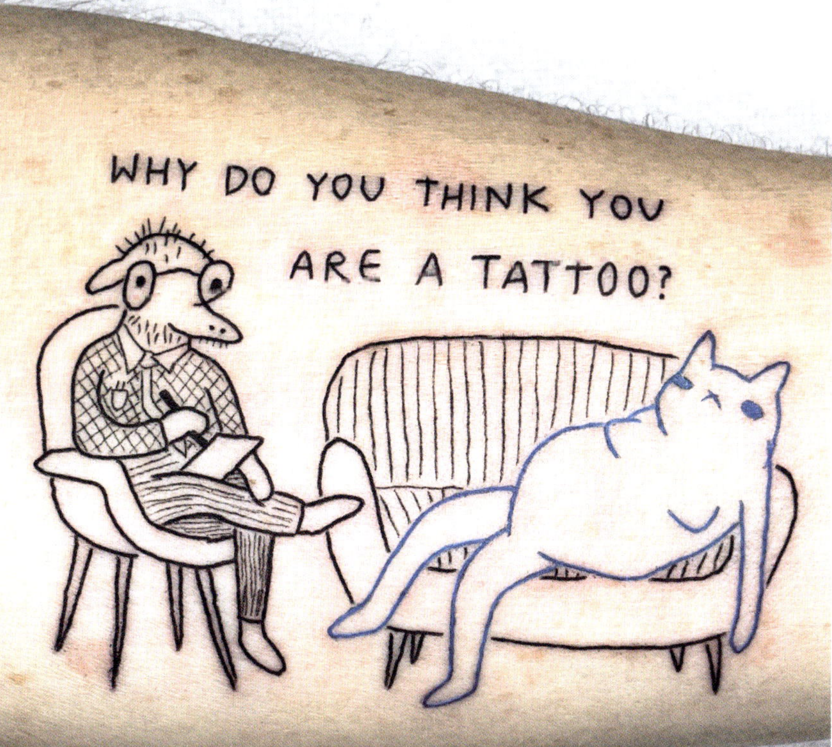
WHY DO YOU THINK YOU
ARE A TATTOO?

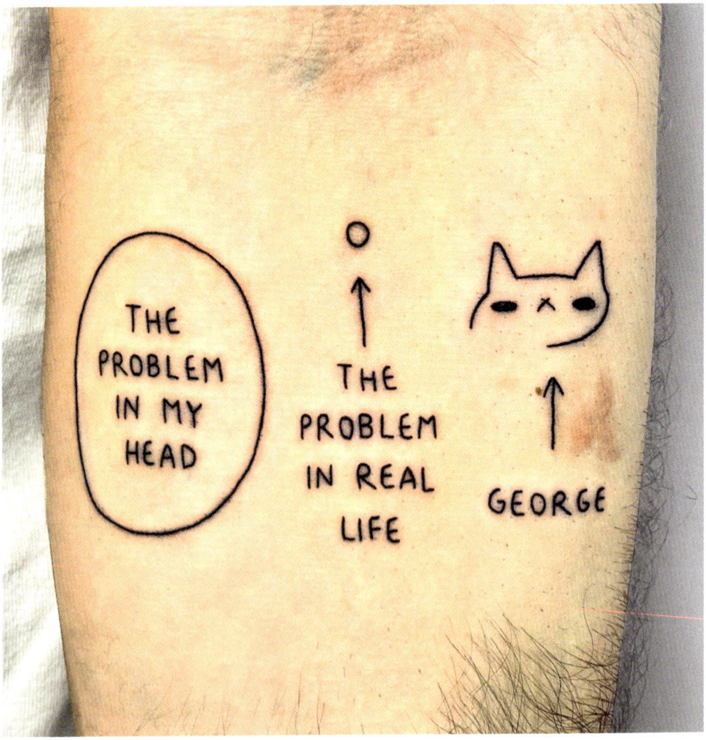

THE
PROBLEM
IN MY
HEAD
O
THE
PROBLEM
IN REAL
LIFE
GEORGE

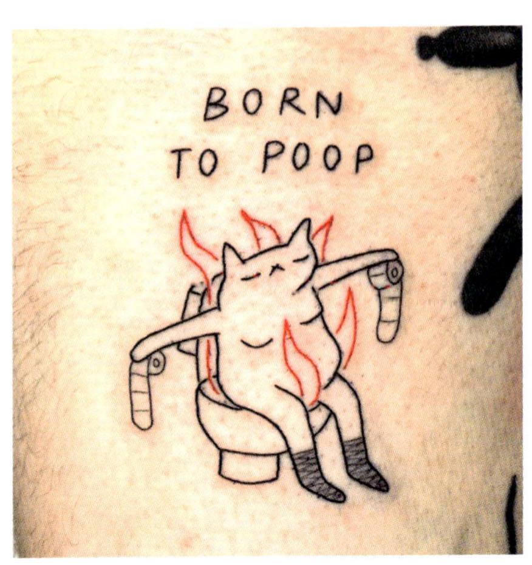
BORN
TO POOP

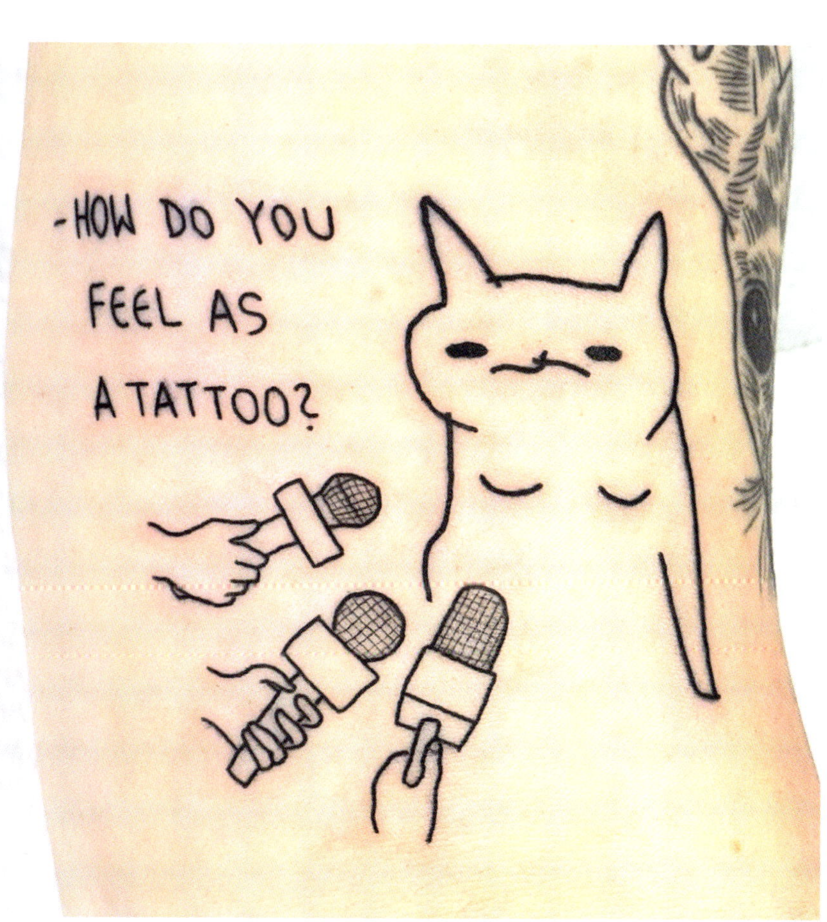
-HOW DO YOU
FEEL AS
A TATTOO?

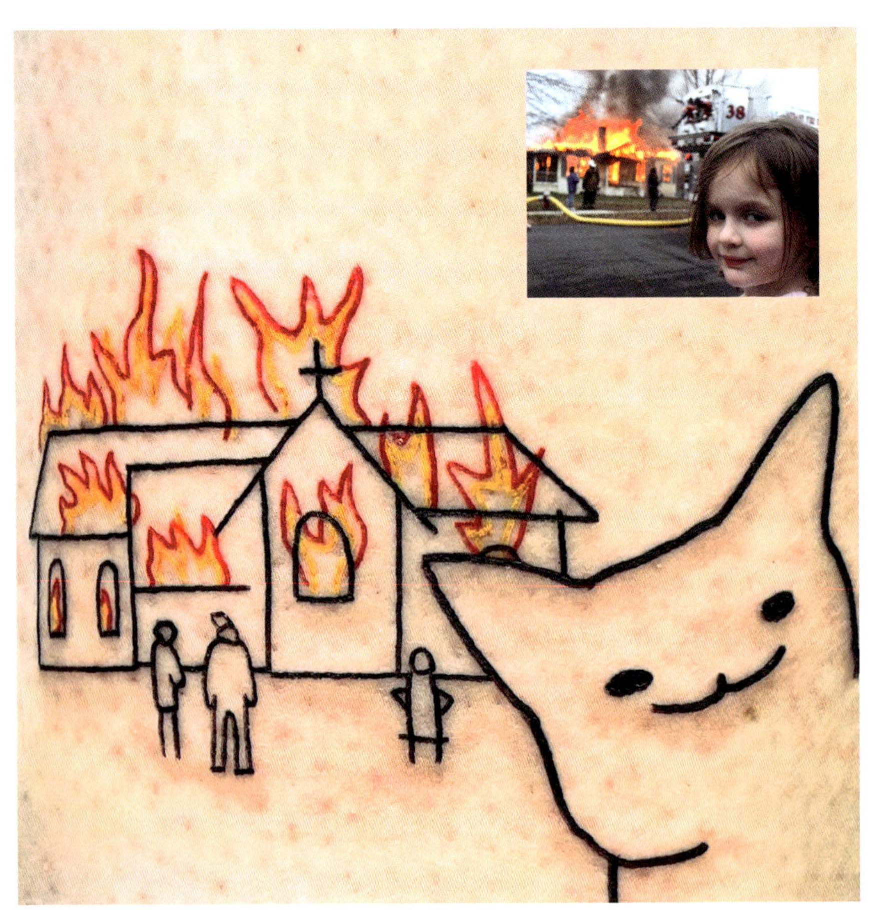
38

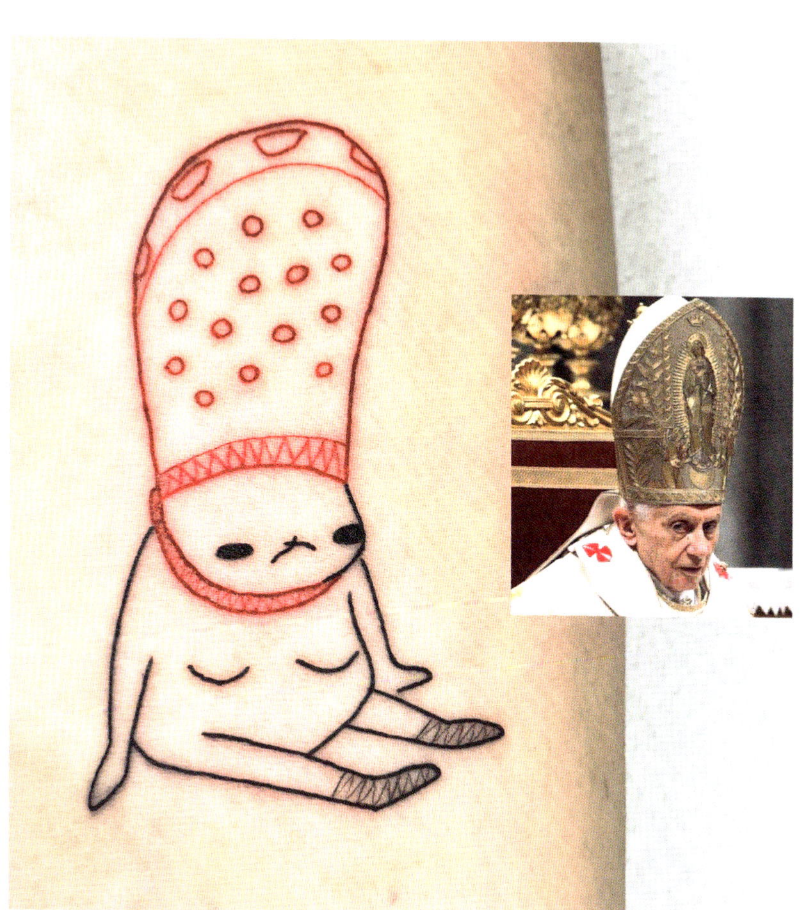

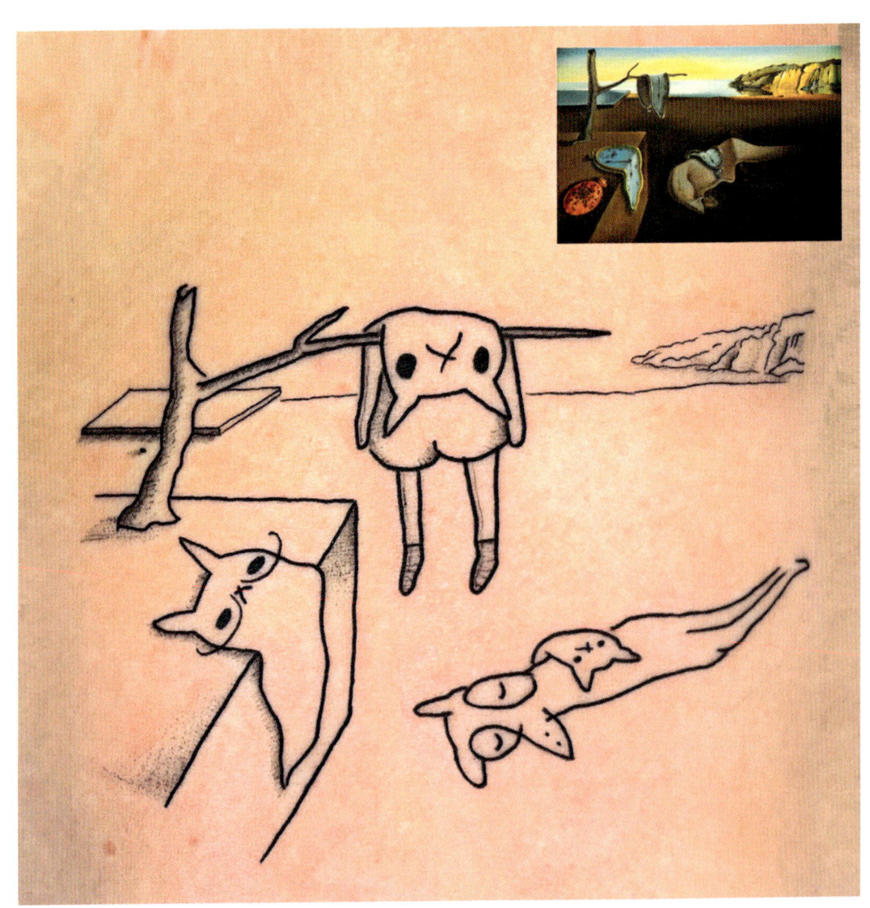

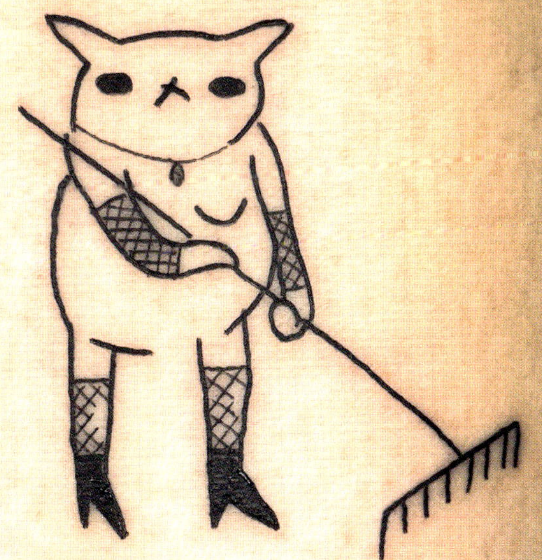
BORN
TO SLAY
FORCED
TO WORK

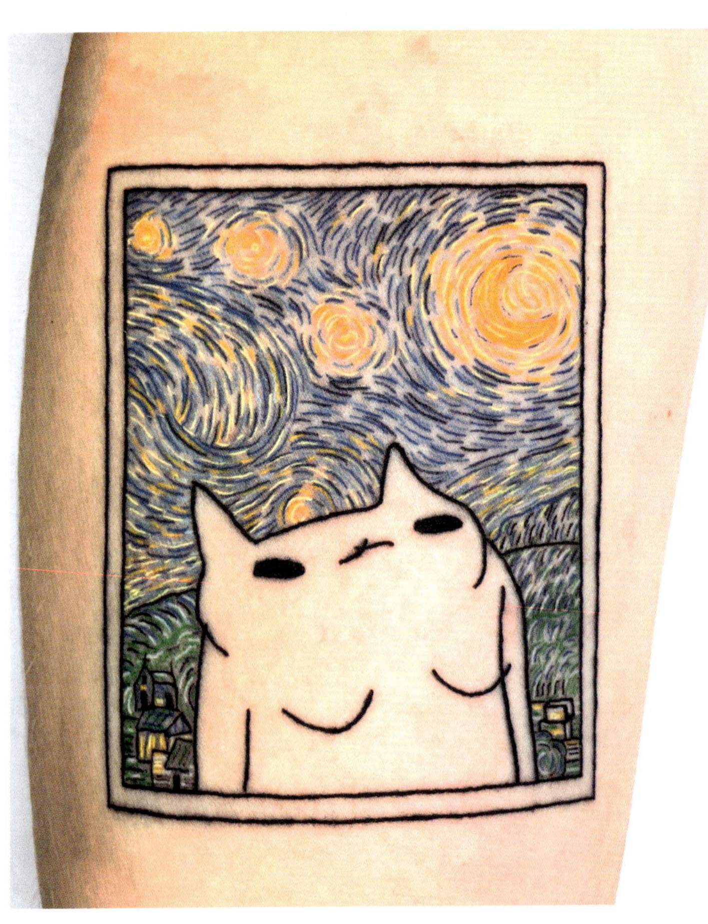

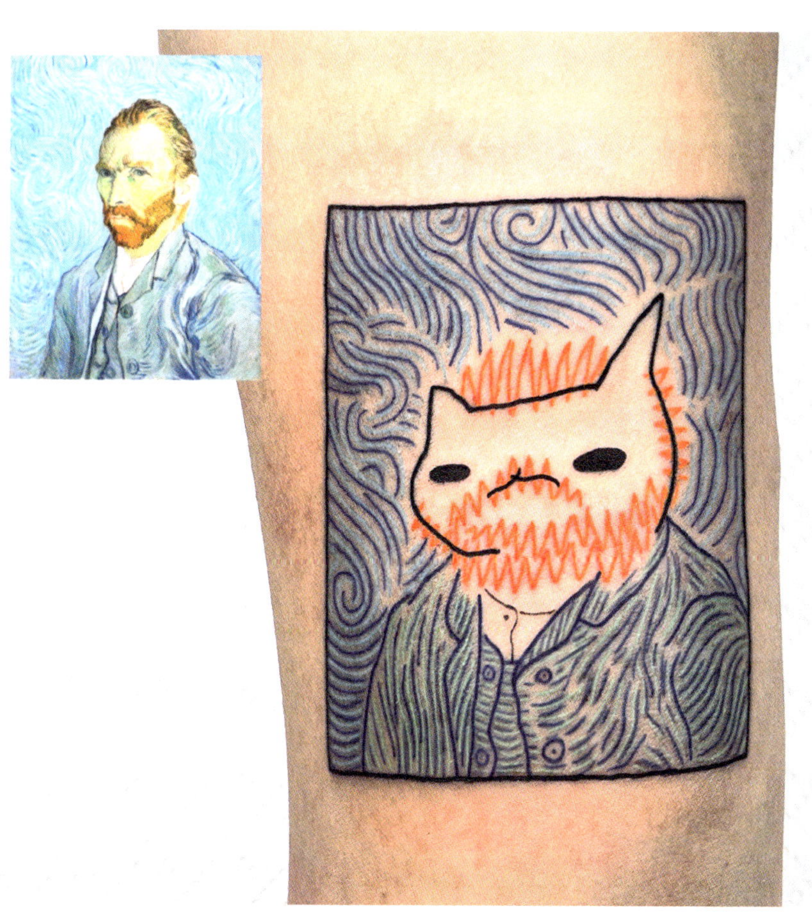

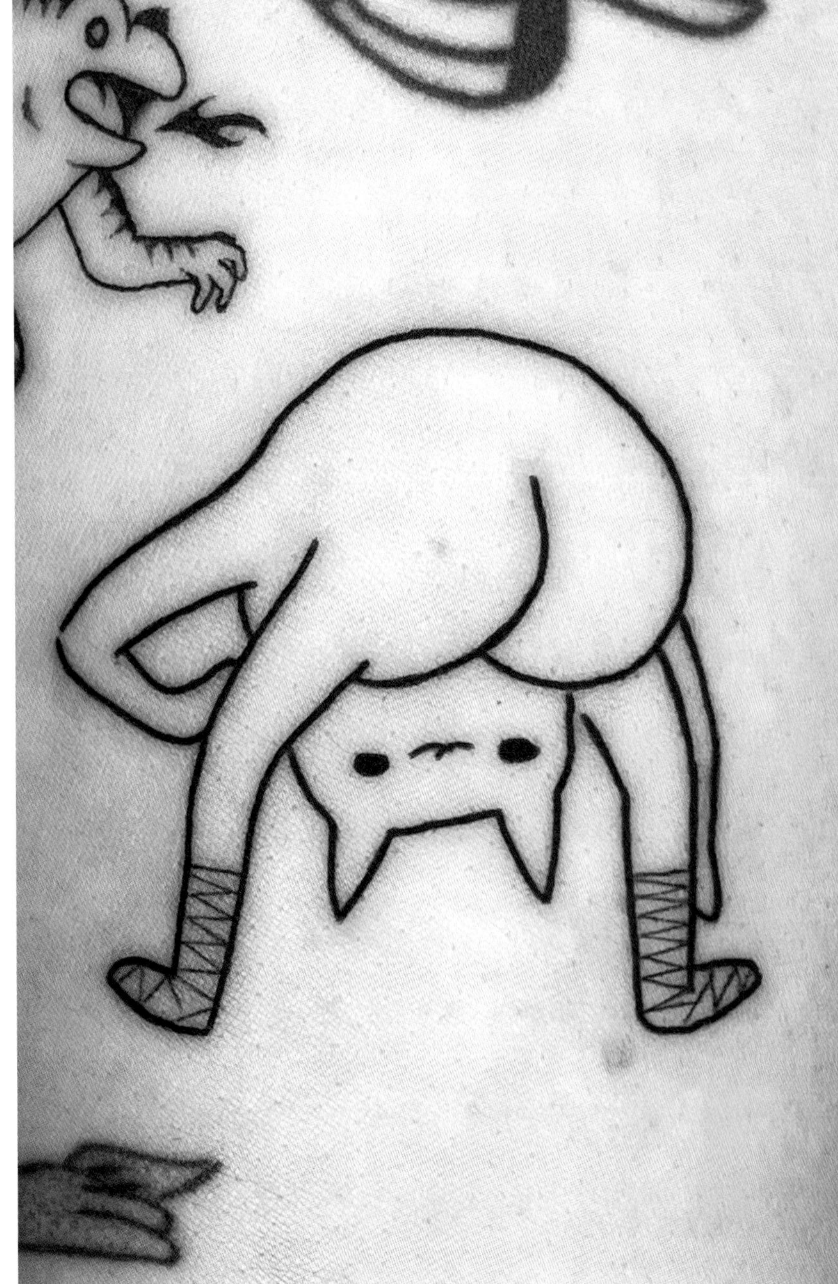

— INTERVIEW

Let's start with a quick introduction. Who are you, and where can people find your work?
My name is Szymon Lipowski, and you can find my work on Instagram under the tag @lipnetattoo. It's a wordplay on my surname – 'lipne' means 'shoddy' or 'dingy' in Polish, which is kind of ironic. In real life people can find me at Europa Tattoo Shop in Kraków, Poland. I've thought about opening my own studio, but I'm just too busy for that at the moment.

What inspired you to start tattooing?
My passion for tattooing started during my time in drug rehab. One of the therapists who had a big impact on my life had self-inked tattoos, which I found impressive. After leaving rehab, I started tattooing myself and my friends – first as a hobby and a form of self-therapy. It helped me stay sober and process my emotions. Over time, I got better and eventually it turned into a career.

I started working in the field before doing an apprenticeship. But to work in a professional studio, I needed to have done one. Even though I was self-taught at first, the apprenticeship gave me valuable knowledge and a new perspective.

What kind of jobs did you have before tattooing?
I've worked in many different fields – waiting tables, bartending, managing bowling alleys, construction – and I even dealt drugs and committed theft to make ends meet. I don't look back on those times fondly and I'm not proud of them.

Besides tattooing, what creative interests bring you happiness?
I love writing stories and creating narratives. Right now, I'm working on a comic book. I'm also very interested in psychology.

What do you find most and least positive about being a tattoo artist?
I love the tattooing process itself. But I hate how exhausting social media management is. You constantly have to post new content to feed the algorithm, and in trying to grab people's attention, it's easy to lose sight of the joy of creating. Sometimes I think it would be nice to go back to tattooing as a hobby without the commercial pressure. Maybe one day I'll be able to support myself through writing instead.

Has tattooing has a positive impact on your life?
Absolutely. I've met so many interesting people - some of my clients have even become good friends. Tattooing has also given me the opportunity to travel and see the world.

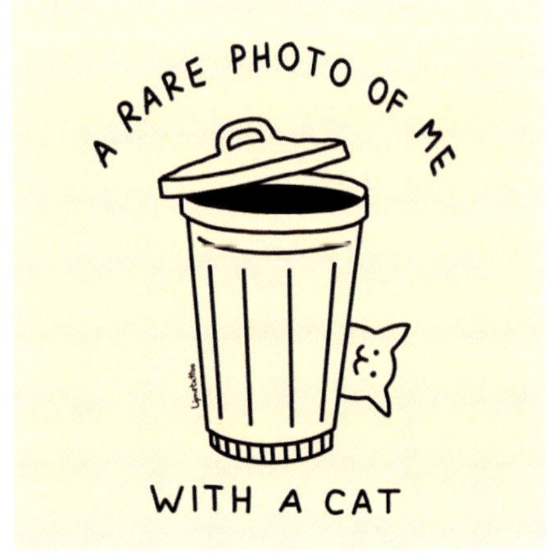

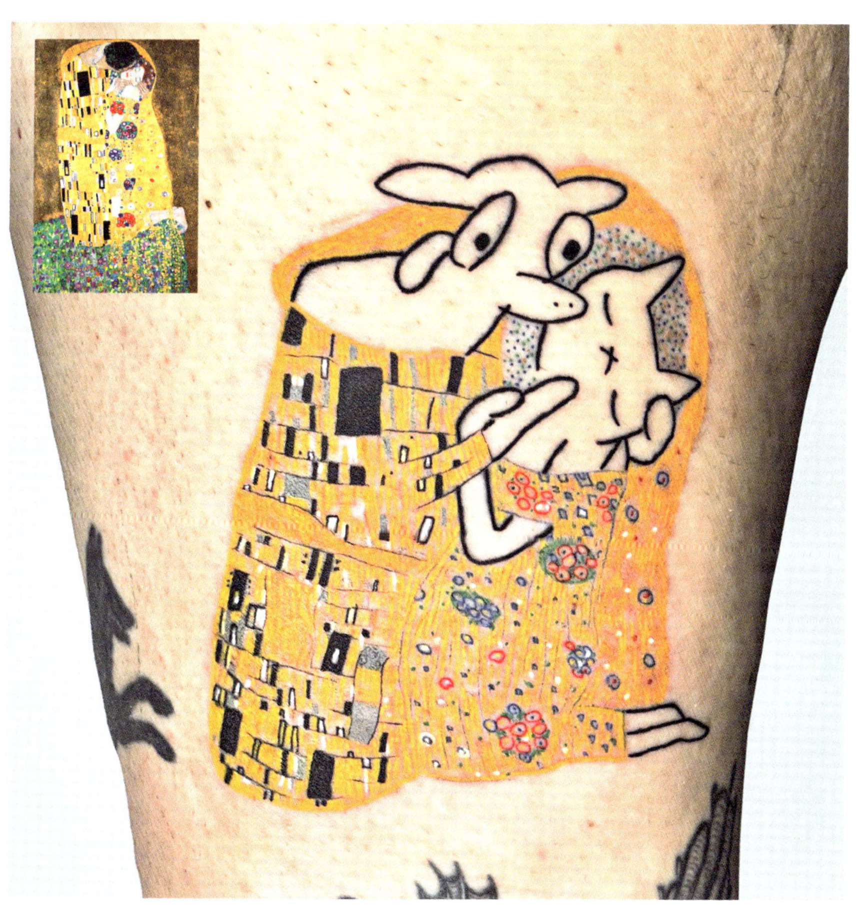

If you weren't tattooing, what do you think you'd be doing?
Honestly, I don't think I'd be in a creative field. I'd probably be doing something I hate.

What kind of tattoos are the most meaningful to you?
I love doing tattoos for charity events. I've done many for causes like animal shelters and cancer research. It's always rewarding to know my work is making a difference.

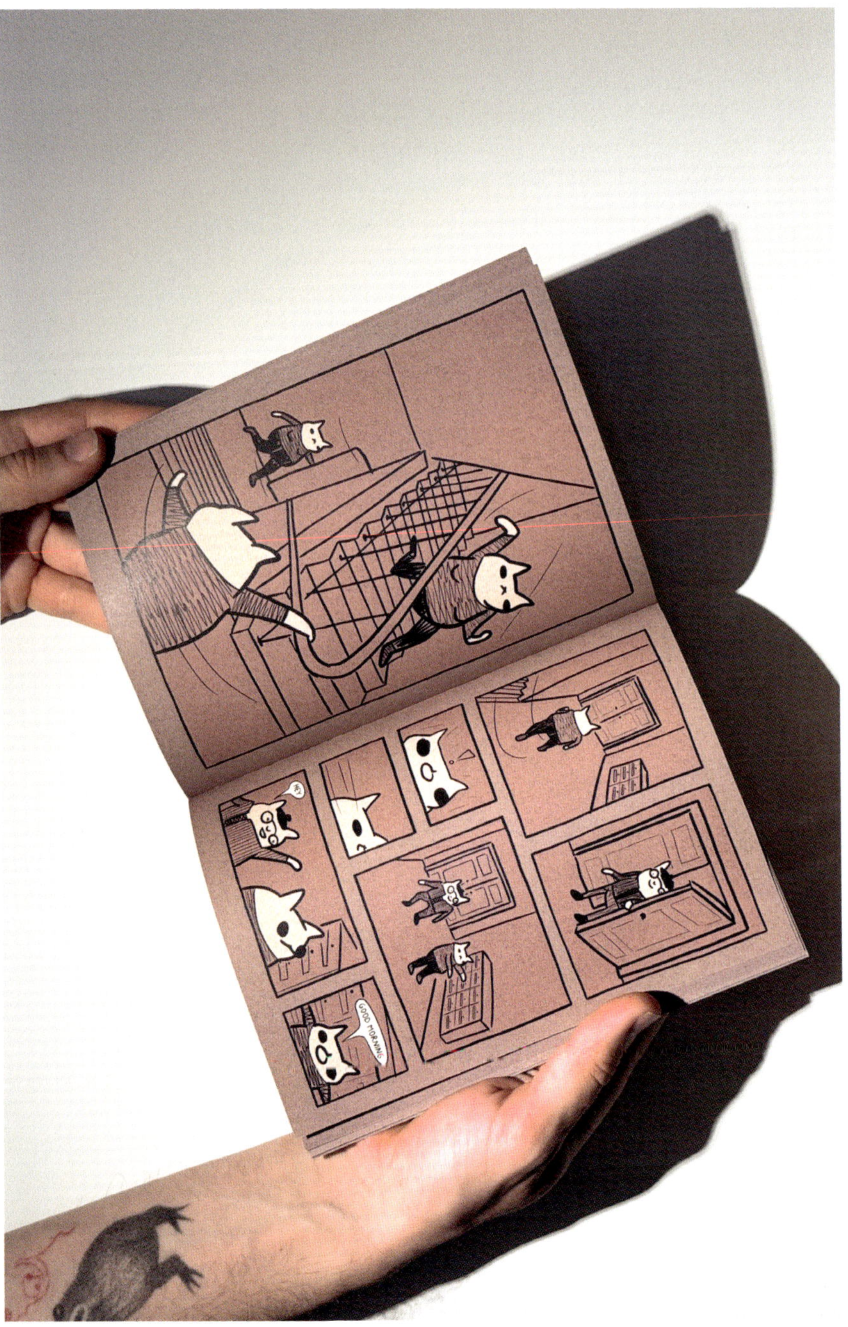
HEY
GOOD MORNING

How would you describe your tattoo style?
I've always loved expressive, minimalist designs - how just a few well-placed lines can say more than a highly detailed piece. My style is about continuous improvement rather than drastic stylistic changes.

Do you remember your first tattoo?
Yes! My first tattoo was on myself in 2015. It took me three days, but it's still in great shape. After that, I didn't tattoo for four years. Once I left rehab, I got serious about tattooing. I can't really recall my first tattoos on other people since I was so nervous - I needed frequent breaks to calm my nerves and avoid a panic attack. But I think they turned out okay for my skill level back then. Hopefully, they still look good!

Do you have any funny client stories?
Too many to count! I could fill an entire book with them. One of the strangest requests I've had was someone asking me to tattoo George the cat coming out of their… well, let's just say I refused that one.

Let's talk about George. What makes him special?
I never really planned to create George - it all started with a few cat drawings. Cats have always been loved in art, and when people responded positively, I kept drawing more. Over time, I found the courage to include more of myself: my anxiety, feelings and struggles.

What began as random sketches gradually became a single character with a distinct personality, moods and emotions. I named him George after my childhood cat - a chubby, slightly goofy cat with crossed eyes whom I adored.

Now, there are thousands of Georges around the world, and I'm incredibly grateful to everyone who has chosen to carry him with them. I'm currently working on a comic book about George, a story about an anxious person struggling with the overwhelming drama of daily life. It's based on my own experiences, and I hope it'll be finished this year.

George isn't just a random meme cat - he's a character with his own story and personality. The more you follow my work, the more you'll understand George. Having him as a tattoo is like carrying around a little friend who will always be with you.

Can you walk us through your creative process for George tattoos?
Sure! Before I start tattooing, I draw each George by hand. Clients can either choose from my free designs or suggest a theme. These are usually memes, short stories or famous photos. We discuss their idea, I sketch, and we refine it together. Then we move on to tattooing.

Do you ever refuse George tattoo requests?
Yes, when an idea is just too questionable.
What was the first tattoo you did on someone else?
It was 'Veni, Vidi, Vici' on my friend's ribs. We did it lying on the carpet in my kitchen, with zero understanding of sanitation. Thankfully, things have changed a lot since then.

Did your family react positively to your career choice?
My parents weren't thrilled. If my father were still alive, I think he'd still see it as a temporary gig - just a way to make beer money until I found a 'real' job.

How do people in Poland view tattoos nowadays?

Things have changed a lot. A decade ago, tattoos were associated with criminals or the mentally ill. Now, most people see them as normal. Only a few stuck-up old folks still hold onto those outdated views.

What inspires your designs?

My life, my emotions, my struggles – everything I go through finds its way into my work.

What values do you think a good tattoo artist should have?

Apart from the obvious – sanitation and hygiene – I'd say patience and humility. In the beginning, you won't get perfect lines, and you won't have a full schedule. You also need curiosity and an artistic drive. It's important to create real art, not just copy others.

Thanks for sharing your story, Szymon. Any final words?

Just that I appreciate anyone who connects with my work. Tattooing has changed my life, and I hope my art can make a difference in others' lives too.

LONELY WEIRDO CLUB

Berlin, Germany

Lonely Weirdo Club is a tattoo artist whose creative journey began in 2009, following an early career running a piercing studio. Deeply inspired by emotion and personal experience, his work explores the full spectrum of feeling - translating it into permanent art.

Known for a style that is raw, emotional and honest, Lonely Weirdo Club celebrates individuality and challenges conformity. His work is a form of rebellion and release - an unapologetic expression of self that embraces what's different, strange or misunderstood. Through subtle irony and bold imagery, he often highlights and mocks societal expectations, using tattooing as a platform for both personal freedom and social commentary.

Currently based in Berlin and working internationally, Lonely Weirdo Club travels the world while tattooing, drawing inspiration from new environments, cultures and human stories. As a nomadic artist, his practice is ever-evolving, but grounded in the belief that true creativity begins where comfort ends.

16.

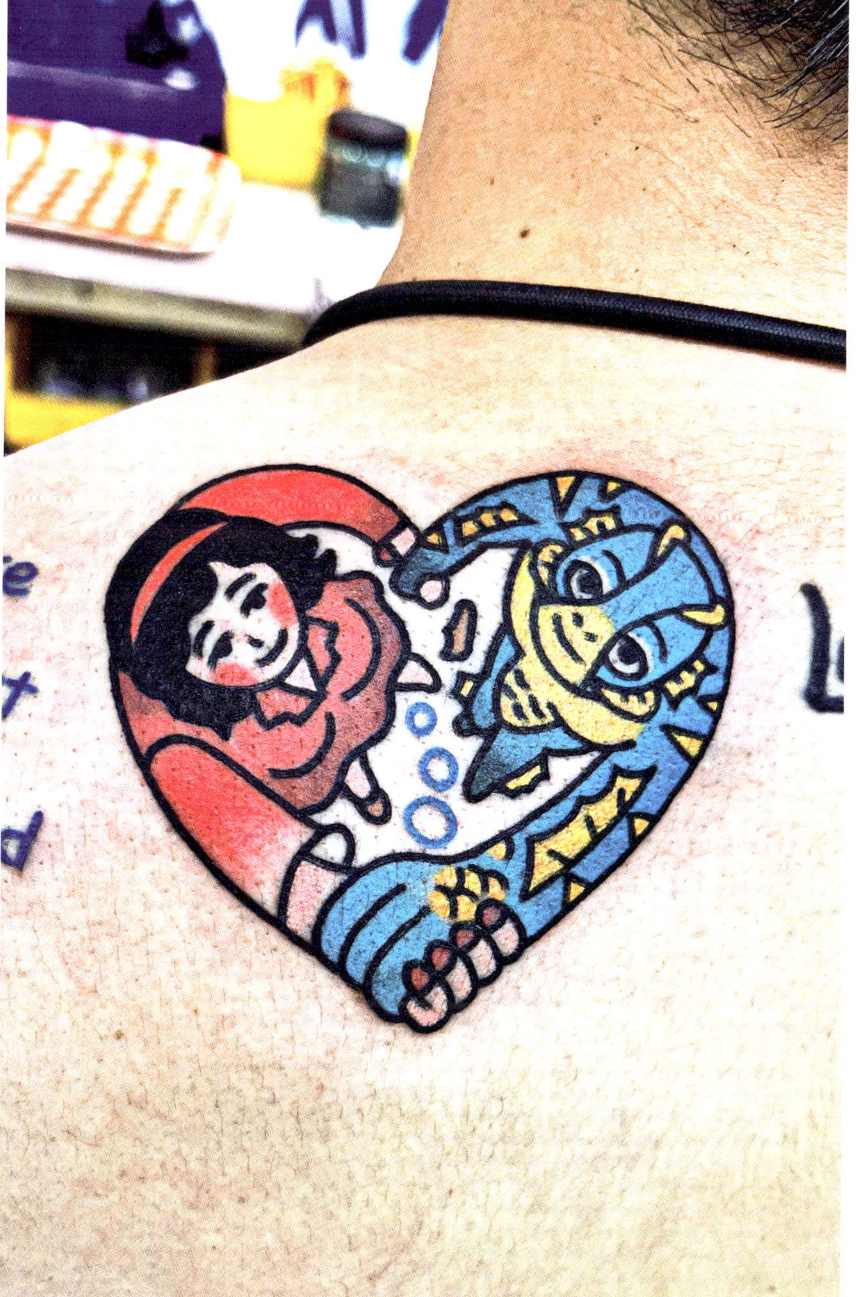

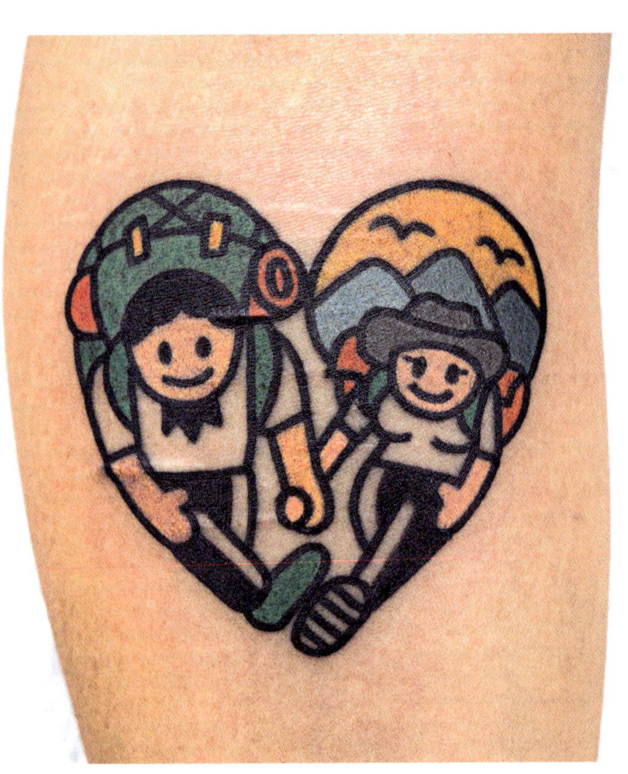

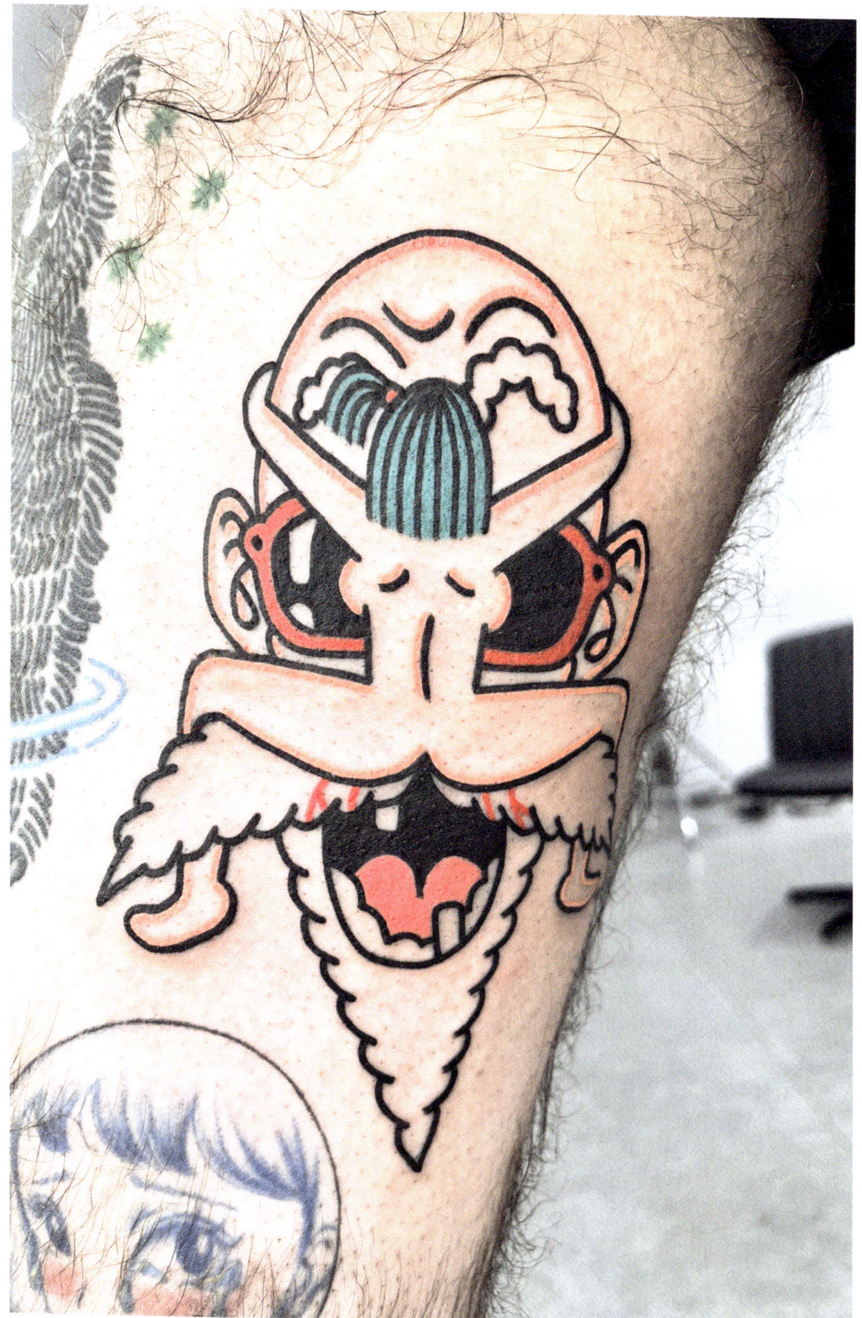

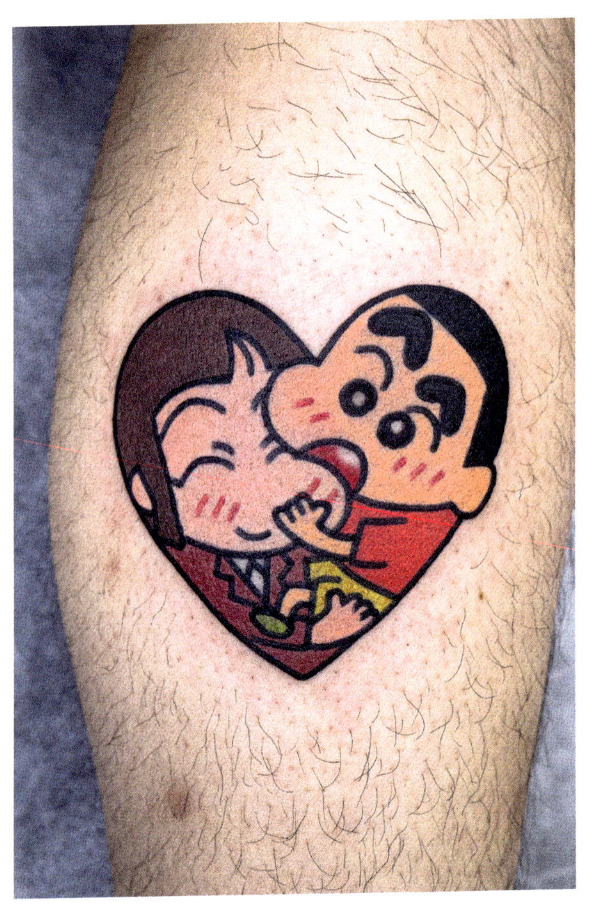

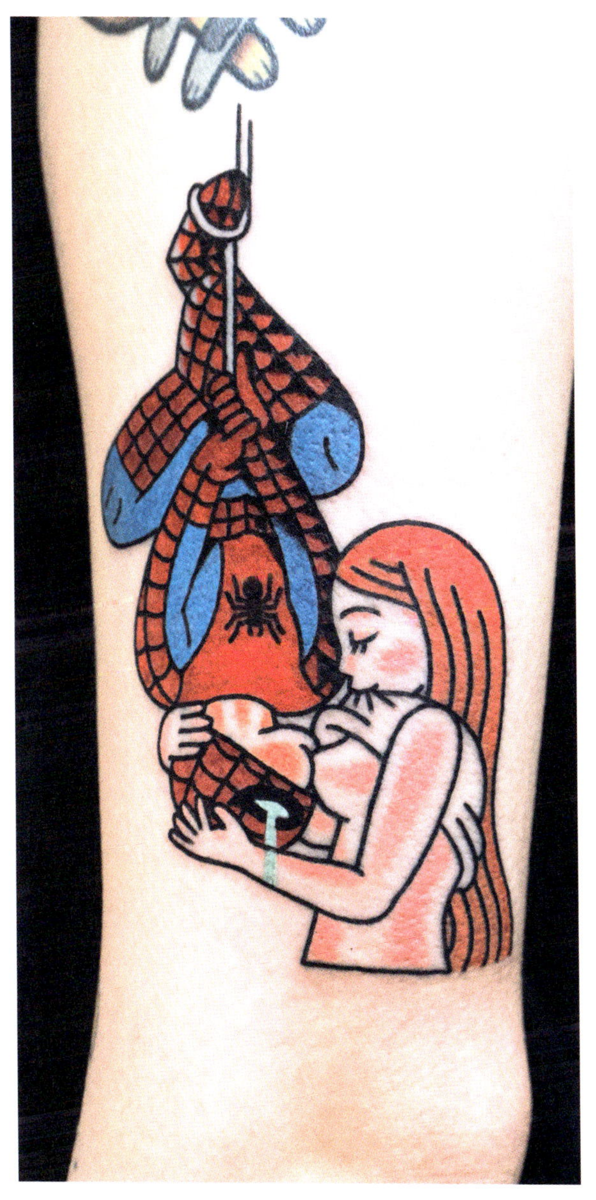

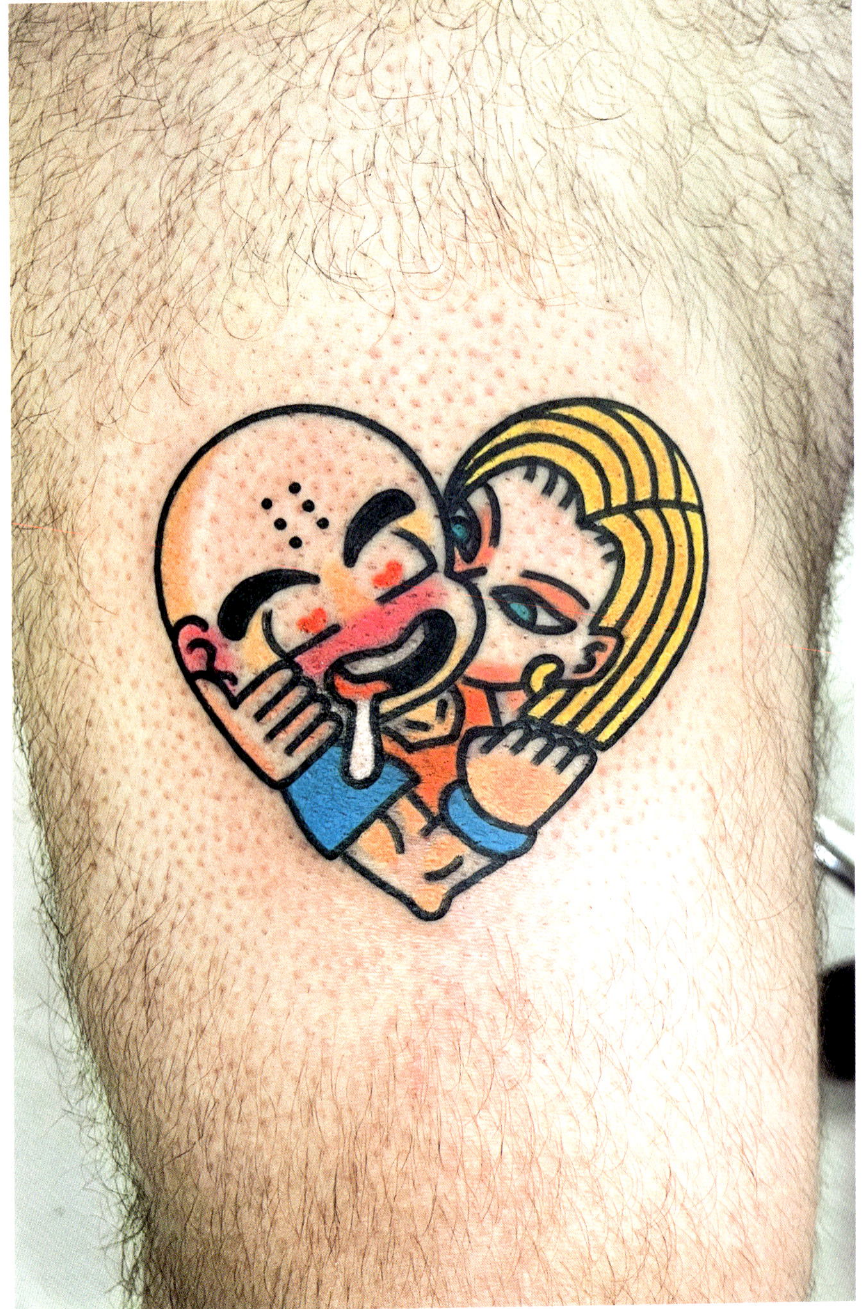

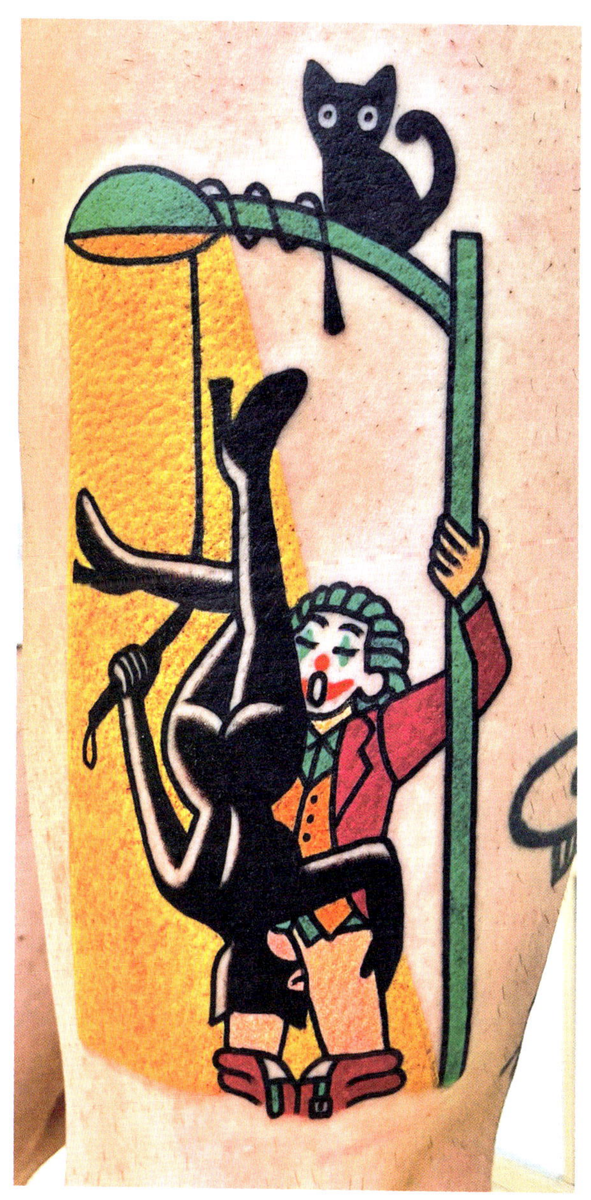

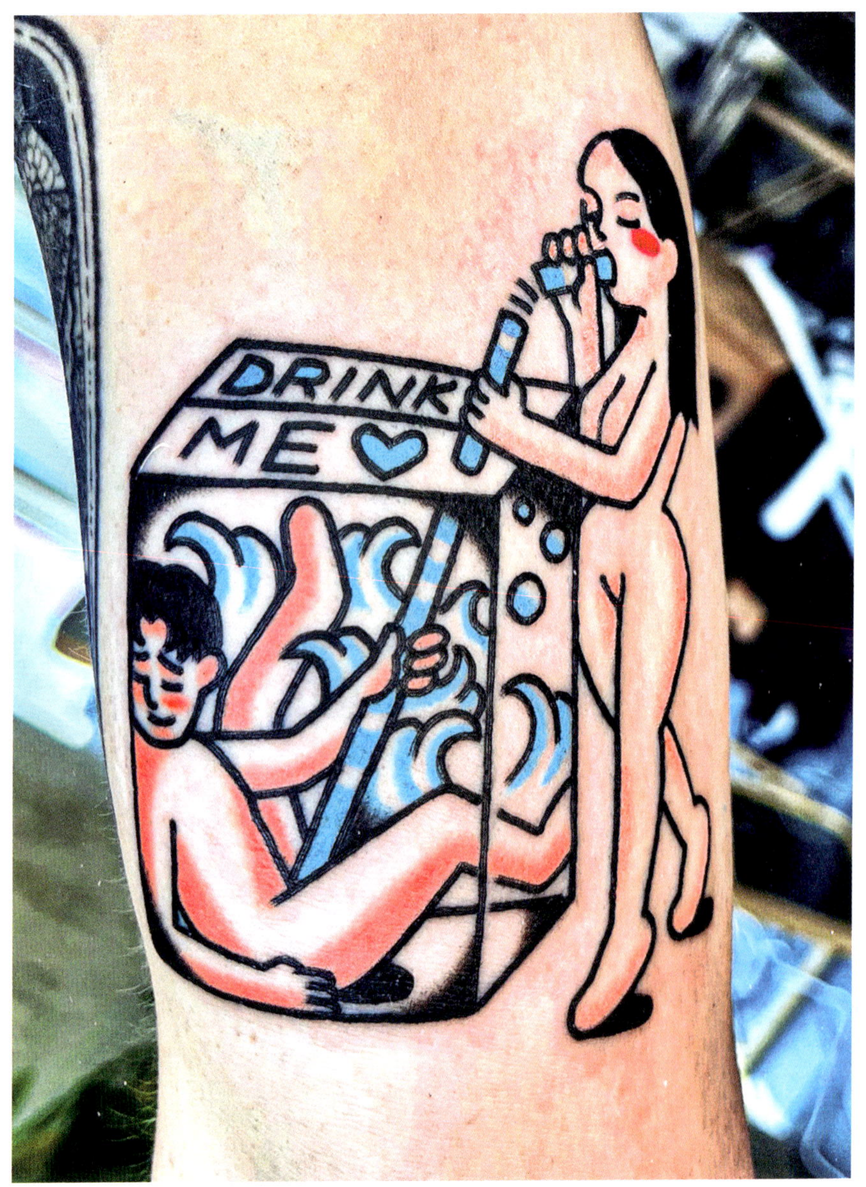
DRINK
ME

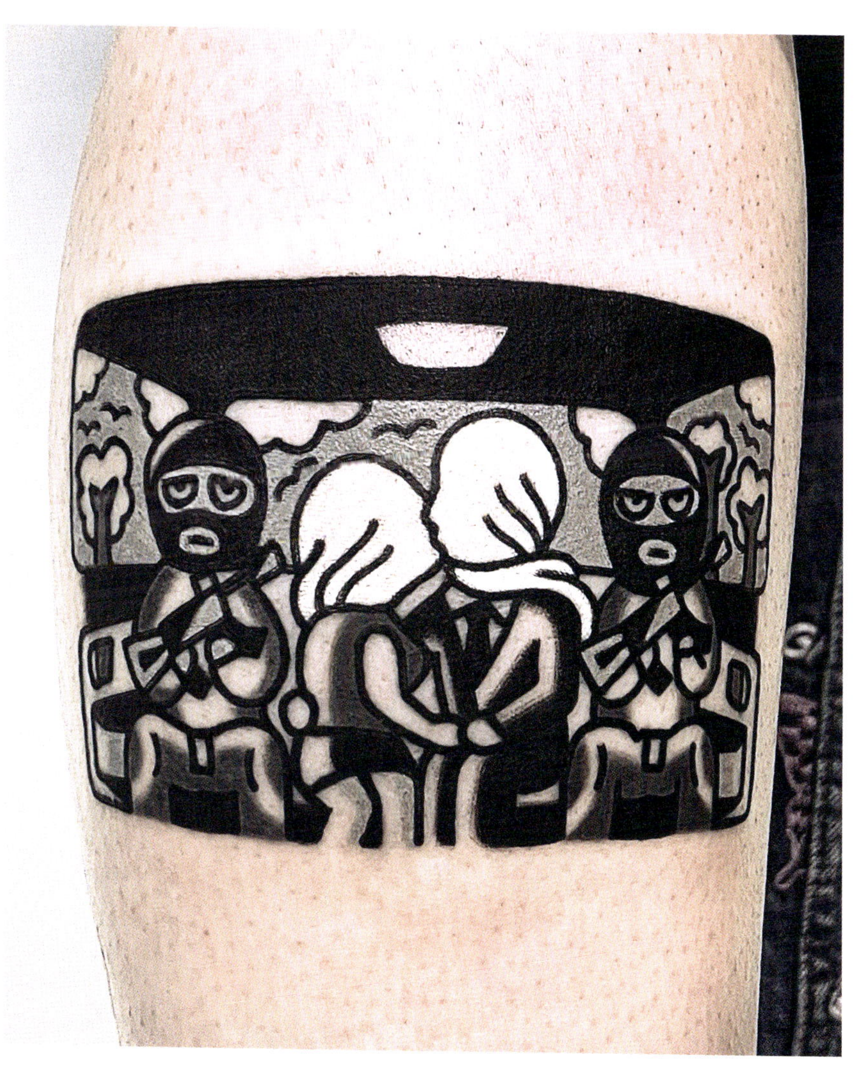

MAMBO TATTOOER

Milan, Italy

Mattia Calvi, professionally known as Mambo Tattooer, is an acclaimed tattoo artist renowned for creating the distinctive 'destrutturato' style. He began his tattooing career in 2010, and by 2016, he had developed and perfected the unique style that has become his signature. In April 2018, Mattia opened Mambo Tattoo Shop in Meda, just 20 kilometres from Milan, where he continues to explore and redefine the art of tattooing.

A lifelong passion for graphic design, logos and icons has deeply influenced Mattia's approach to tattoo art. The simplicity of logos and the precision they embody played a key role in shaping the destrutturato style.

Mattia's process starts with a basic concept provided by the client, which he then refines until the balance between bold black lines and vibrant colour is harmoniously achieved. His goal is to craft tattoos where the interaction between these elements creates a compelling visual story. For Mattia, a tattoo is not just an image but a narrative, and when the balance of form and colour is perfect, he considers the tattoo complete and harmonious.

17.

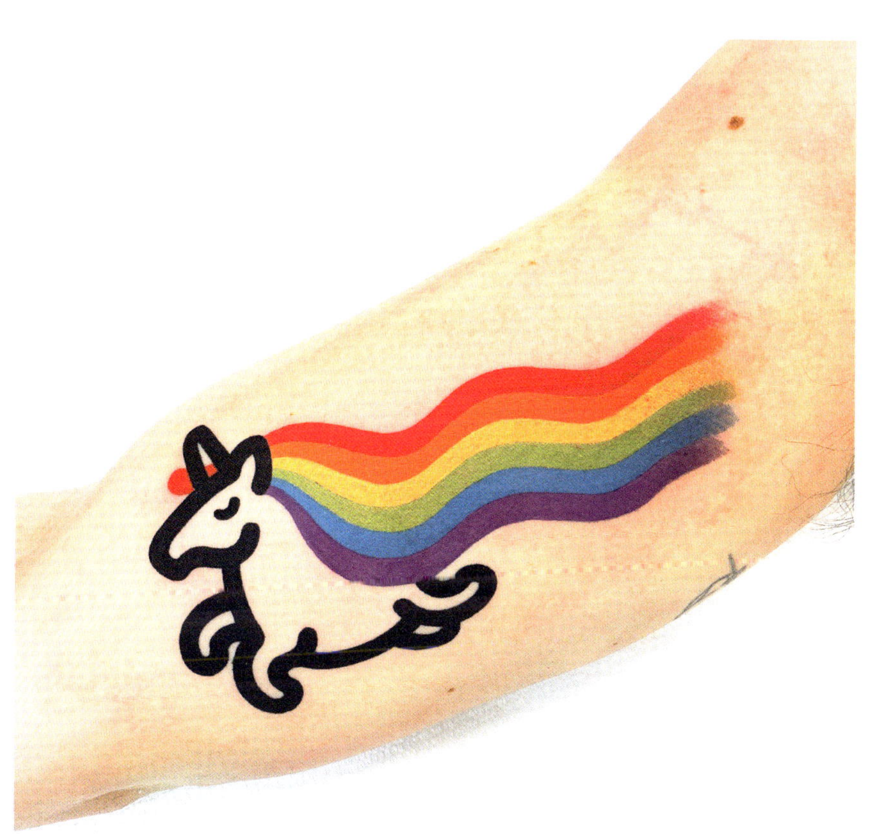

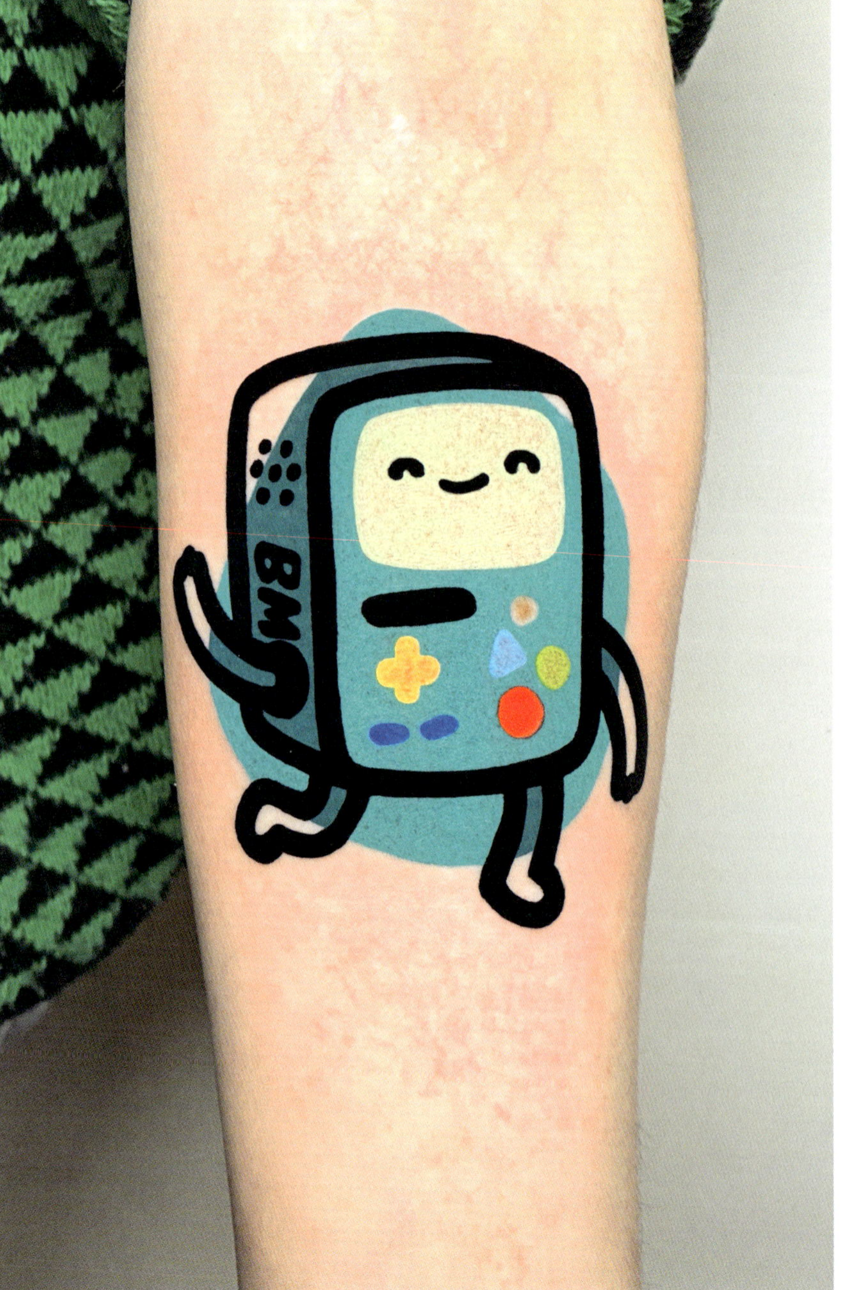
BM

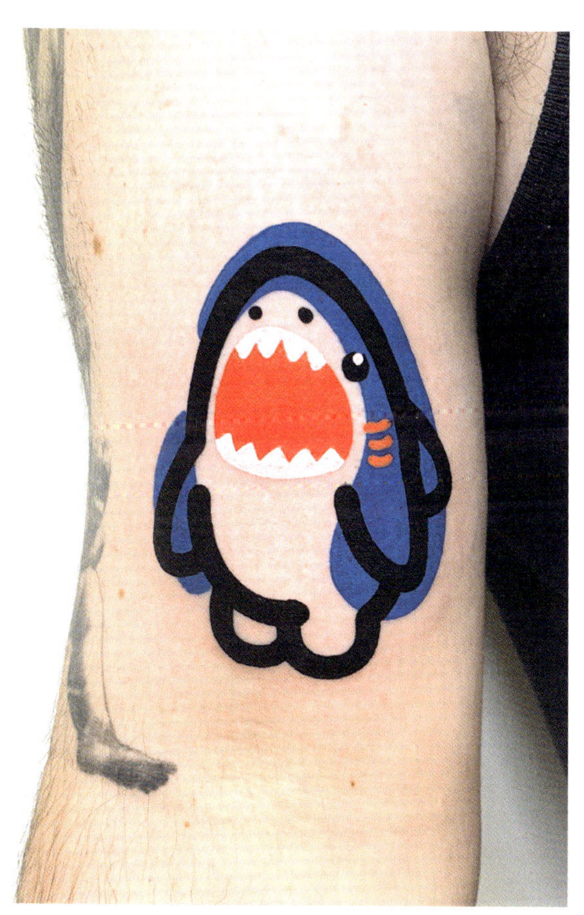

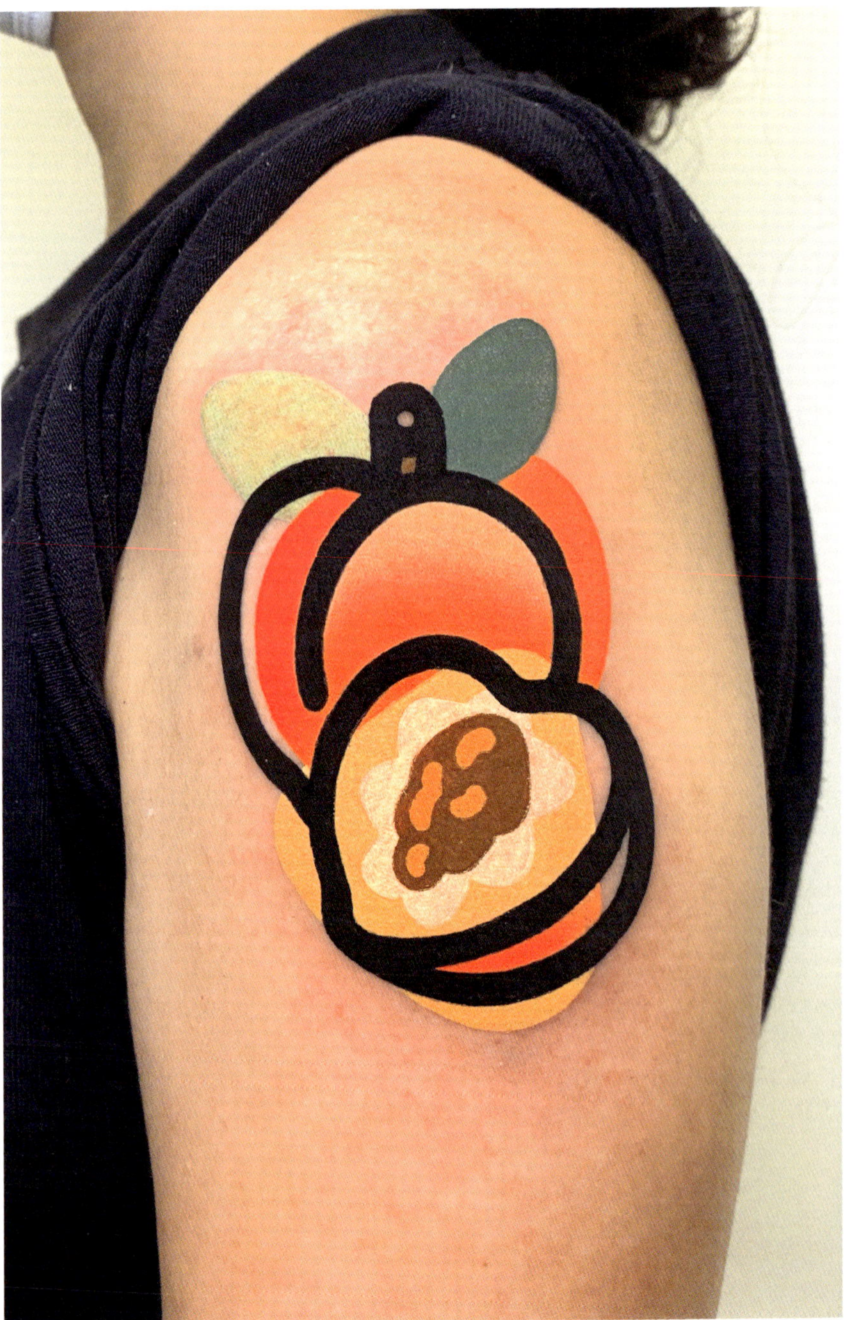

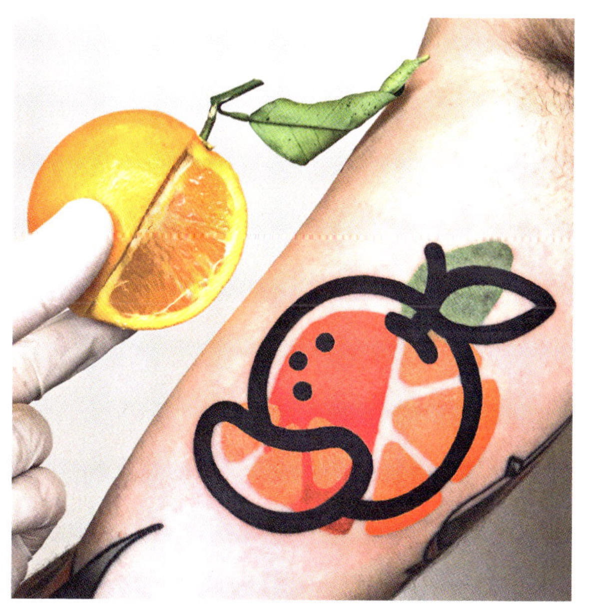

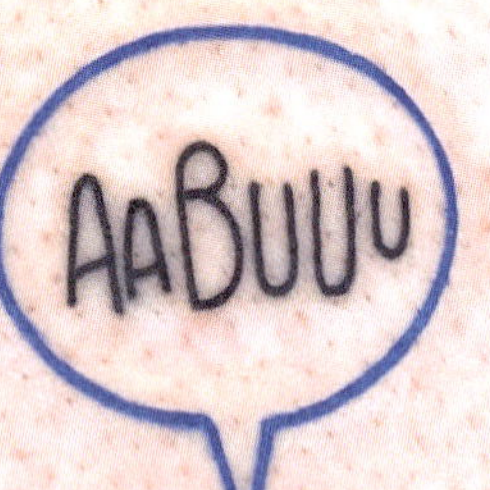
AABUUU

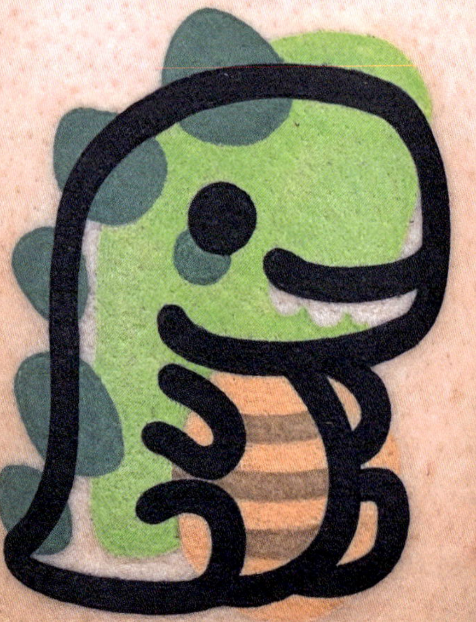

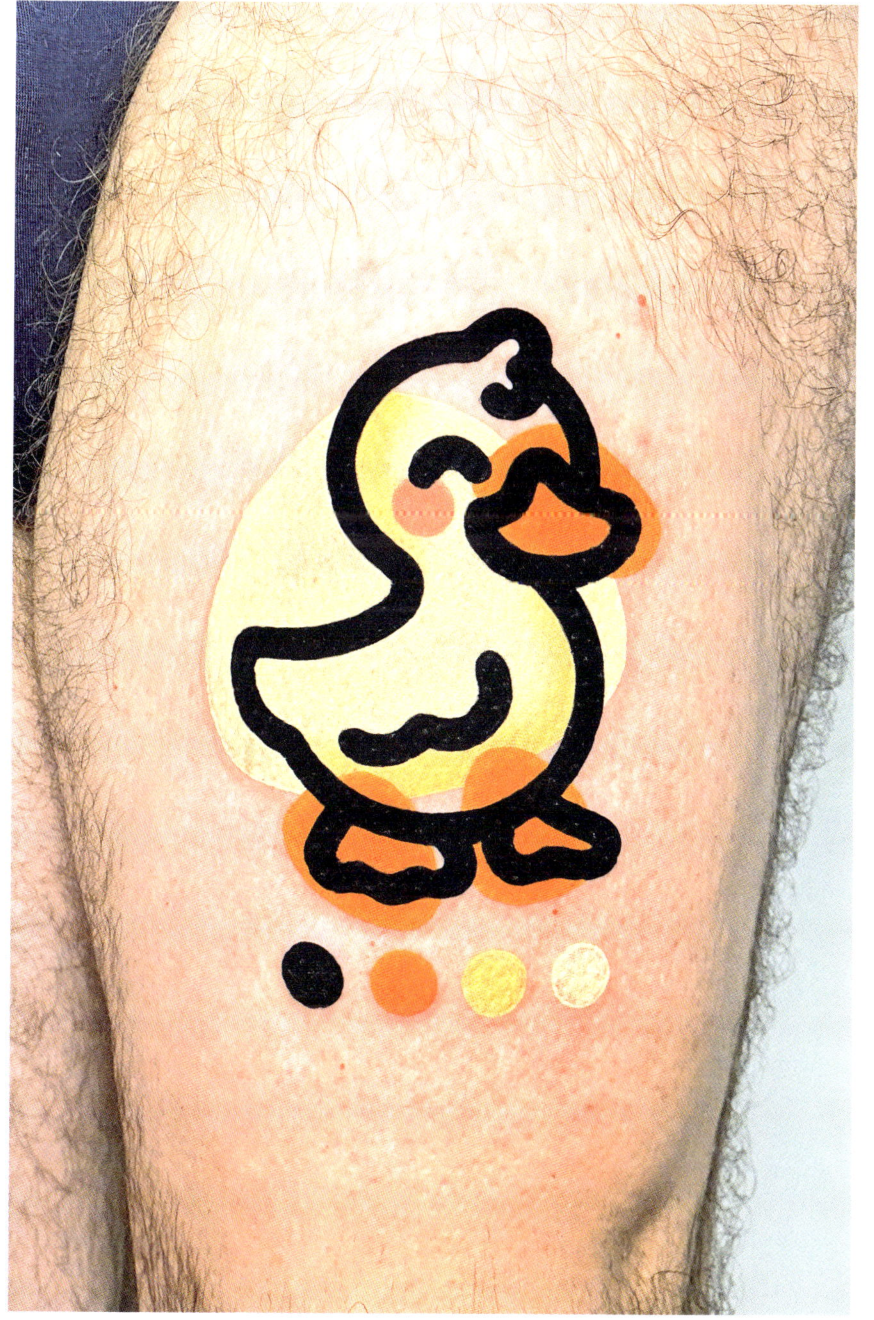

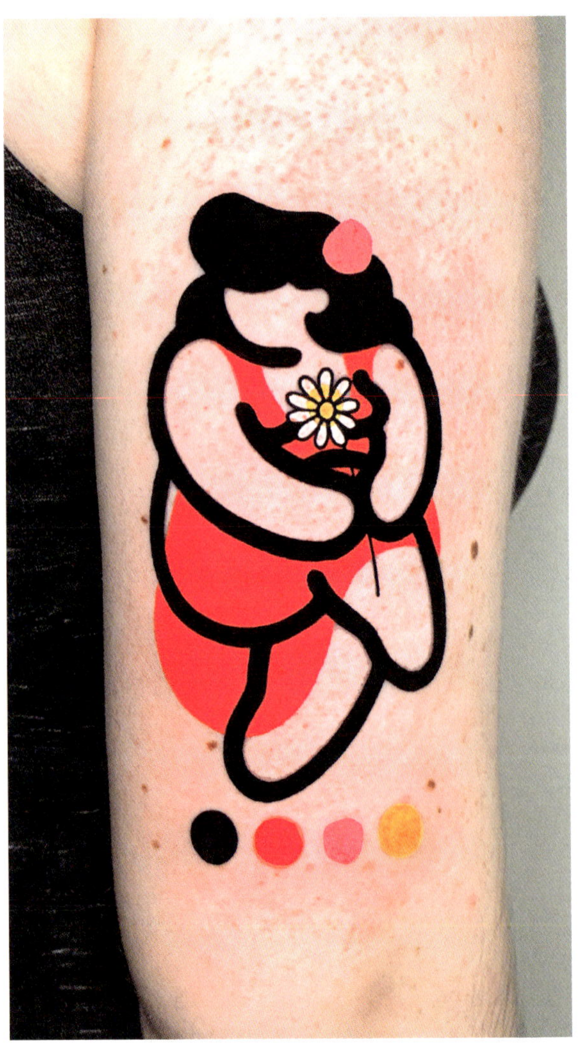

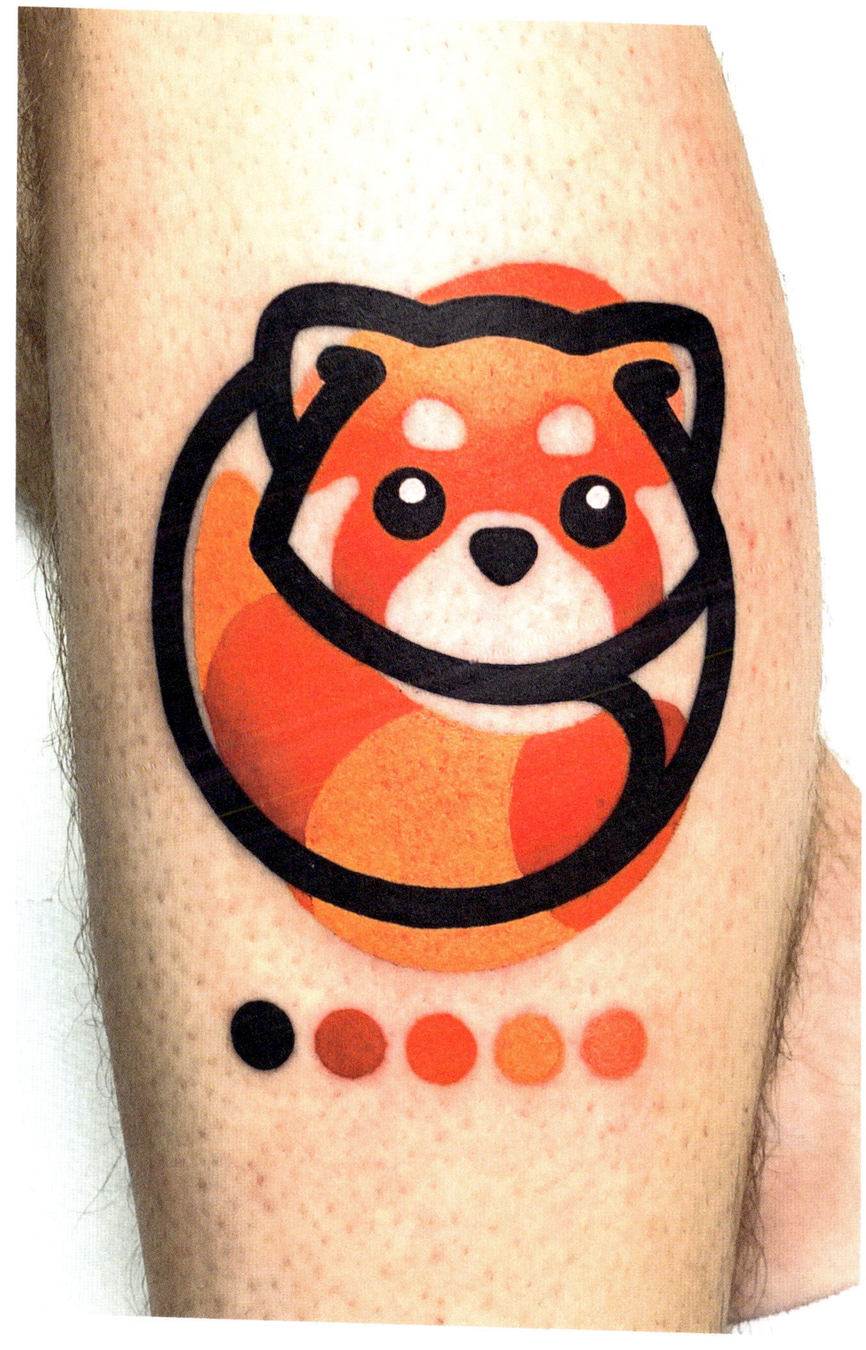

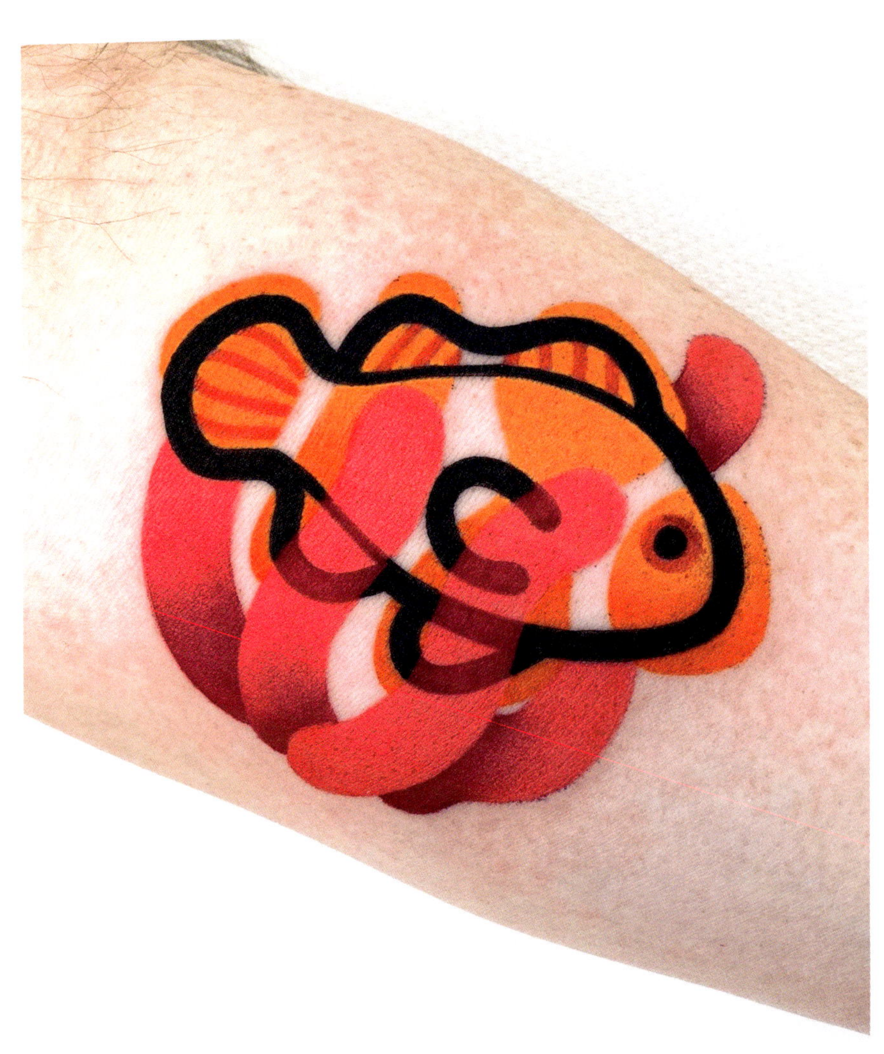

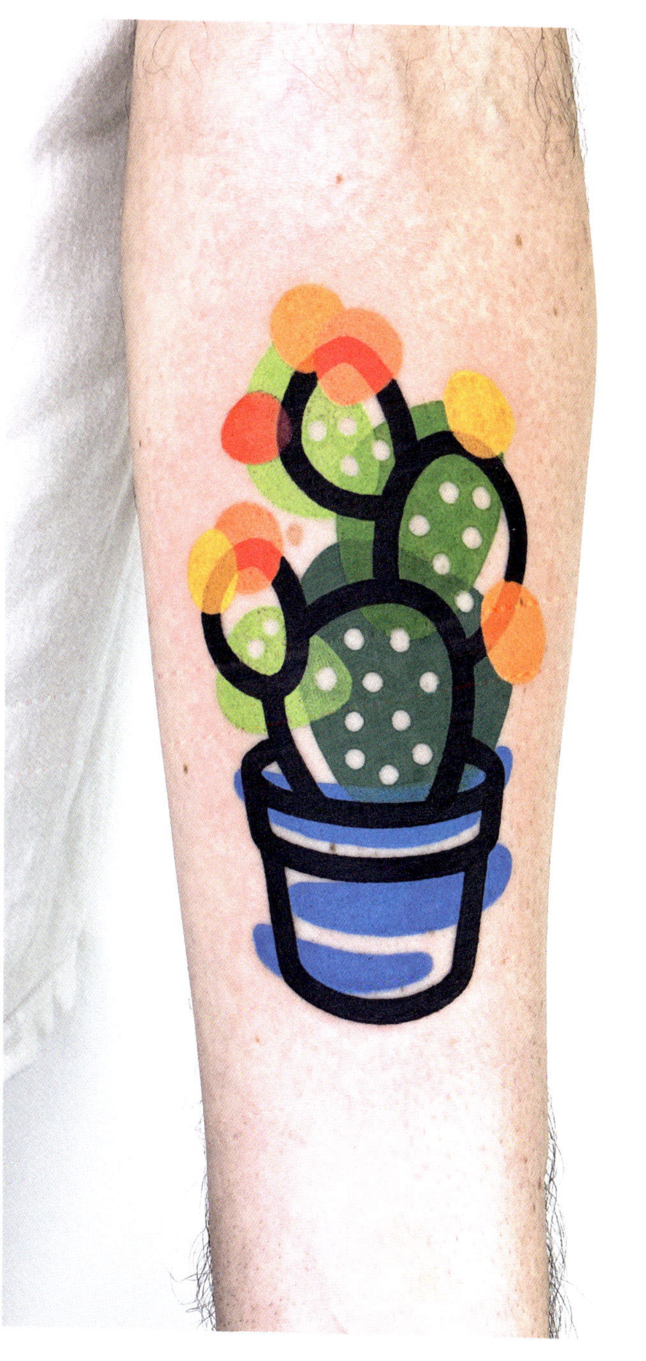

MR. HEGGIE

USA

Born in London, England, Mr. Heggie is a multidisciplinary artist with a lifelong passion for art, storytelling and visual experimentation. He began tattooing in 2007, building on an already well-established career in the arts. His work has appeared in gallery exhibitions and across various media, including design projects for bands, books, television and film.

Now based in the United States, Mr. Heggie is constantly on the move, drawing inspiration from weird situations, ambiguous moments, daily life, his dog, and the people he meets on his travels across Australia, New Zealand, Asia, Europe and beyond.

Whether through tattooing, illustration or design, Mr. Heggie's approach remains grounded in a distinctive blend of humour, melancholy and irony. At the heart of it all is a simple philosophy: make art, explore the world - and if it brings joy to others, all the better.

18.

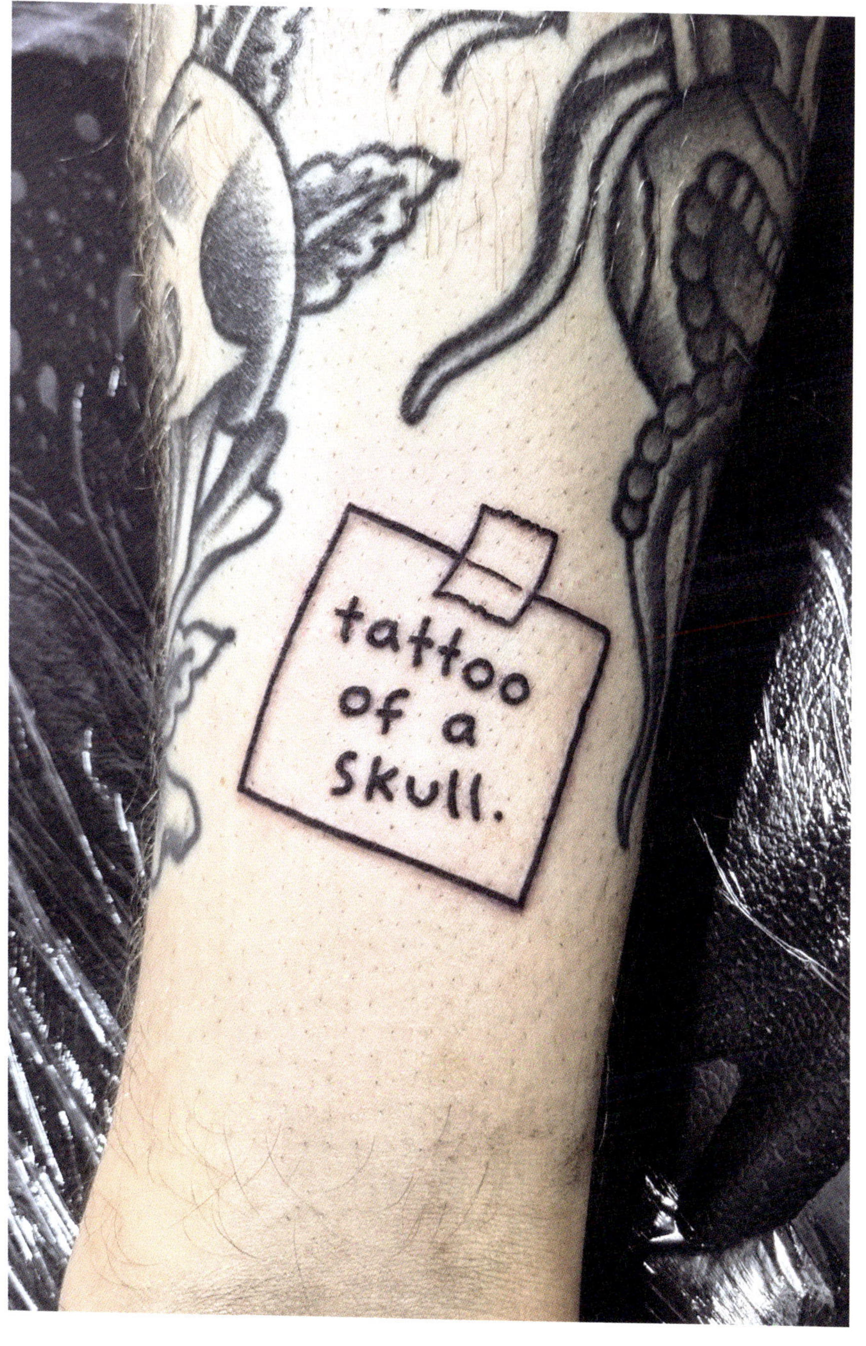
tattoo
of a
skull.

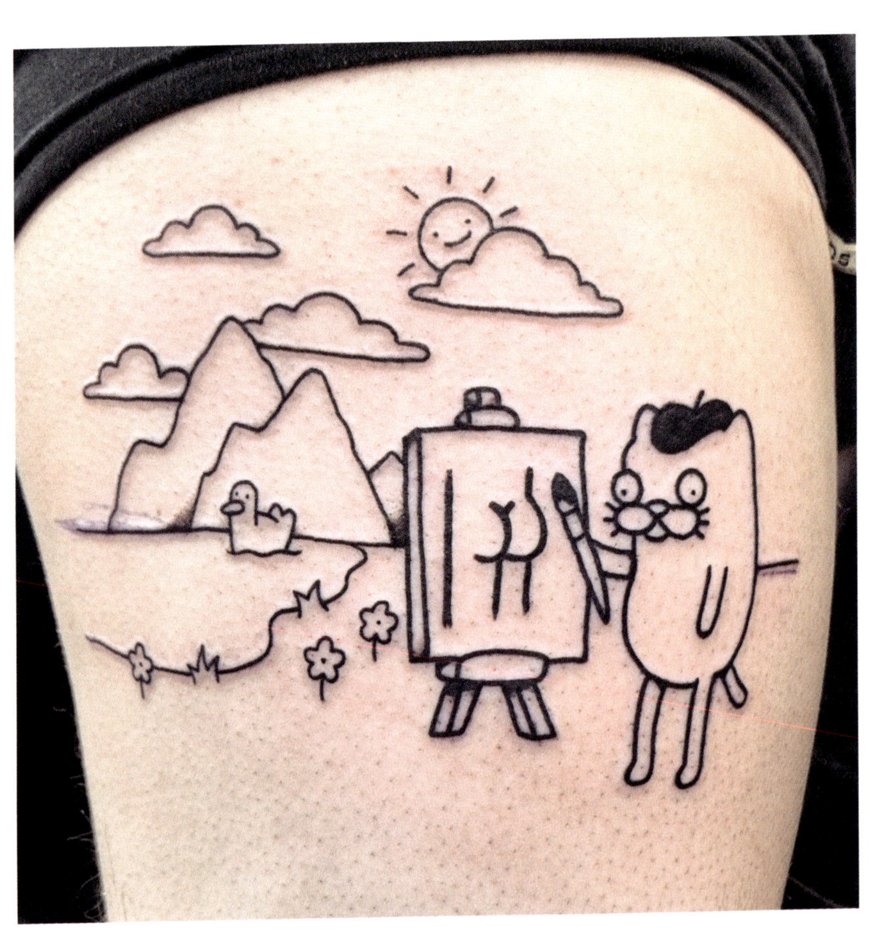

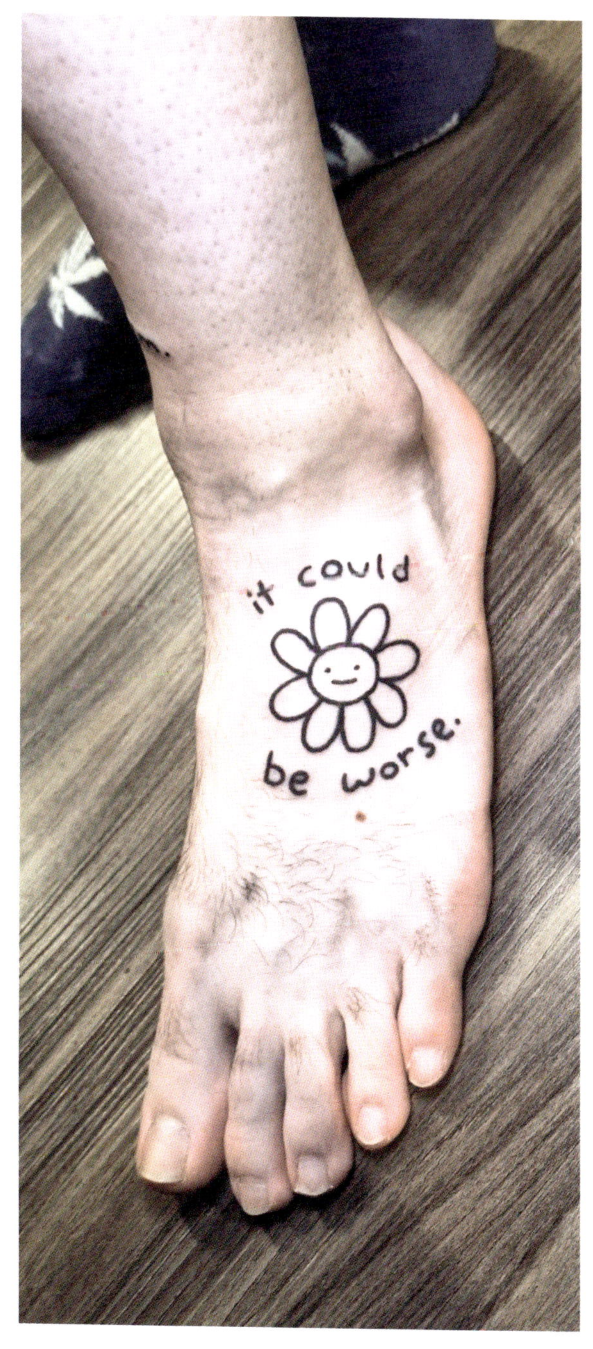
it could
be worse.

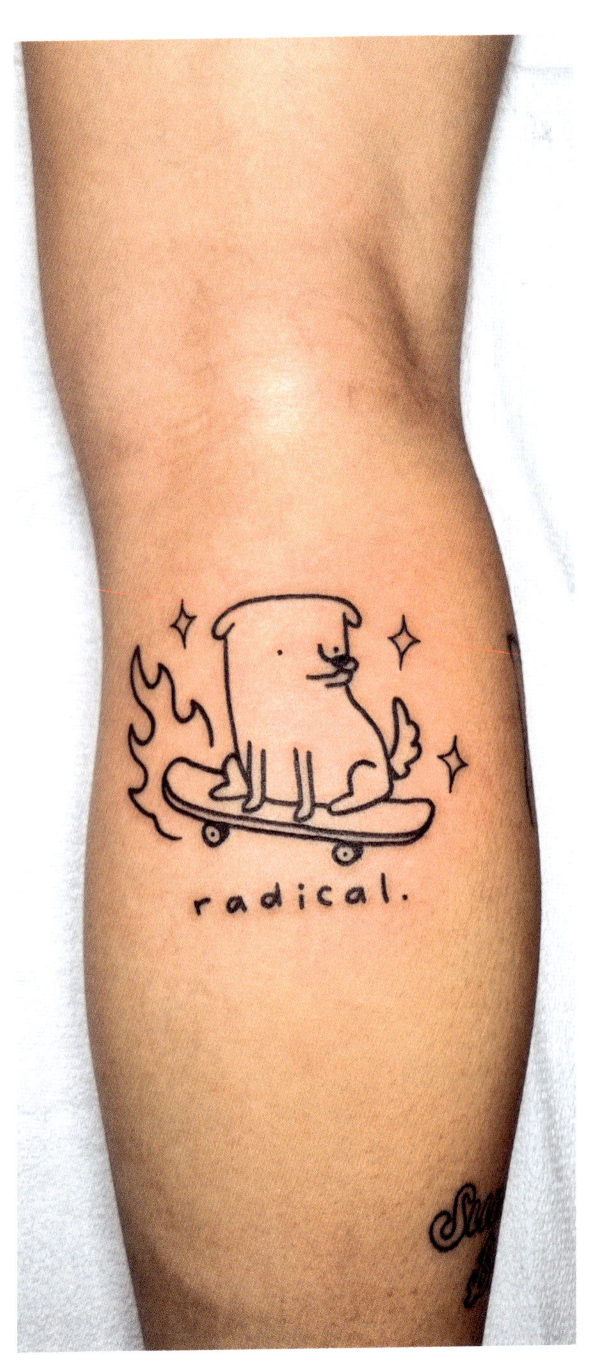
radical.

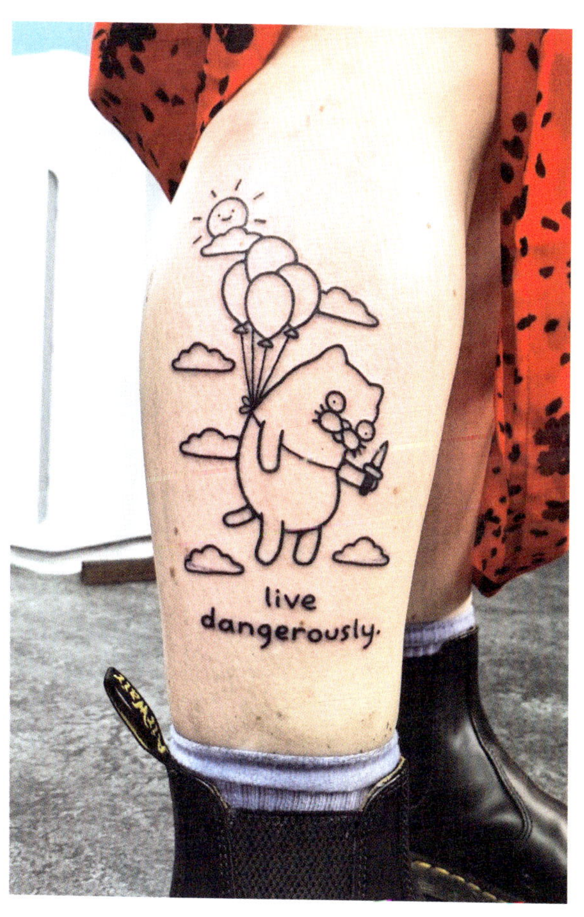
live
dangerously.

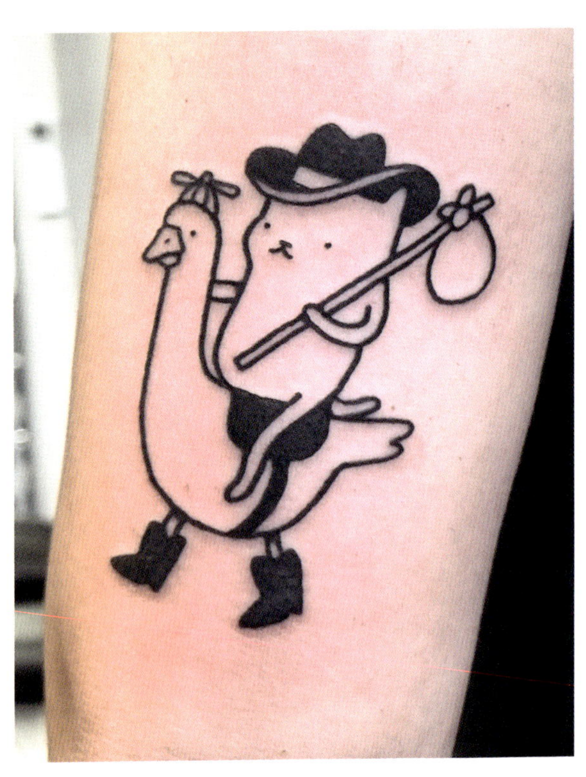

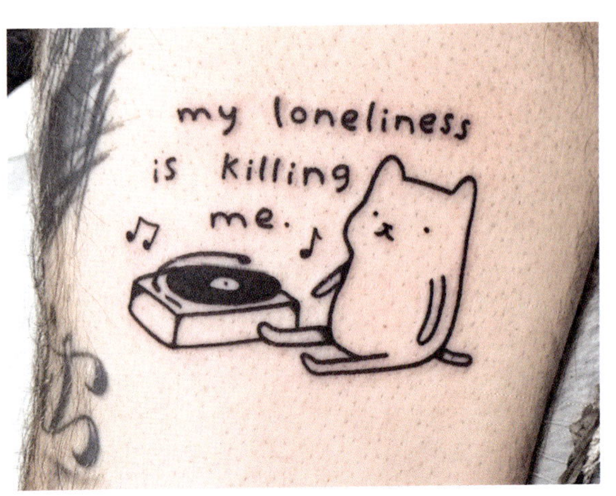
my loneliness
is killing
me.

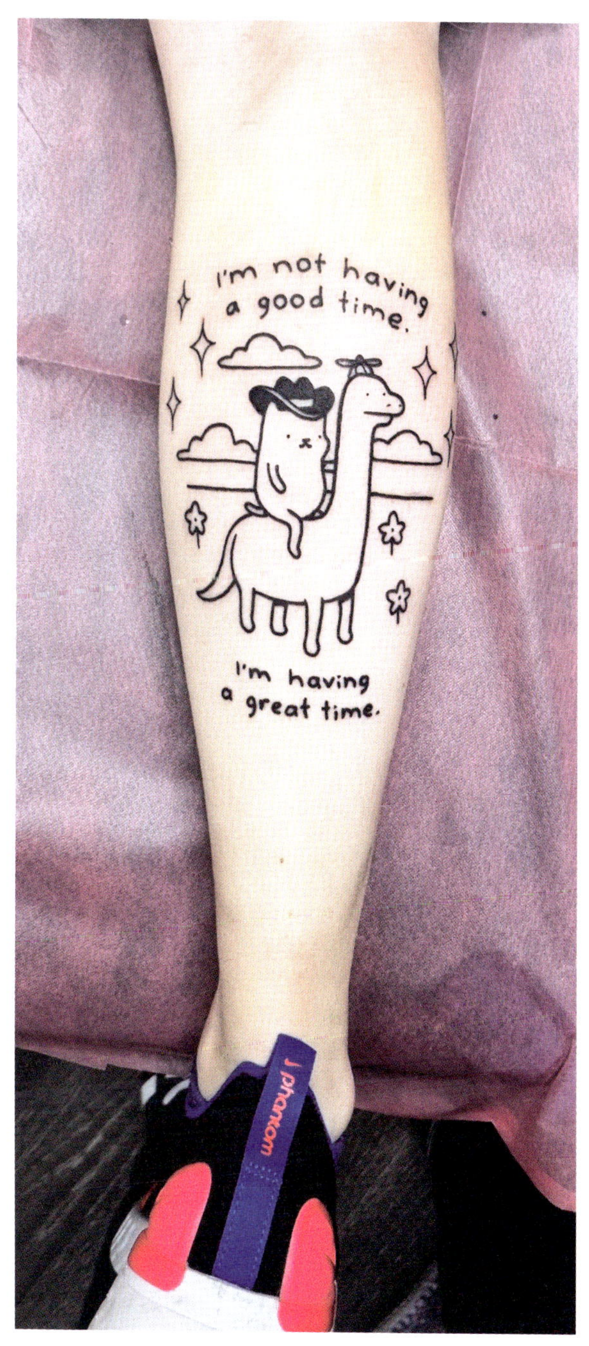
I'm not having
a good time.
I'm having
a great time.
phantom

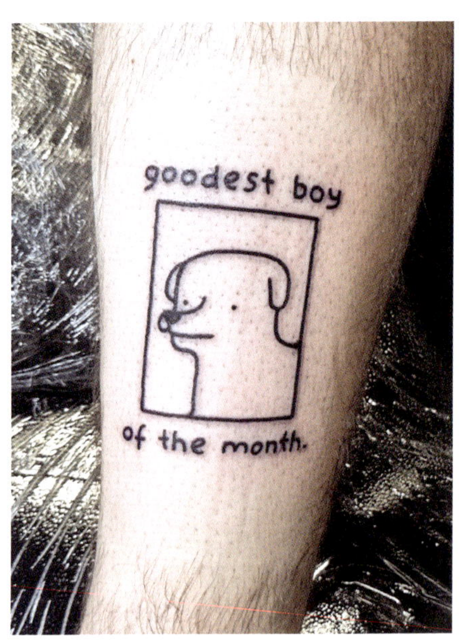
goodest boy
of the month.

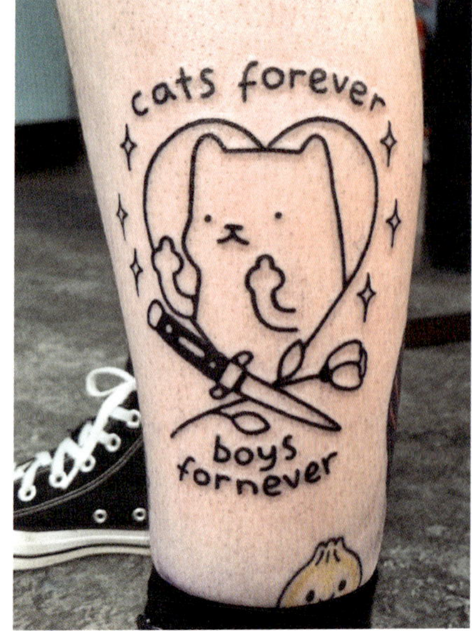
cats forever
boys
fornever

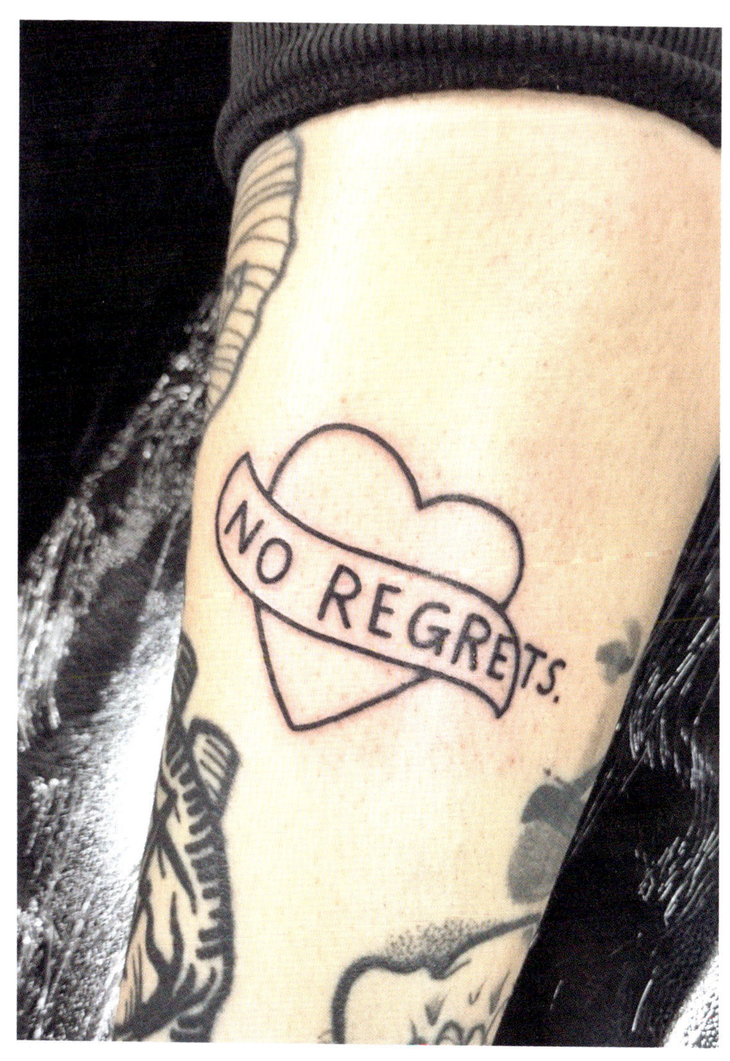
NO REGRETS.

NANCY-DESTROYER

Barcelona, Spain

Based in Barcelona, Nancydestroyer is a self-taught tattoo artist and illustrator known for her raw, unconventional 'ignorant' style of tattoos - bold, full of personality, and often infused with dark humour and quirky charm. Rejecting the notion that tattoos must always carry deep meaning, she embraces the idea that sometimes they're just meant to make you smile.

Drawing inspiration from indie films, illustrations, art exhibitions, cartoons and song lyrics, Nancydestroyer transforms seemingly random phrases and images into offbeat, unexpected designs. Her work attracts a crowd that shares her love for the weird and wonderful, making her creative process all the more enjoyable.

For her, tattooing is about having fun and experimenting, resulting in playful, bizarre and joyfully absurd pieces.

19.

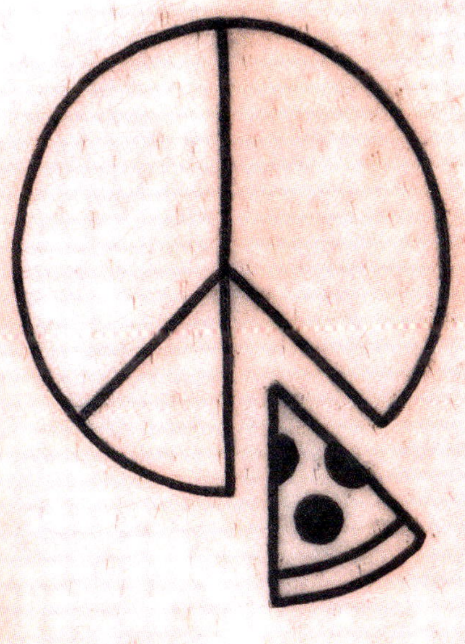
FIND YOUR
INNER PIECE

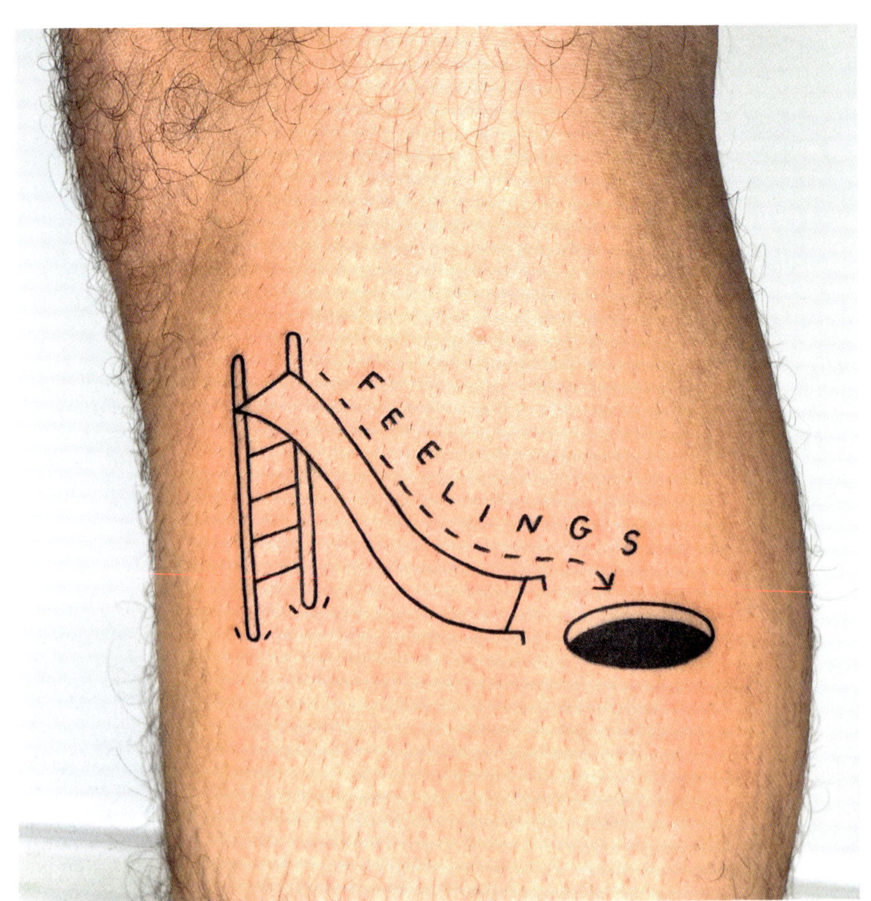
FEELINGS

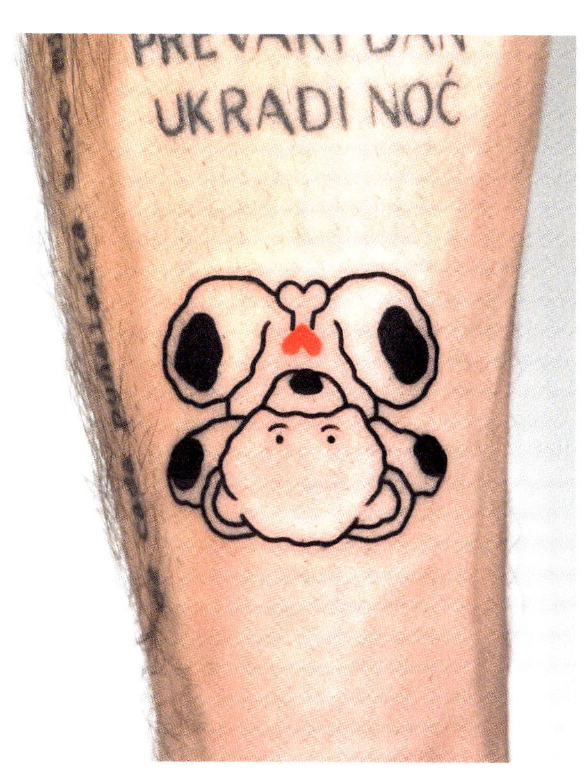
UKRADI NOĆ

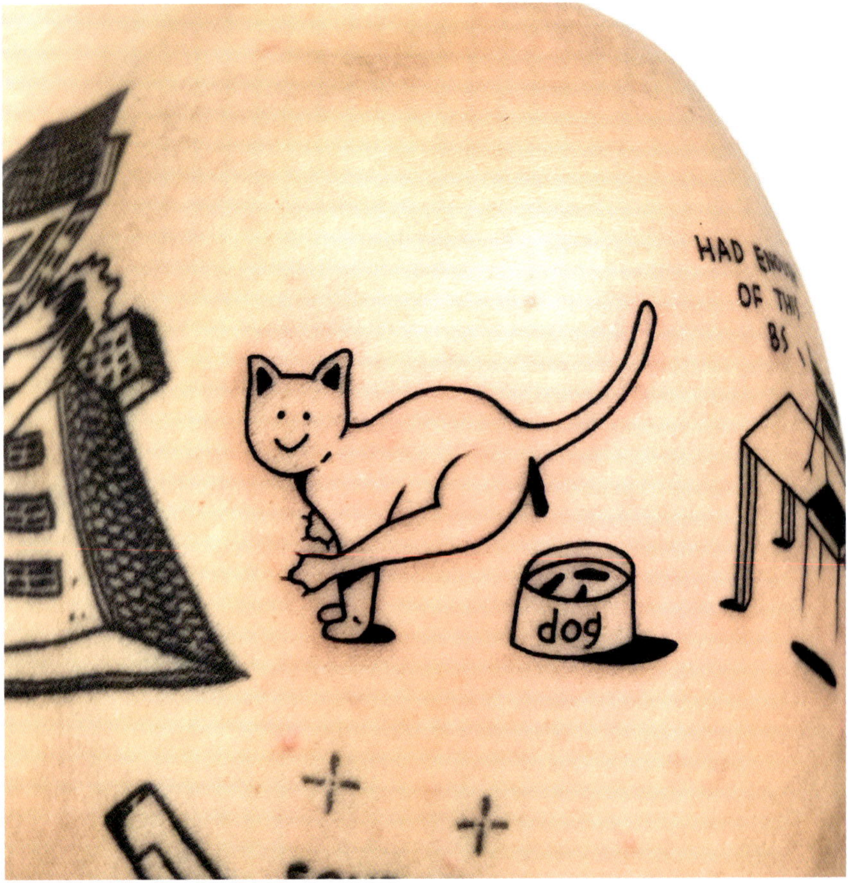

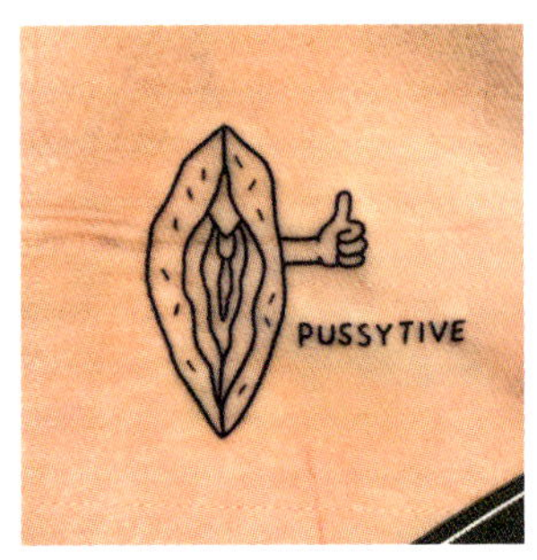
PUSSYTIVE

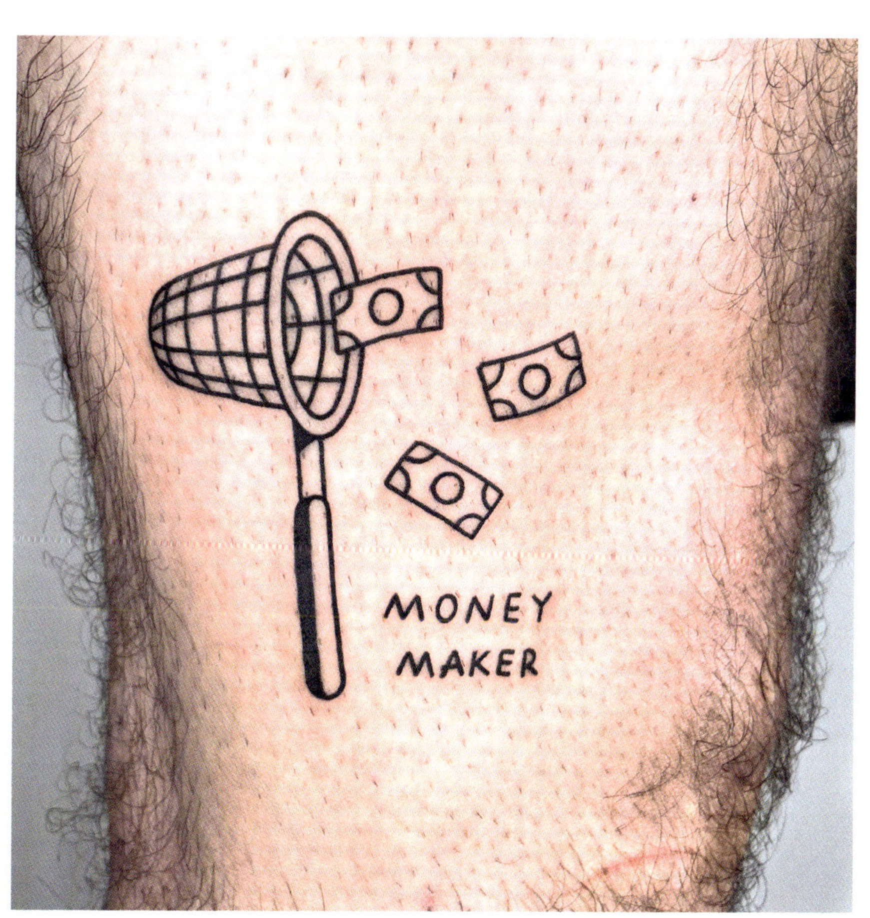
MONEY
MAKER

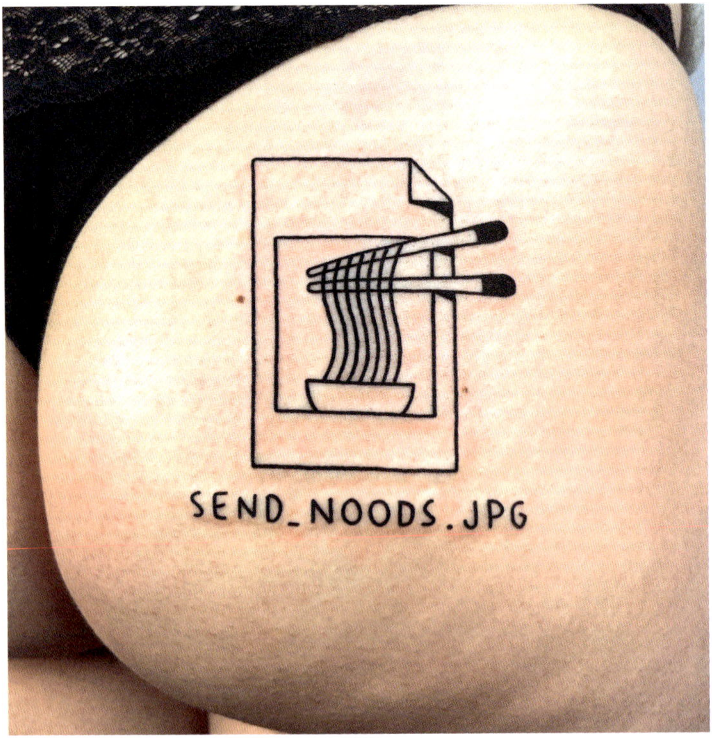

SEND_NOODS.JPG

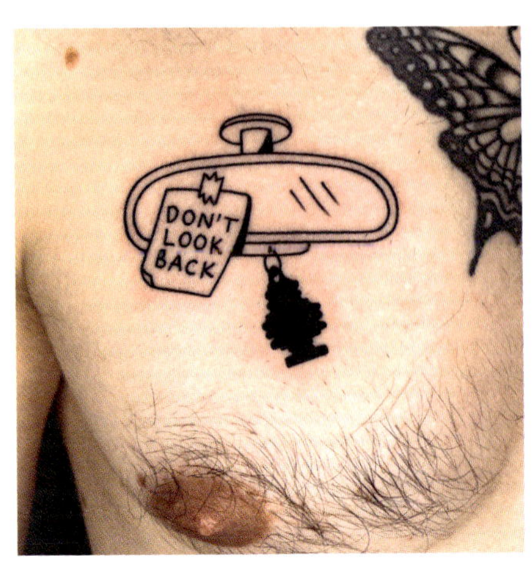
DON'T
LOOK
BACK

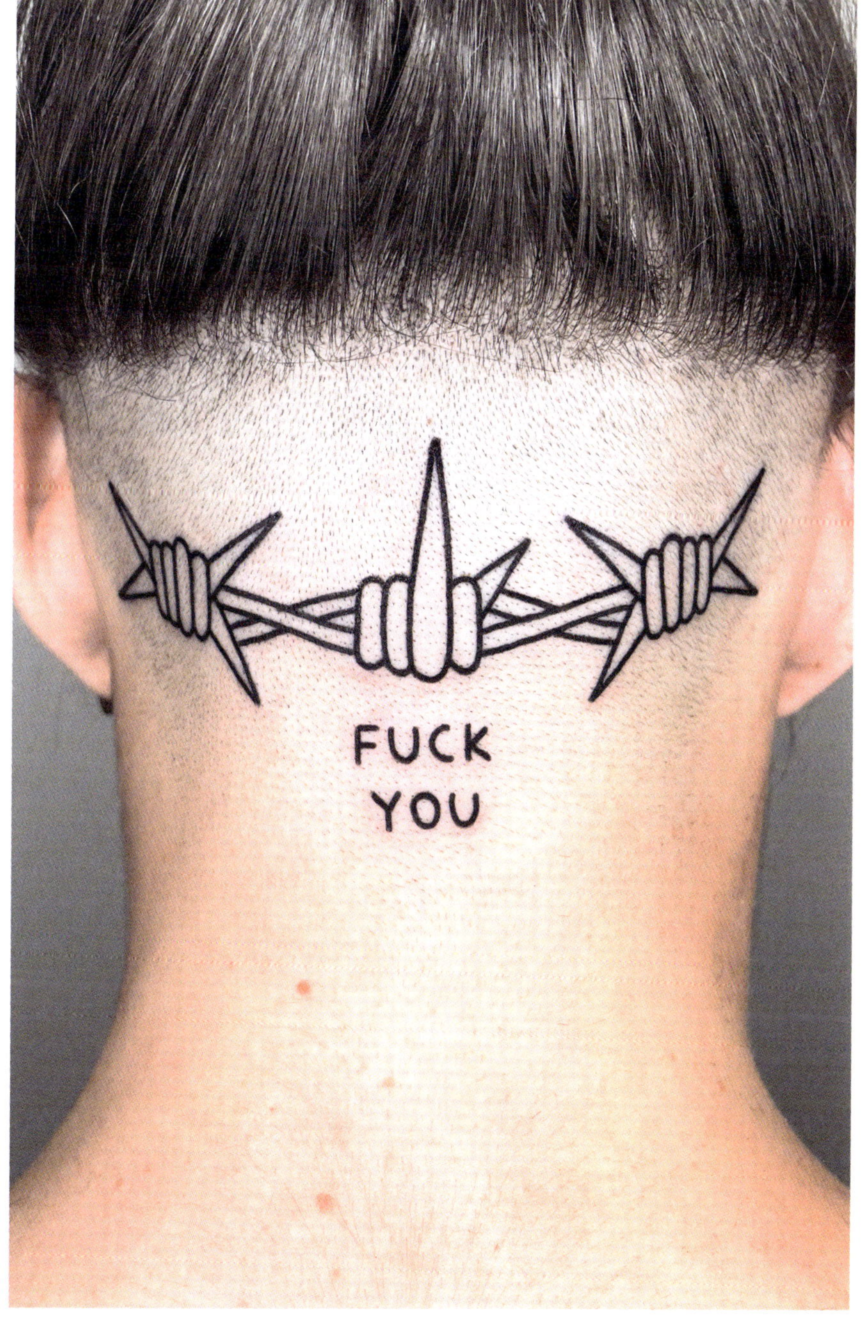
FUCK
YOU

PISATCHÉ

Seoul, South Korea

PISATCHÉ is a Seoul-based tattoo artist known for a unique fusion of contrasting aesthetics, combining robust battle suit designs in gleaming chrome with soft, stylised animal motifs. These striking, armoured figures are balanced by charming representations of clients' pets, forming a unique visual contrast between strength and softness.

Inspired by childhood memories, cartoons and early doodles, PISATCHÉ's work balances strength and playfulness, creating a distinct visual identity. Originally studying visual design at Incheon National University, PISATCHÉ realised that true creative fulfilment came not from structured design work, but from freely drawing and expressing personal ideas. This realisation led to a bold decision to leave university after a year to pursue a more authentic artistic path.

After completing military service, PISATCHÉ discovered a deep passion for tattooing in 2018. Since then, PISATCHÉ has continued refining an artistic voice that merges the cute with the edgy, the delicate with the daring, crafting tattoos that surprise and captivate.

20.

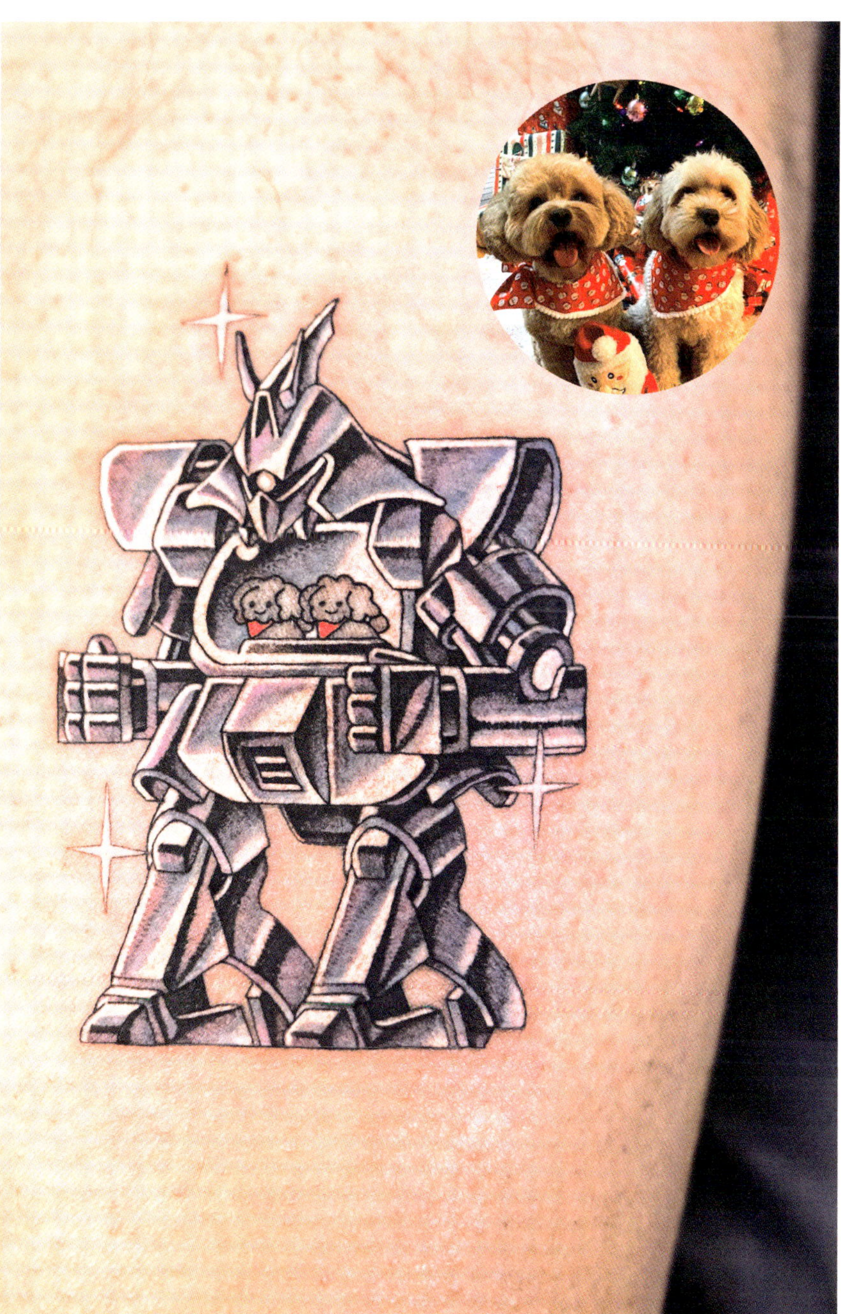

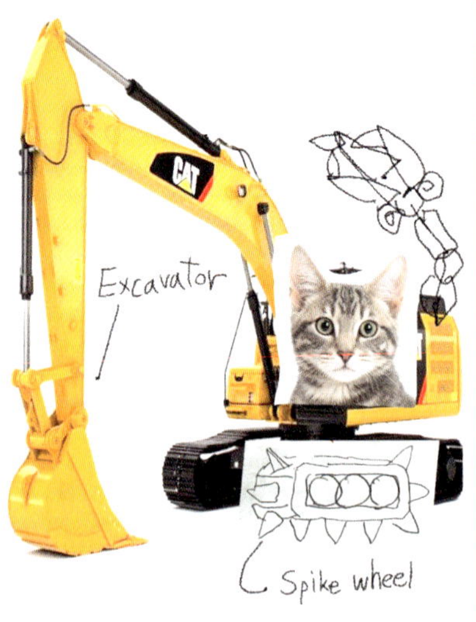
CAT
Excavator
Spike wheel

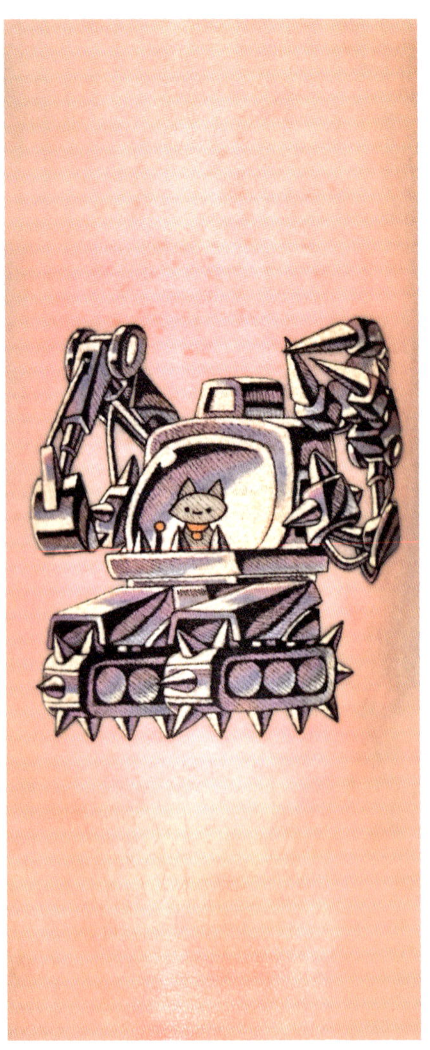

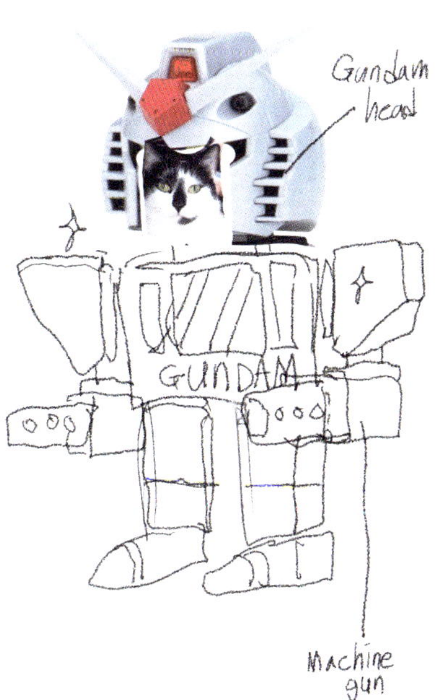
Gundam
head
GUNDAM
Machine
gun

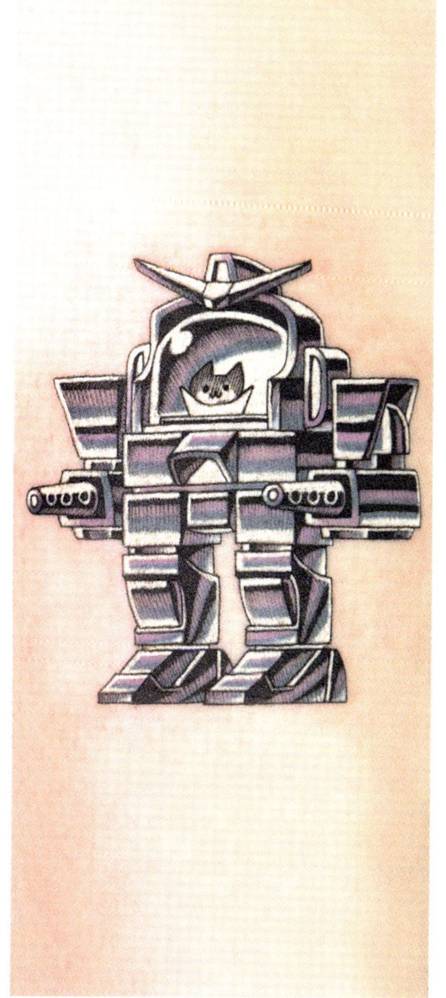

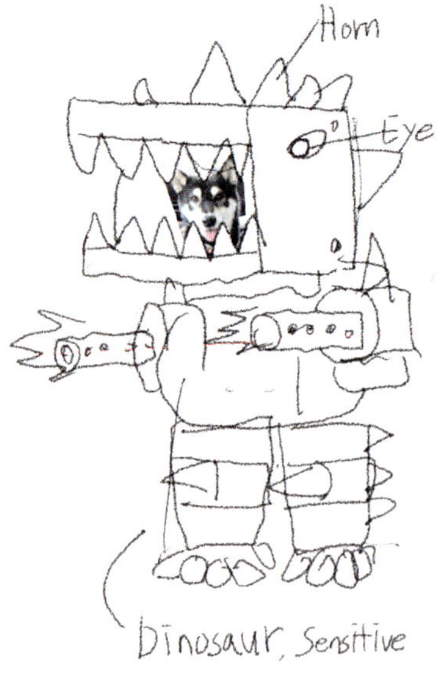
Horn
Eye
Dinosaur, Sensitive

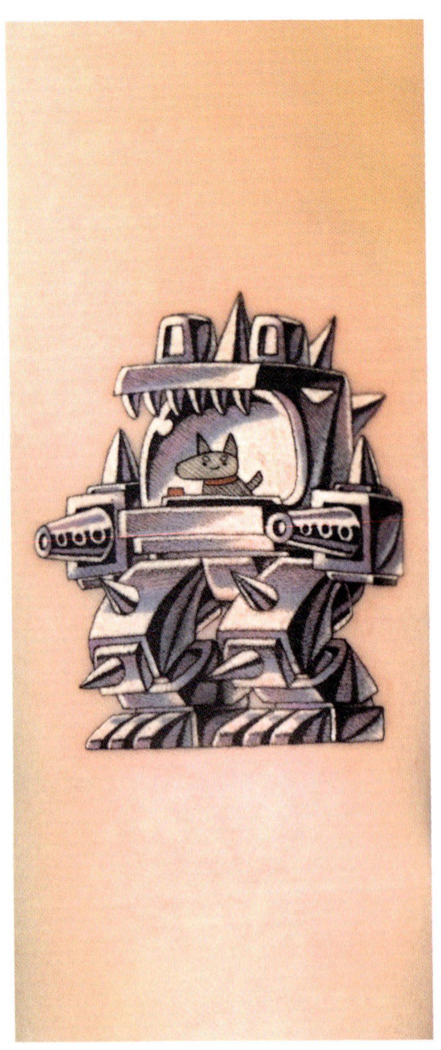

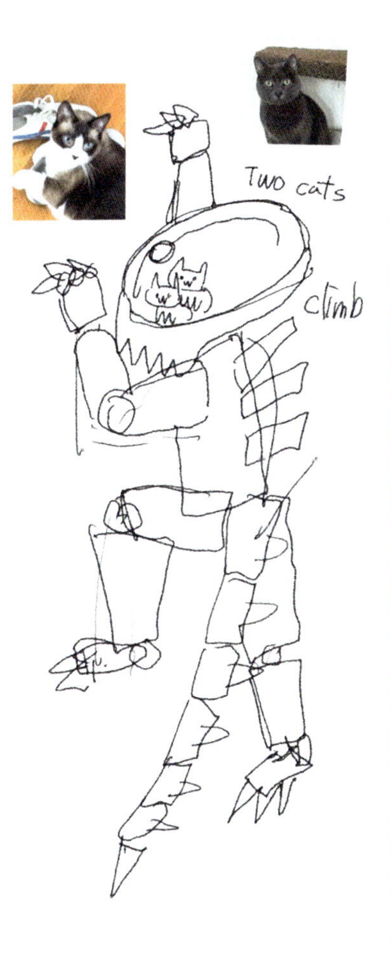
Two cats
climb

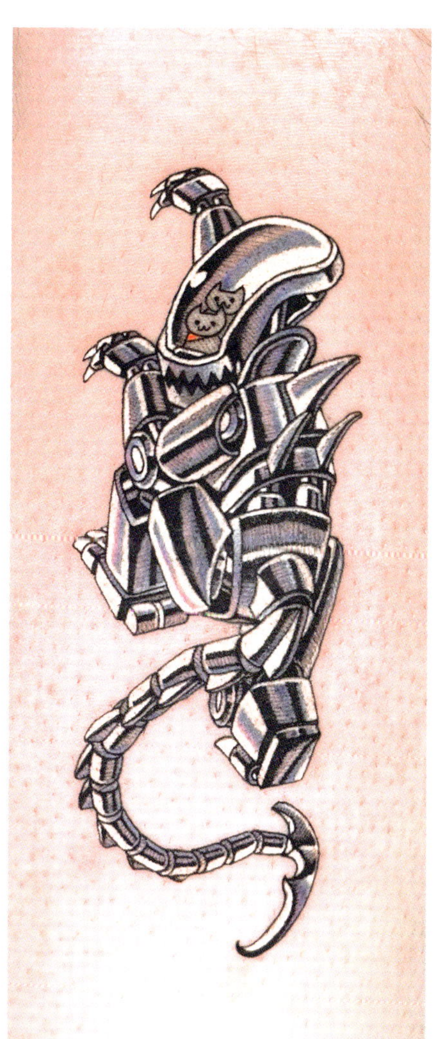

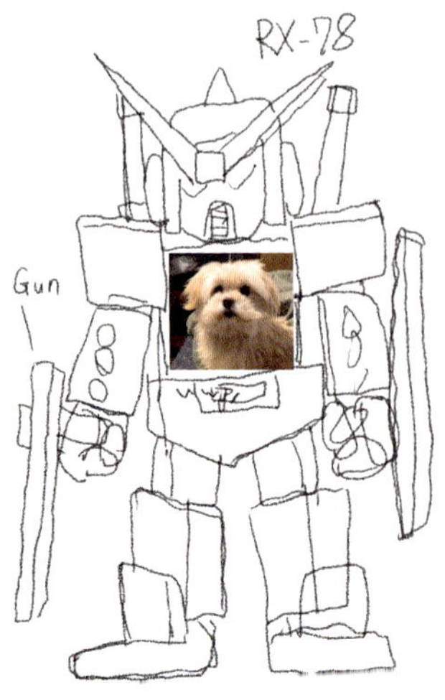
RX-78
Gun

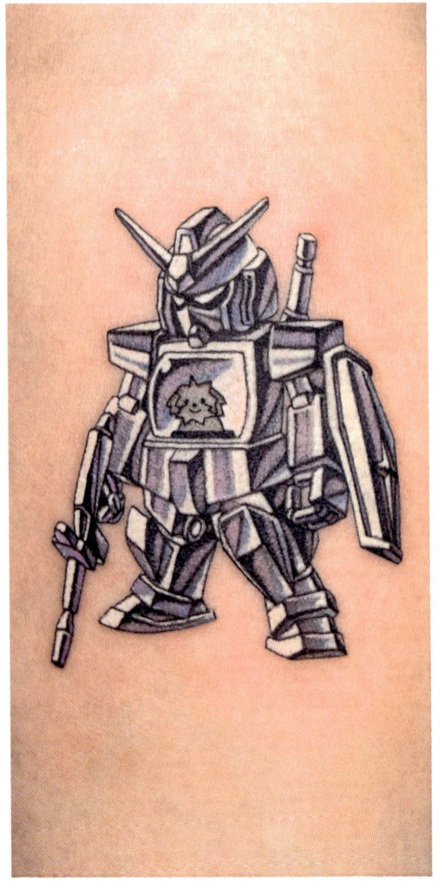

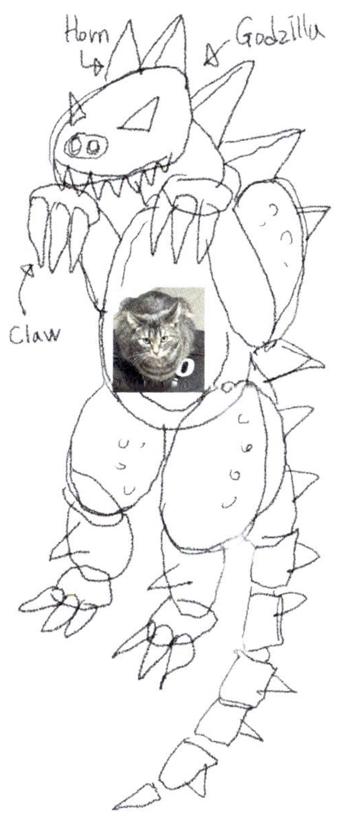
Horn
Godzilla
Claw

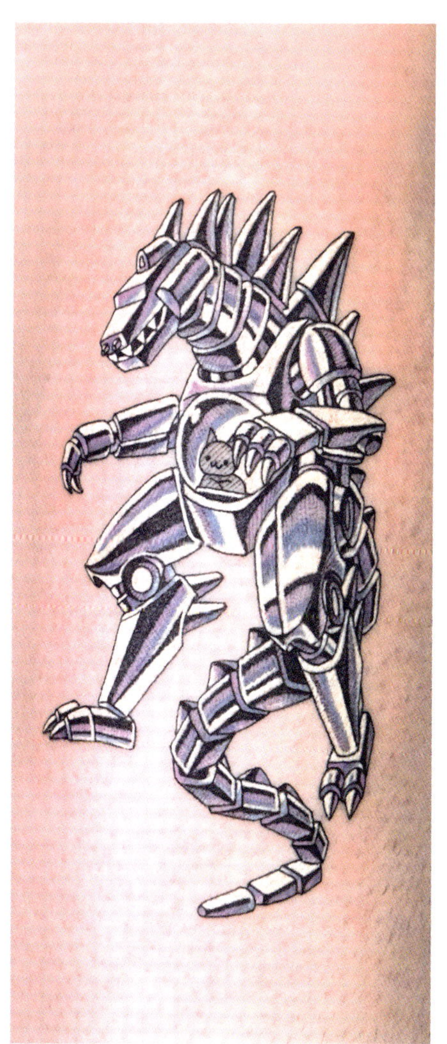

ROOOOSE-BLUE

Taipei, Taiwan

Roooooseblue, also known as Rose, is a tattoo artist based in Taipei, Taiwan. Renowned for her refreshingly offbeat style, her designs are quirky, humorous and full of personality. After graduating from Shih Hsin University, she began her tattooing journey in 2023.

Rose currently works out of her own private studio in Taipei, where she also enjoys creating merchandise that complements her artistic vision.

She has a deep love for wolves and a passion for the unusual - elements that shine through in her work. With a background in design and her hands-on attitude, Rose brings both creativity and a strong work ethic to her craft.

Inspired by daily life, photography and illustration, she continues to create one-of-a-kind designs that offer her clients a memorable and personal experience.

21.

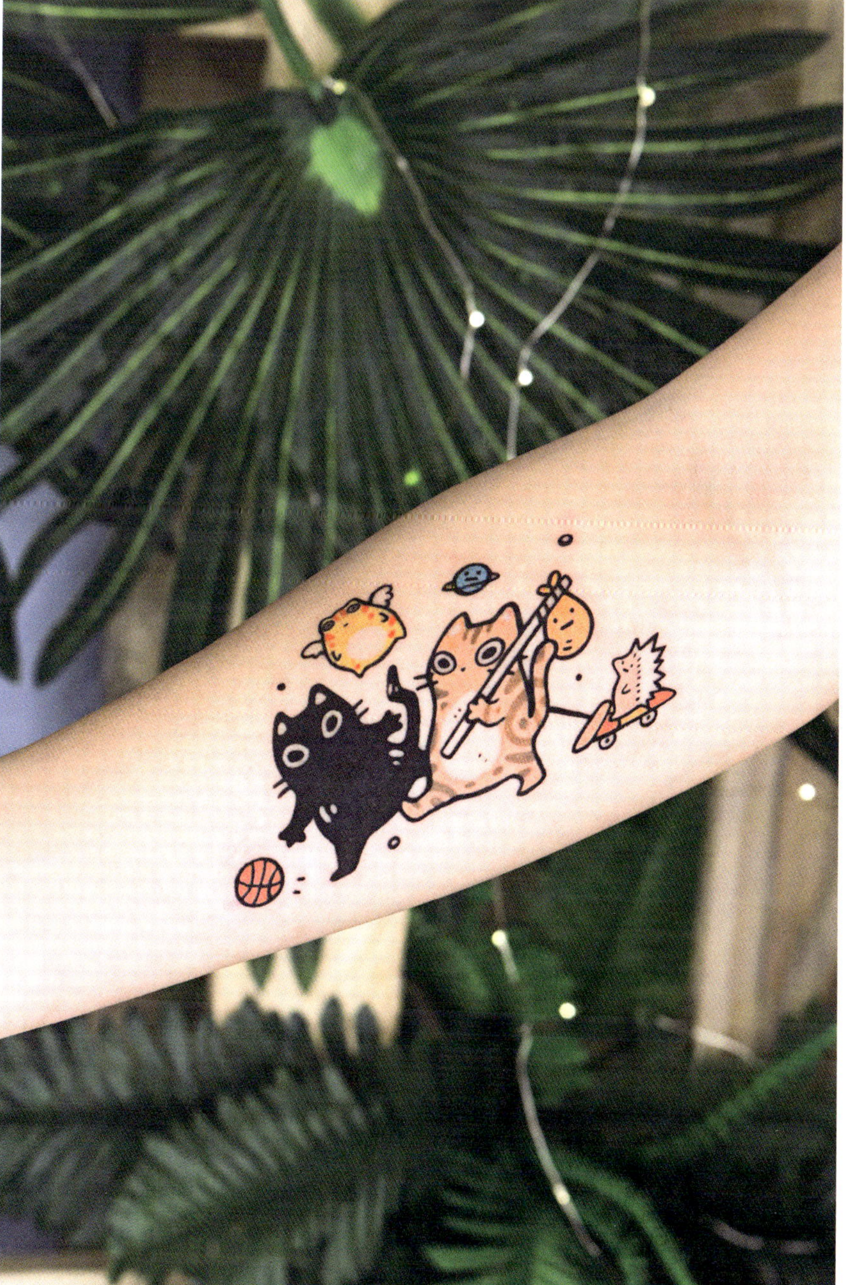

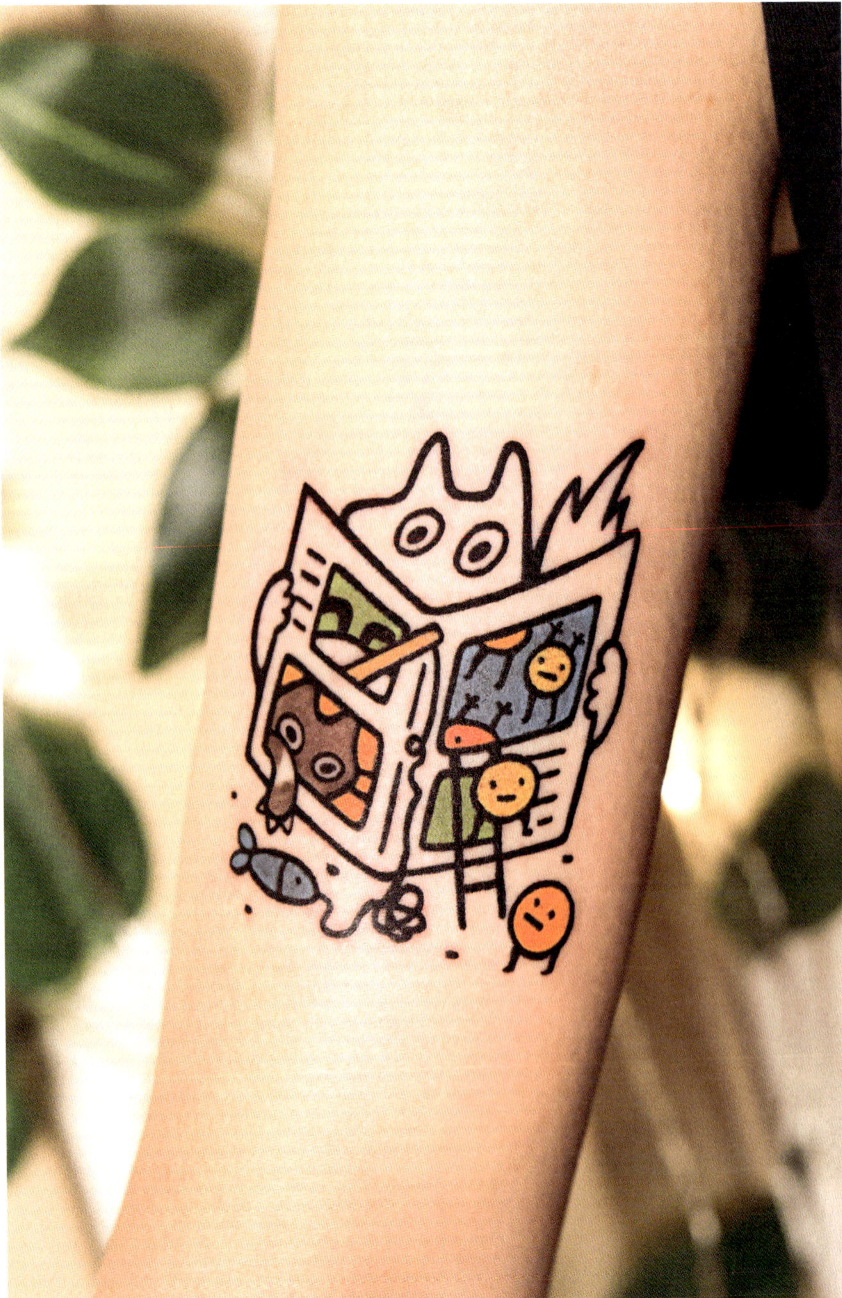

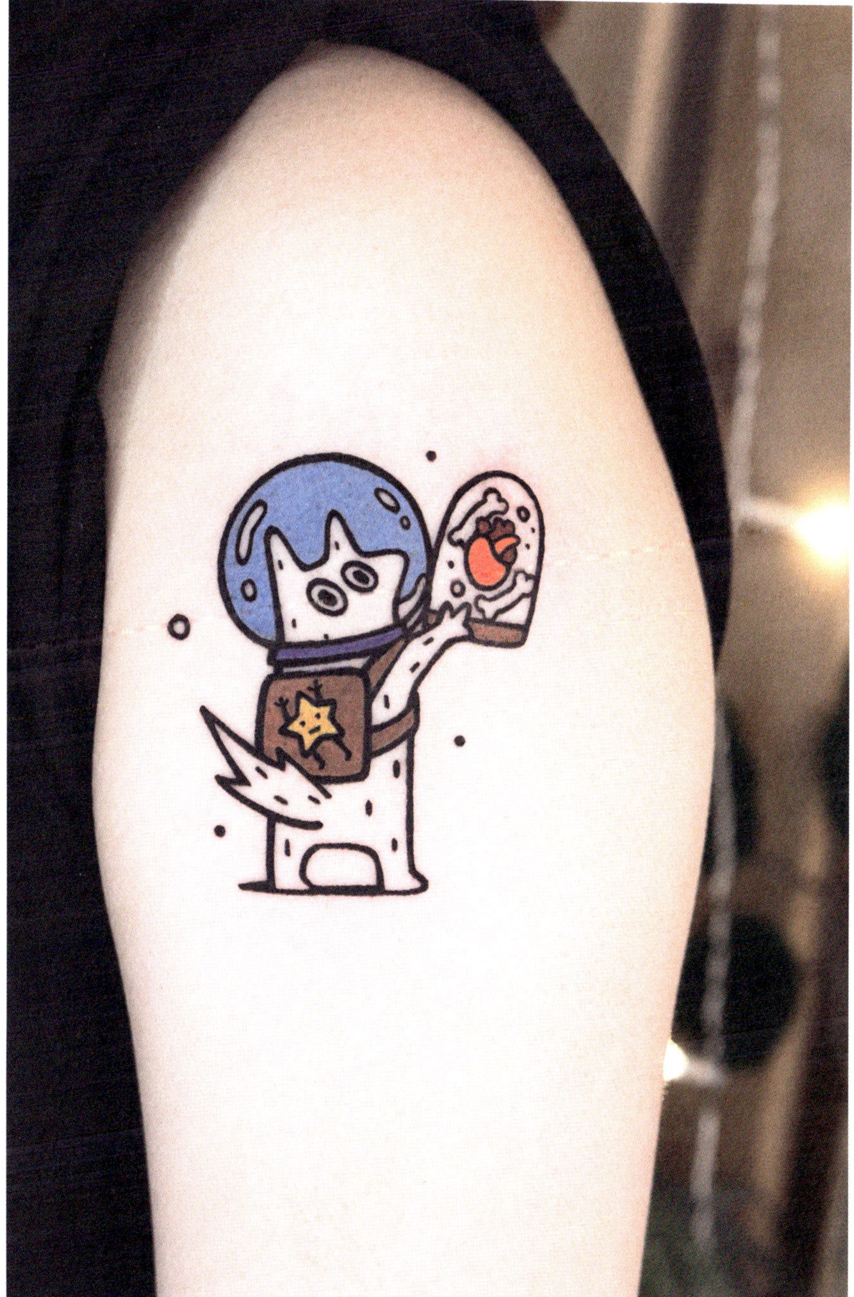

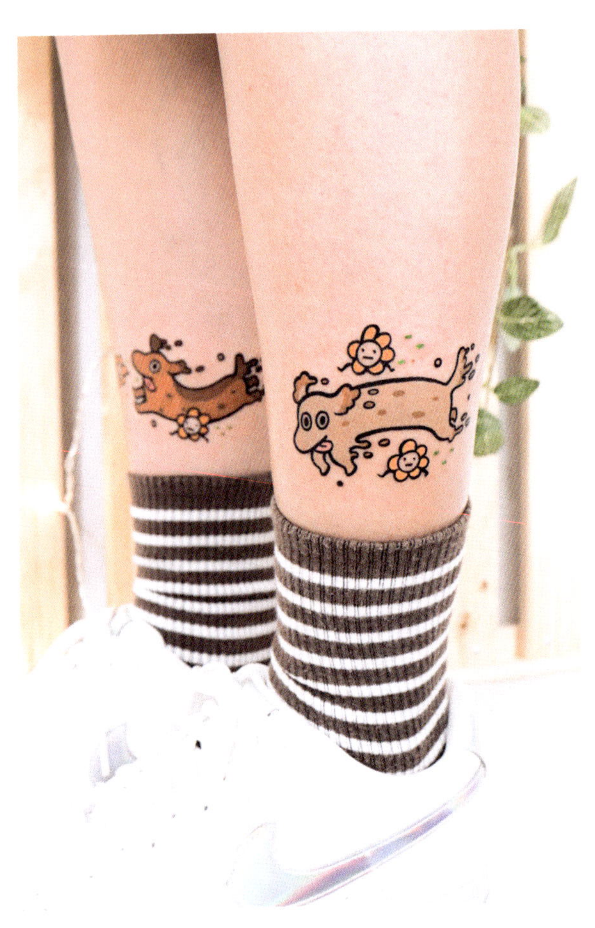

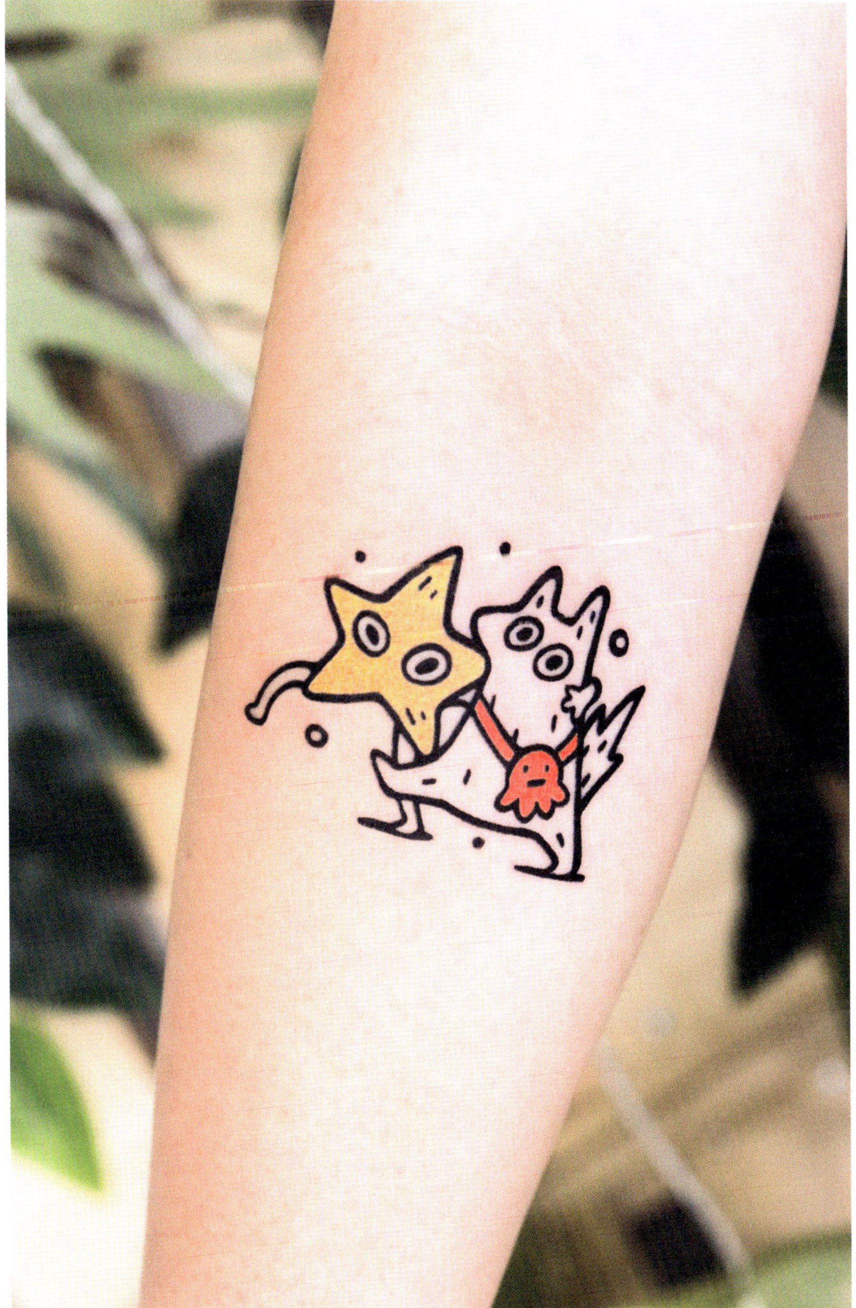

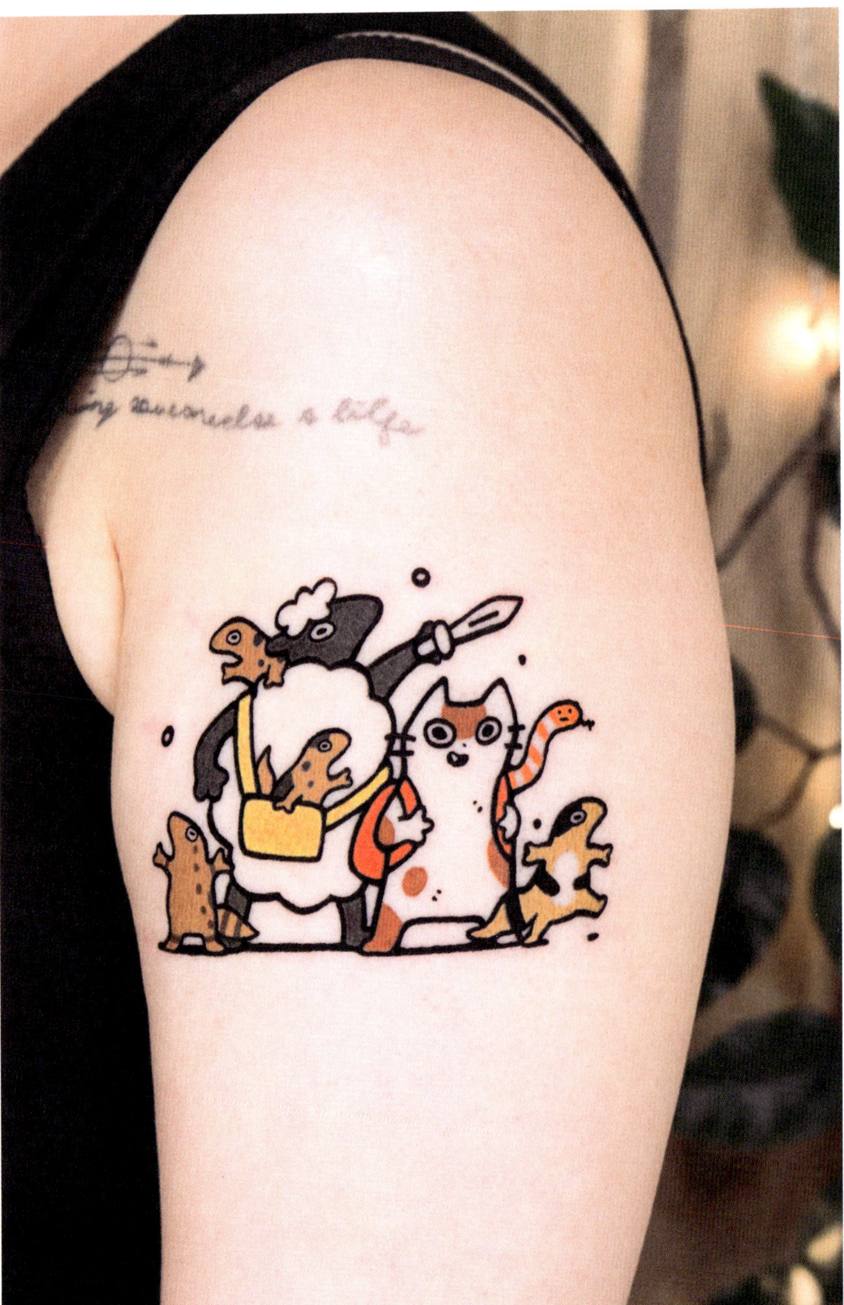

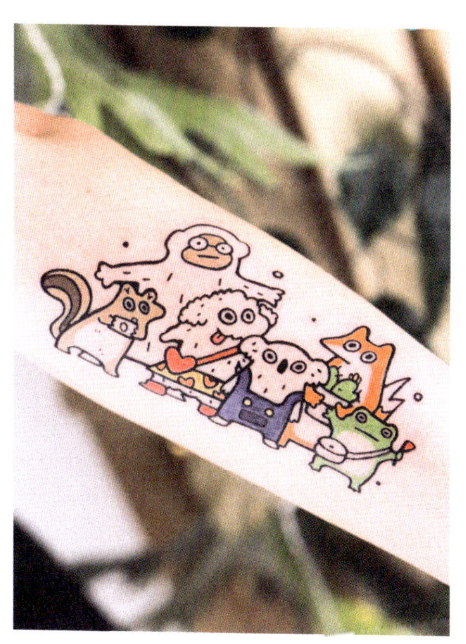

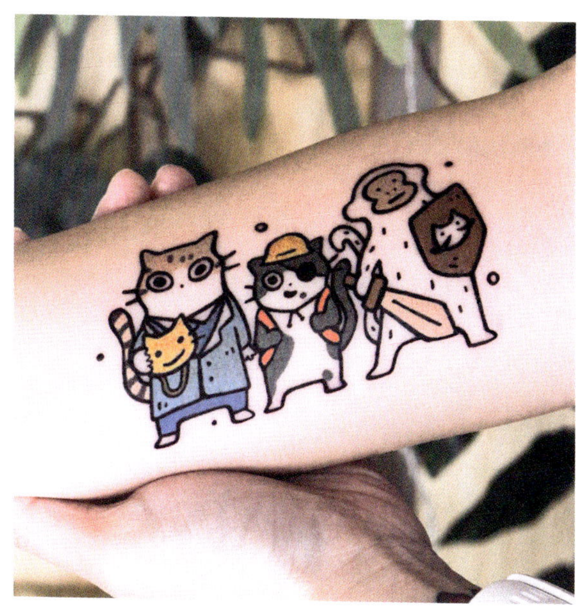

SSUN_ FROM_LOVE

Berlin, Germany

Ssun_from_Love is a Korean tattoo artist, currently living in Berlin with her husband - also a tattooer - and their three-year-old son. Although Berlin is their base, the family leads a largely nomadic life, moving with inspiration and creative purpose. Tattooing became Ssun's first true platform for expressing her thoughts and philosophy, a natural extension of her lifelong love for making things by hand and working with focus and care. It's a craft she continues to feel grateful for every day.

Her tattoo designs often carry messages she wants to share with the world - moments that are sweet, beautiful or quietly reflective. Many feel like small fairy tales: intimate, thoughtful and warm. Rooted in an appreciation for life's slower, easily missed details, her work invites a gentle pause from the fast pace of the world.

What matters most to her is connection. If someone can look at one of her tattoos during a difficult time and feel even a little lighter, that's the true reward. 'I believe my story can become your story,' she says, 'and that it can grow into a warm kind of energy that connects all of us.'

22.

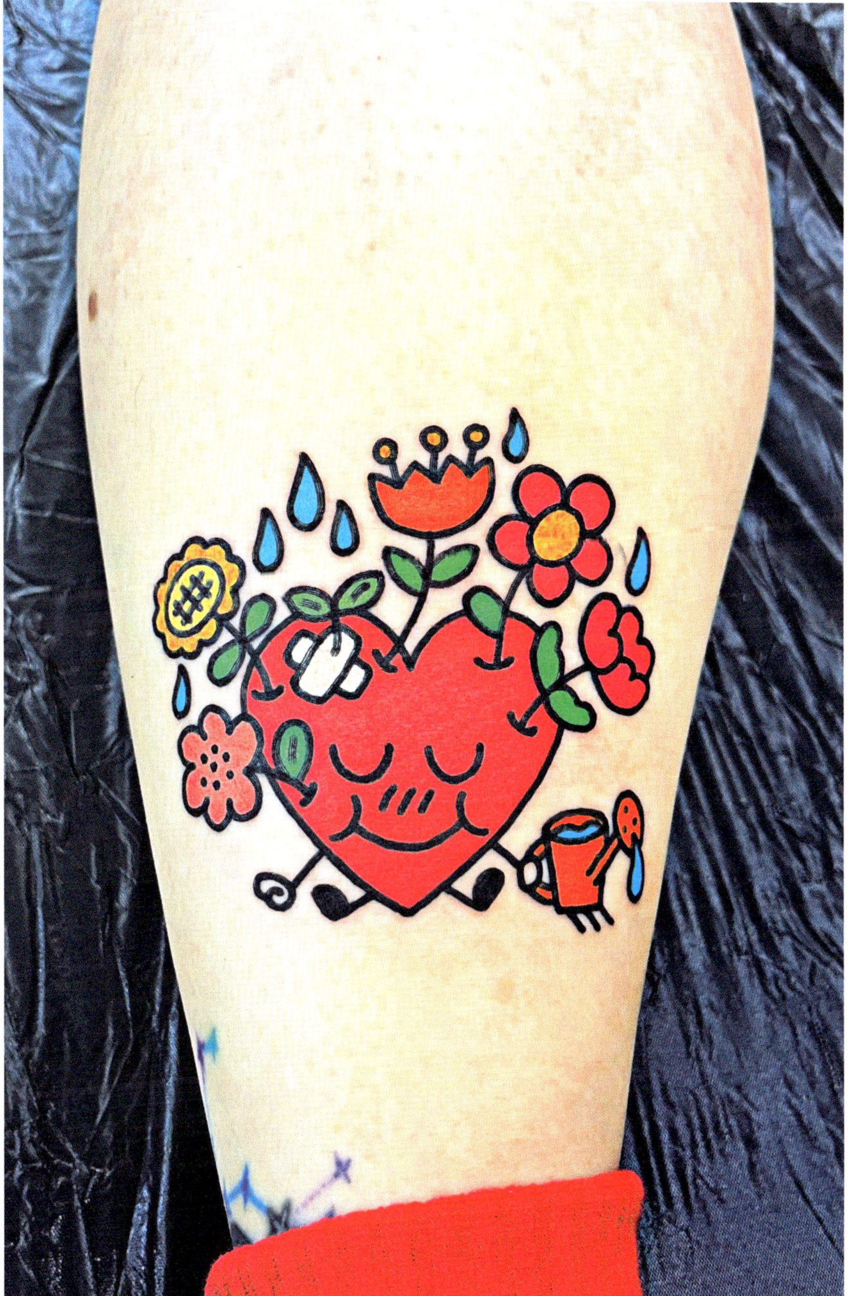

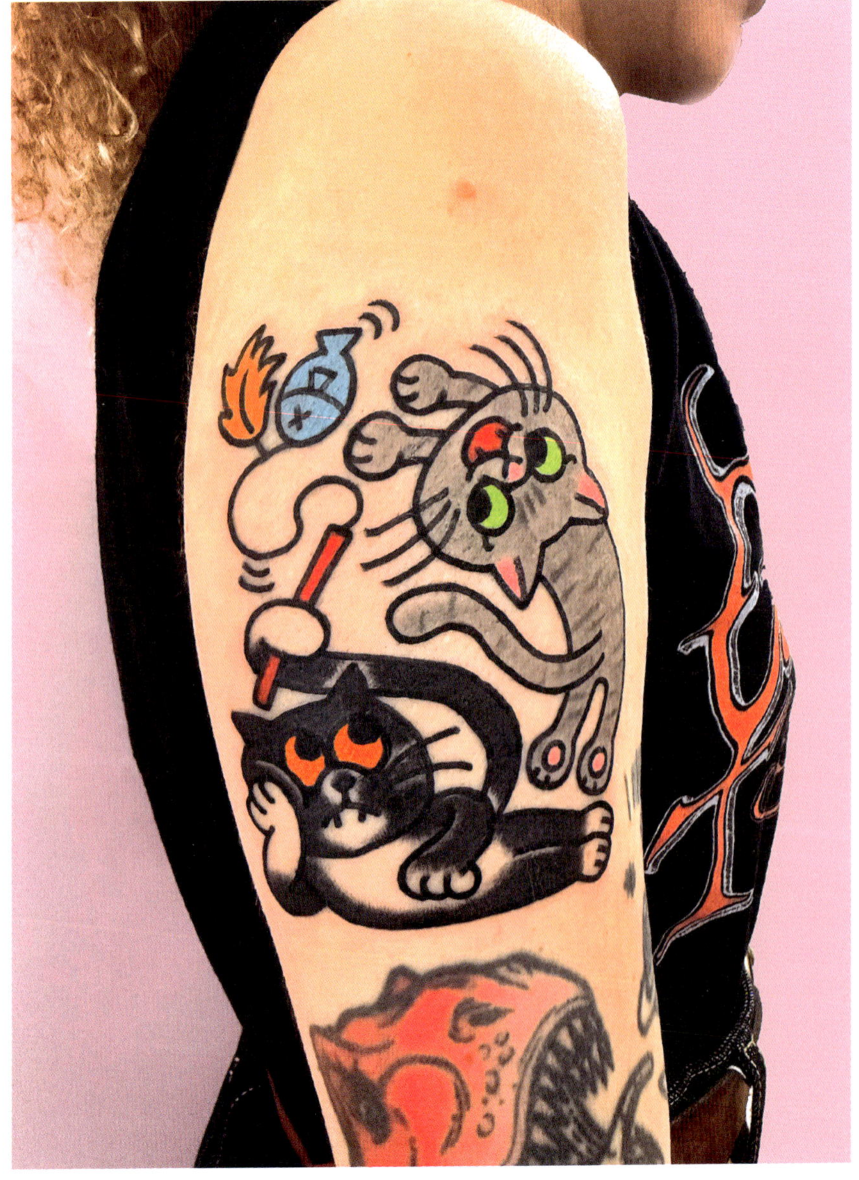

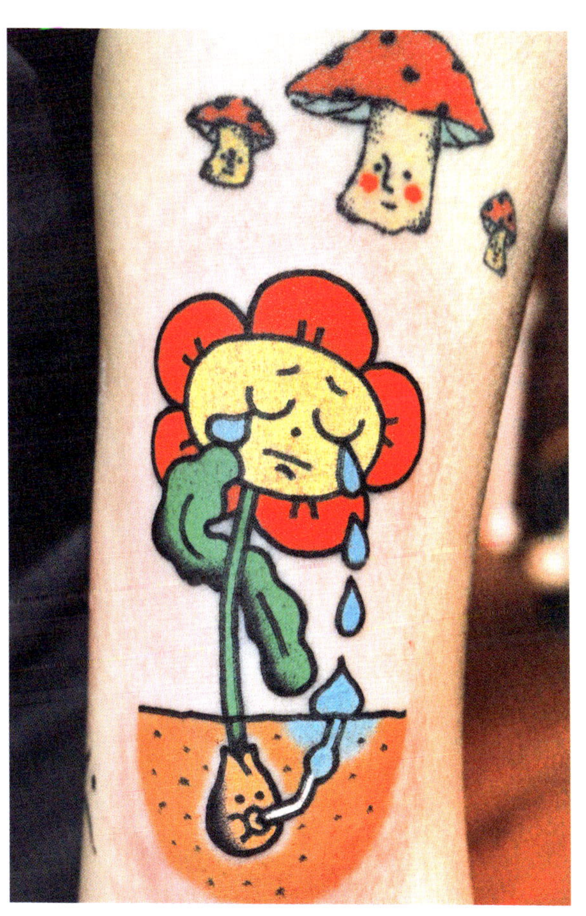

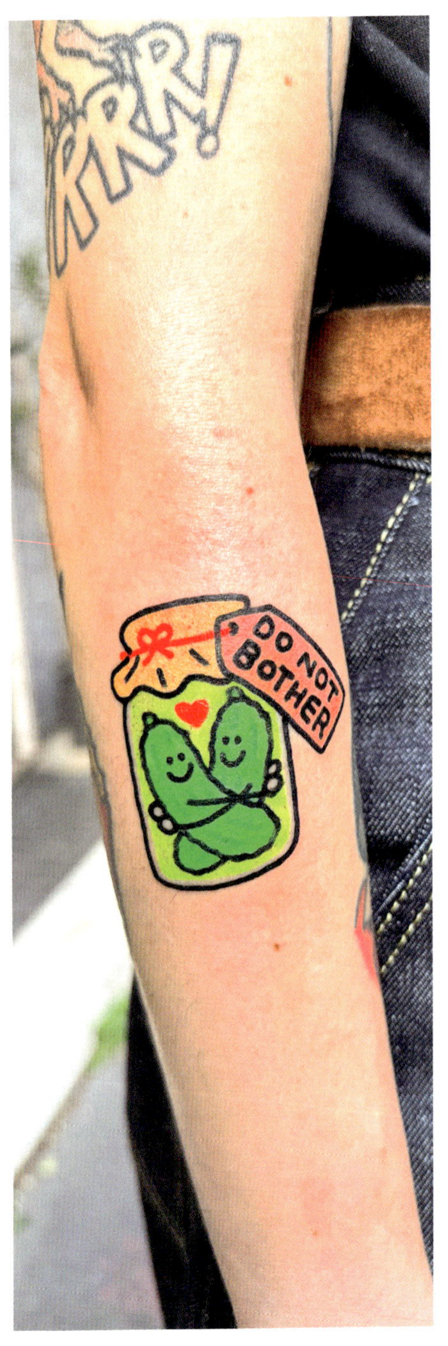
RR!
DO NOT BOTHER

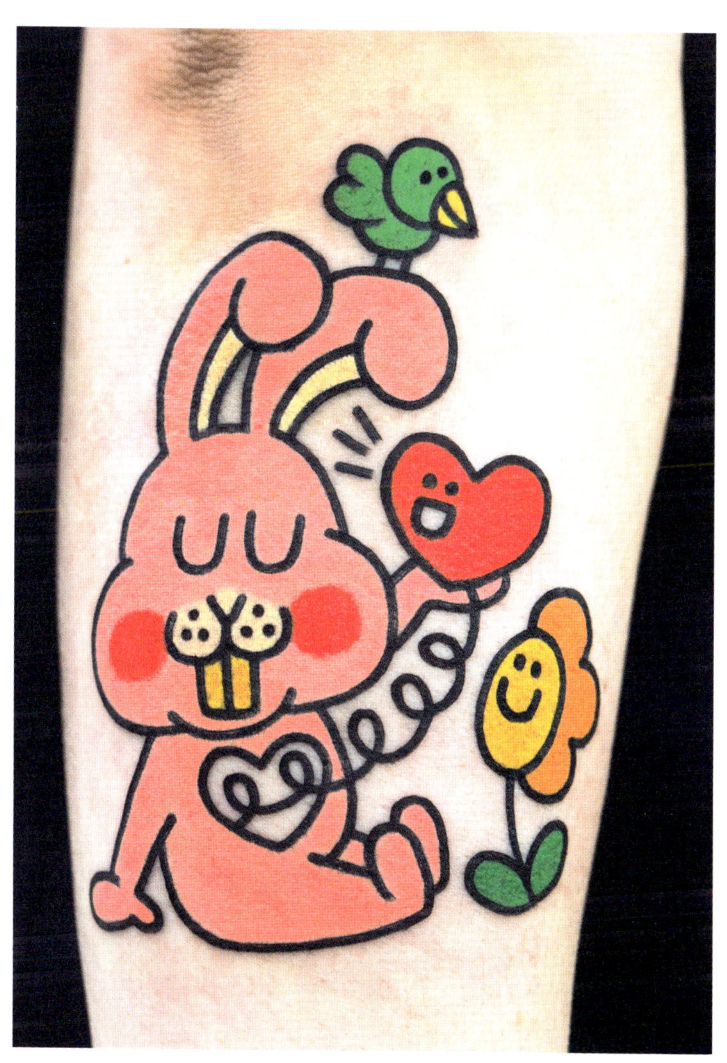

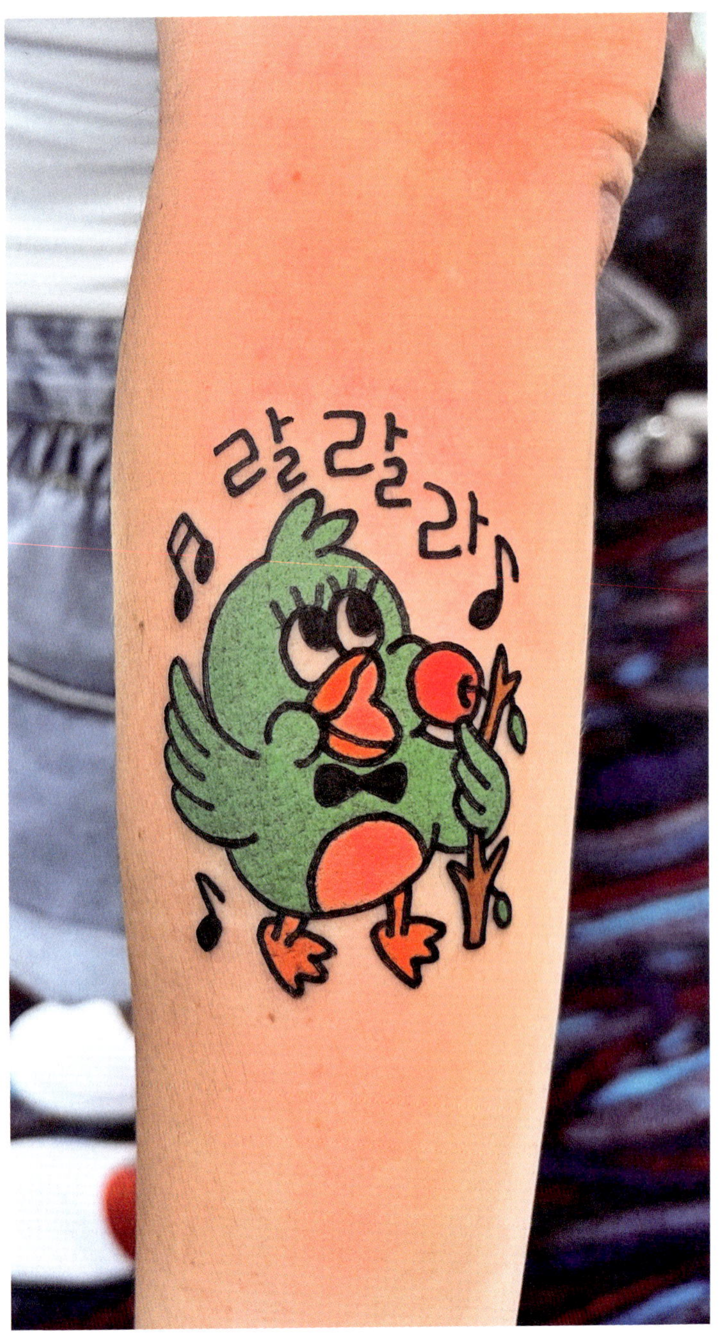
랄랄라

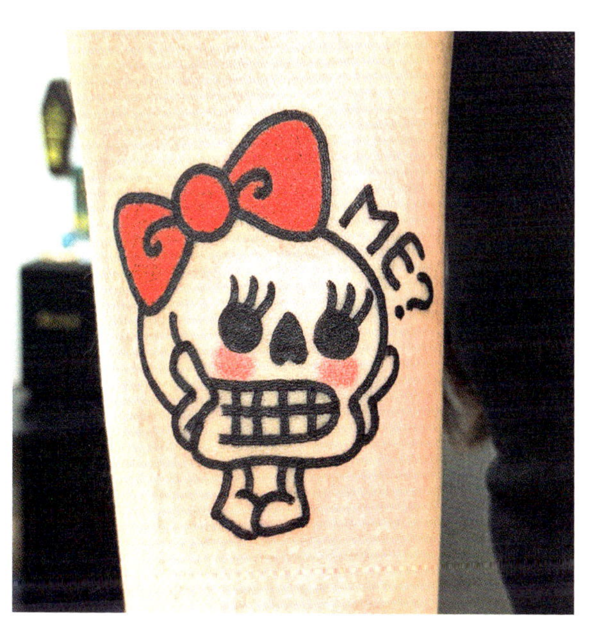
ME?

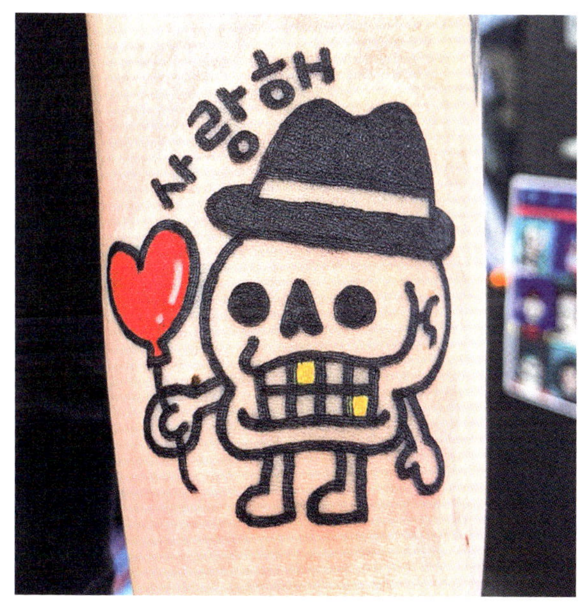
사랑해

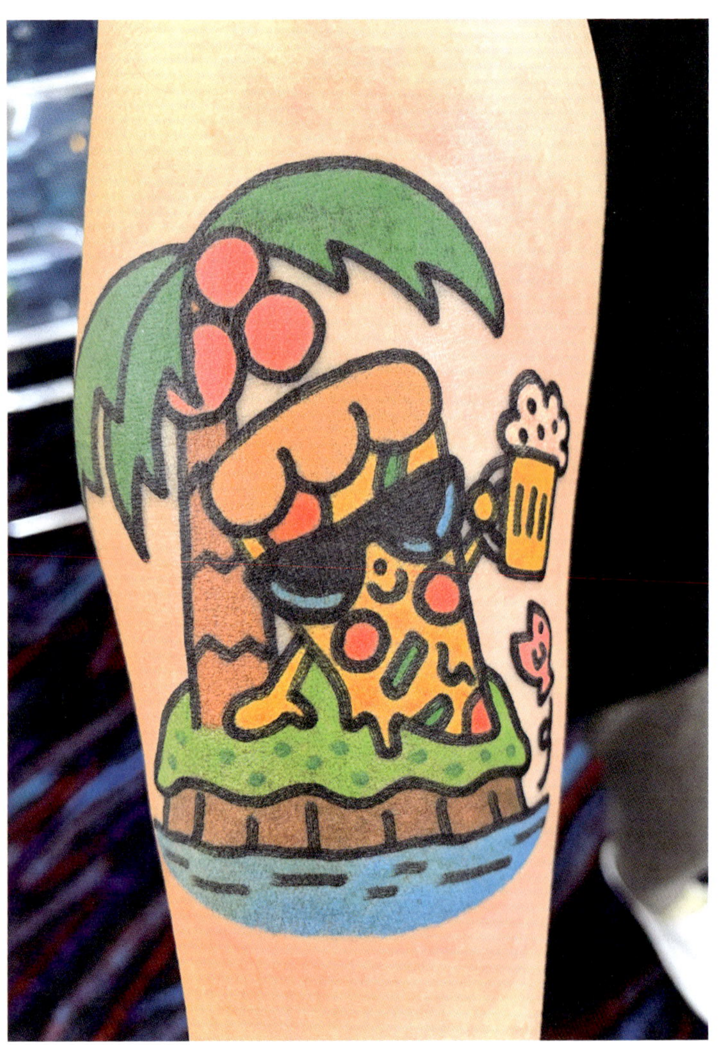

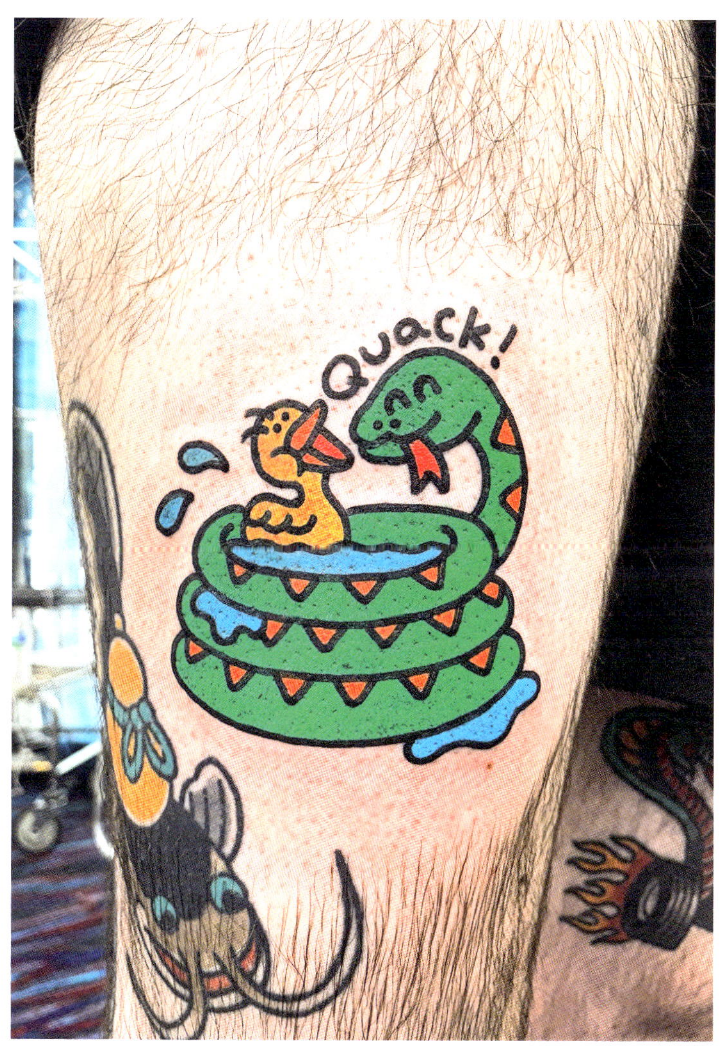
Quack!

U_OOOOPS

Seoul, South Korea

Yuwon Jung, known professionally as u_oooops, is a tattoo artist based in Seoul, Korea, specialising in soft, pastel-toned designs. Yuwon started her tattoo career in 2017, and her art is dedicated to creating delicate, airy designs that add warmth and lightness to the skin.

With a background in the electronic devices industry, Yuwon's path to tattooing was unconventional. However, the realisation that tattoos can be a meaningful source of comfort and self-expression led to a deep passion for the craft. Clients often describe Yuwon's work as 'soft cotton candy', and many have even remarked that the colours look 'delicious' - a testament to the dreamy, ethereal aesthetic that defines the style.

A passionate traveller, Yuwon draws inspiration from visiting new places and observing other tattoo artists in their environments. Each journey brings fresh perspectives, shaping an ever-evolving artistic approach. Beyond technique, Yuwon finds fulfilment in the connection with clients, believing that the experience of tattooing is just as meaningful as the art itself.

23.

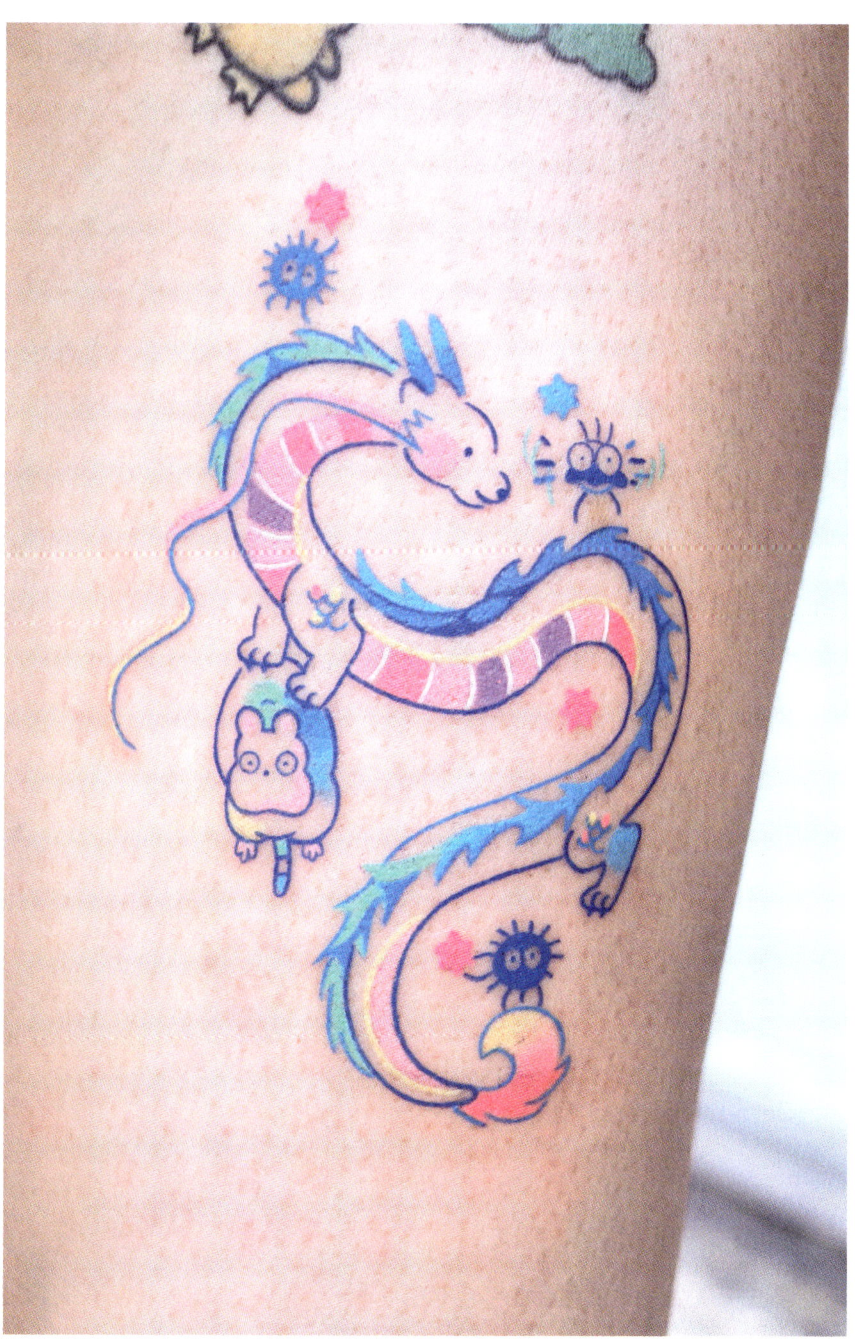

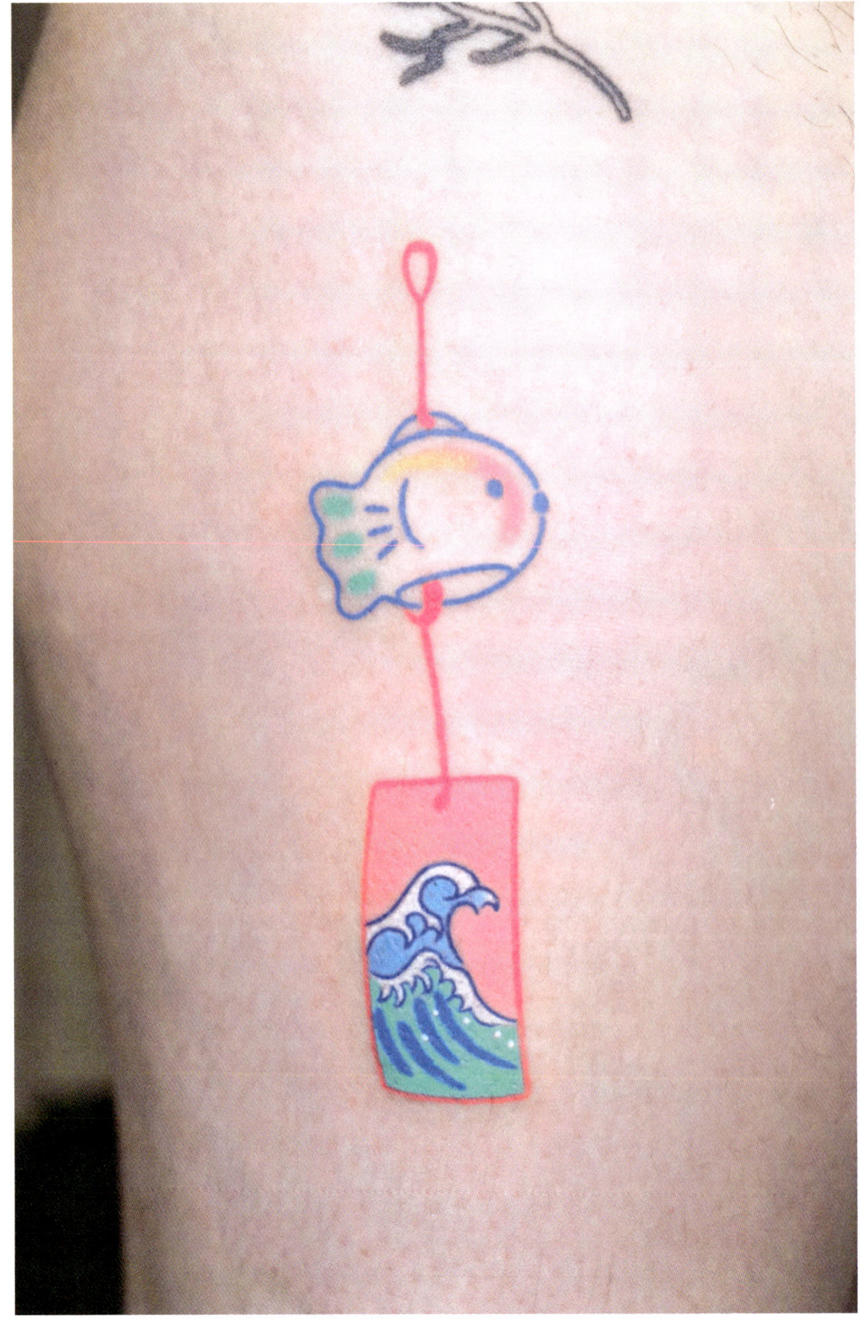

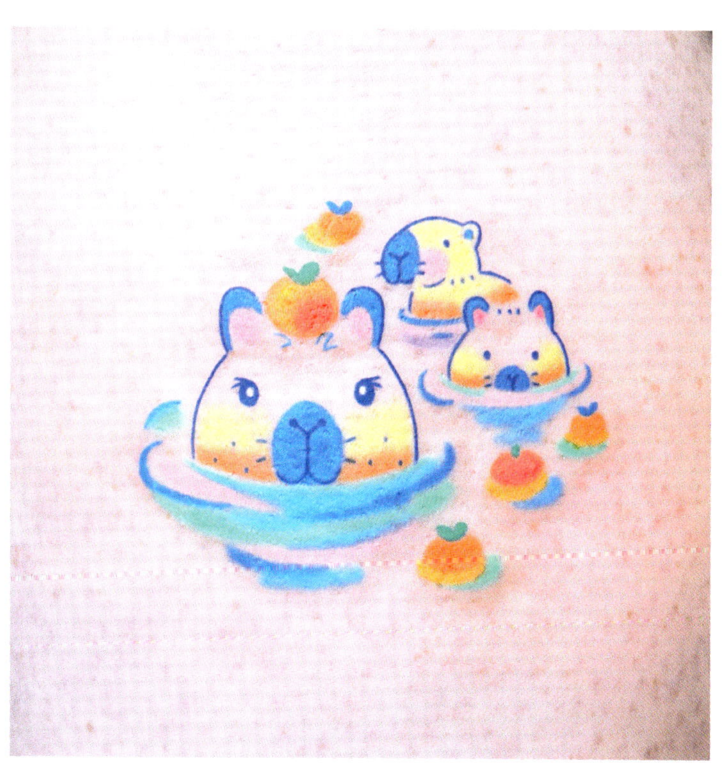

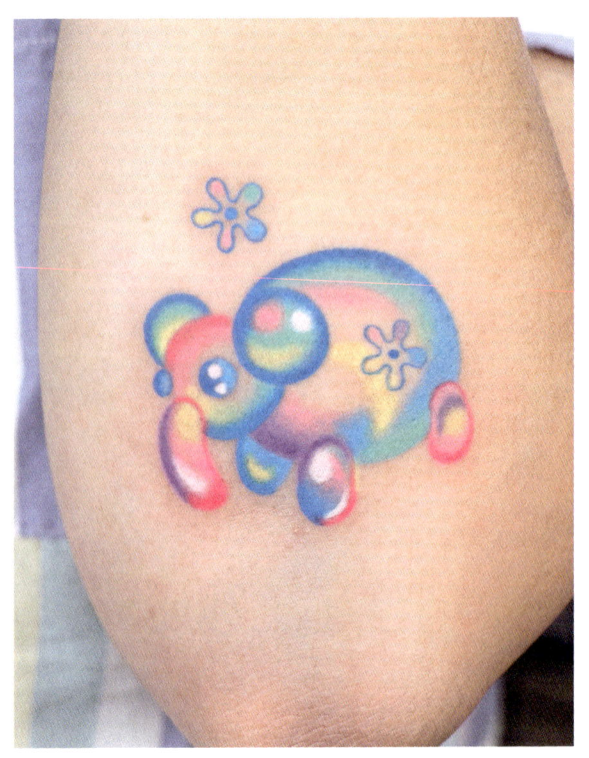

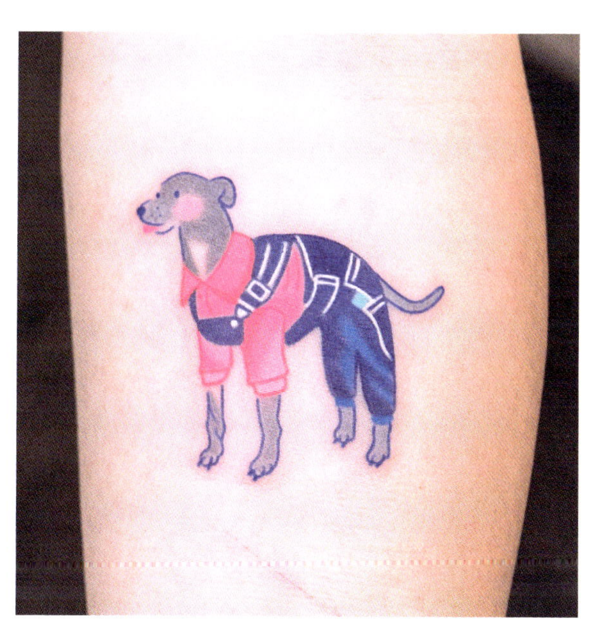

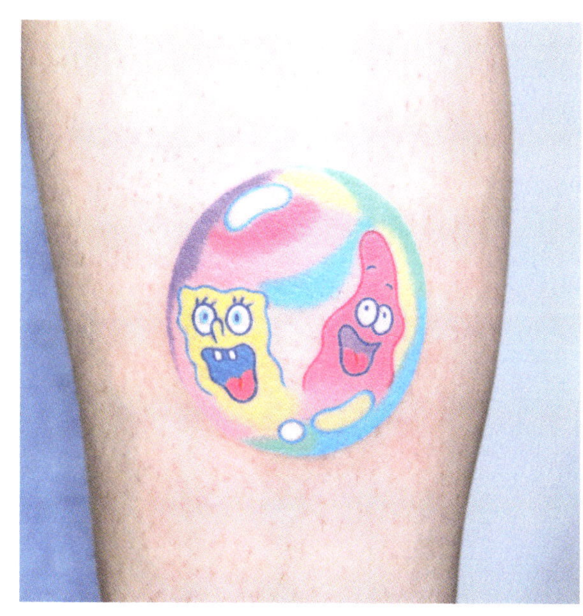

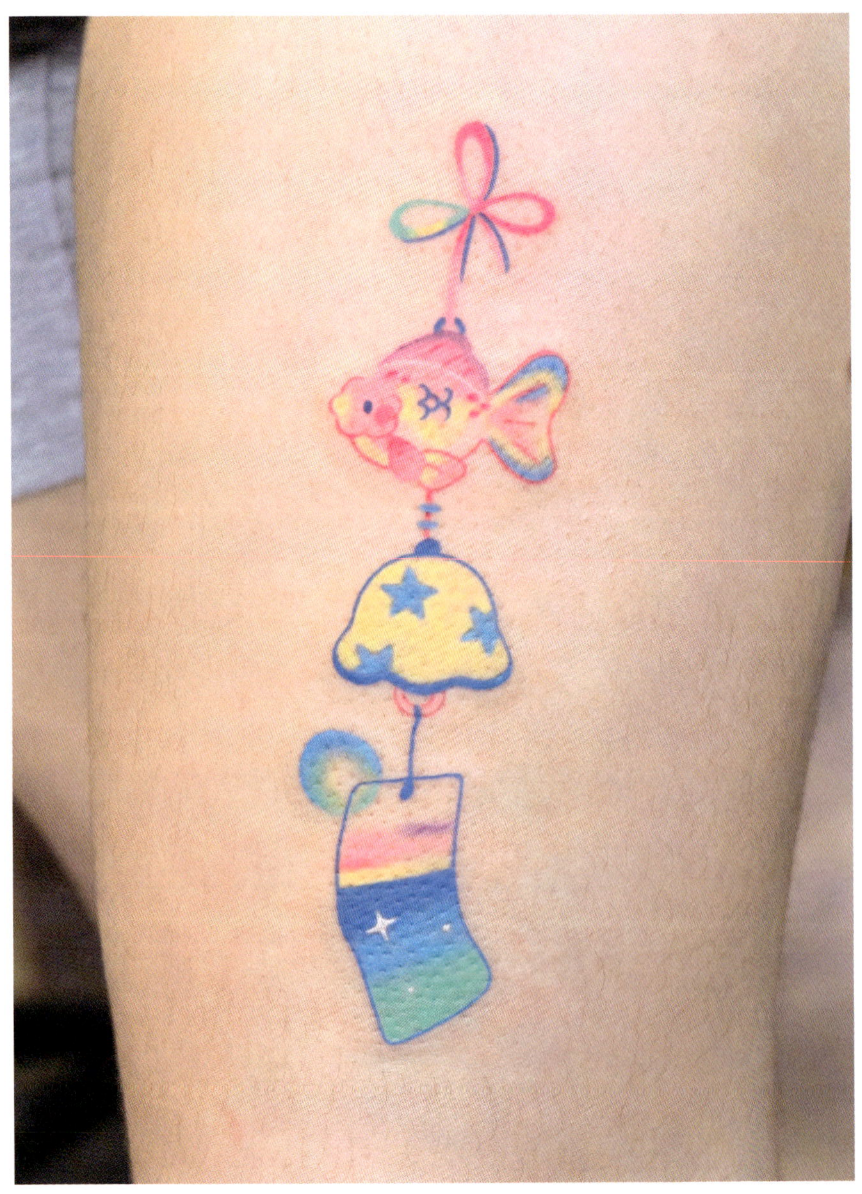

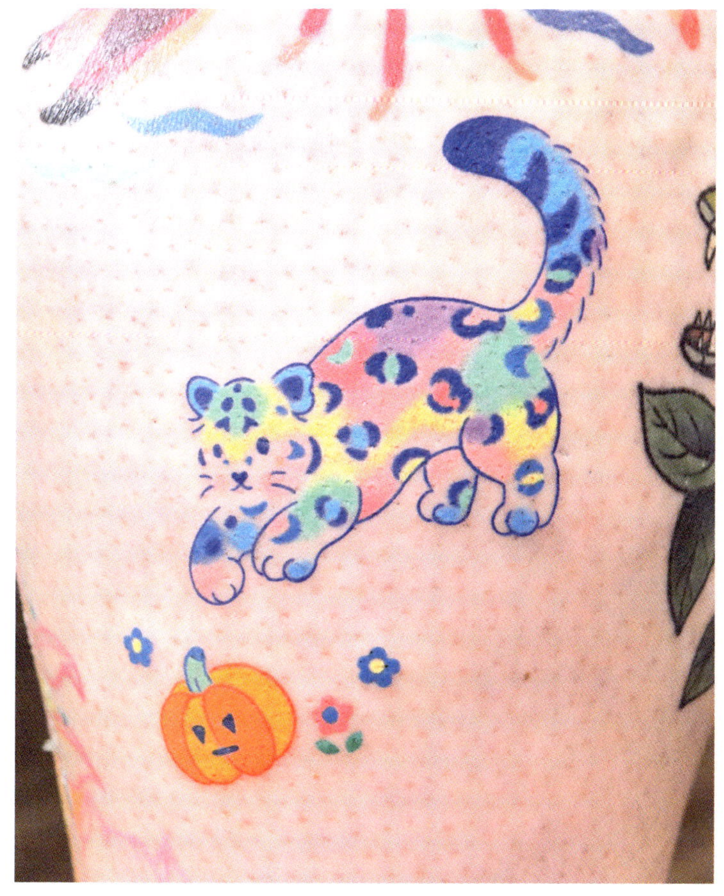

WINSTON THE WHALE

Portland, USA

Based in Portland, Oregon, Winston the Whale is a tattoo artist at Dental Bonez Clubhouse, known for his bold, colourful designs with thick, striking lines. A lover of rainbow hues, he has a playful, eye-catching style that incorporates vibrant colour palettes and dynamic compositions into most of his work, aiming to create tattoos that radiate joy, fun and positivity.

Winston began tattooing in 2015. Prior to that, he focused primarily on painting and illustration, with a strong emphasis on street art and murals - an influence that continues to shape his tattooing style today.

When he's not tattooing, Winston enjoys spending time with friends, being out in nature and focusing on self-work.

24.

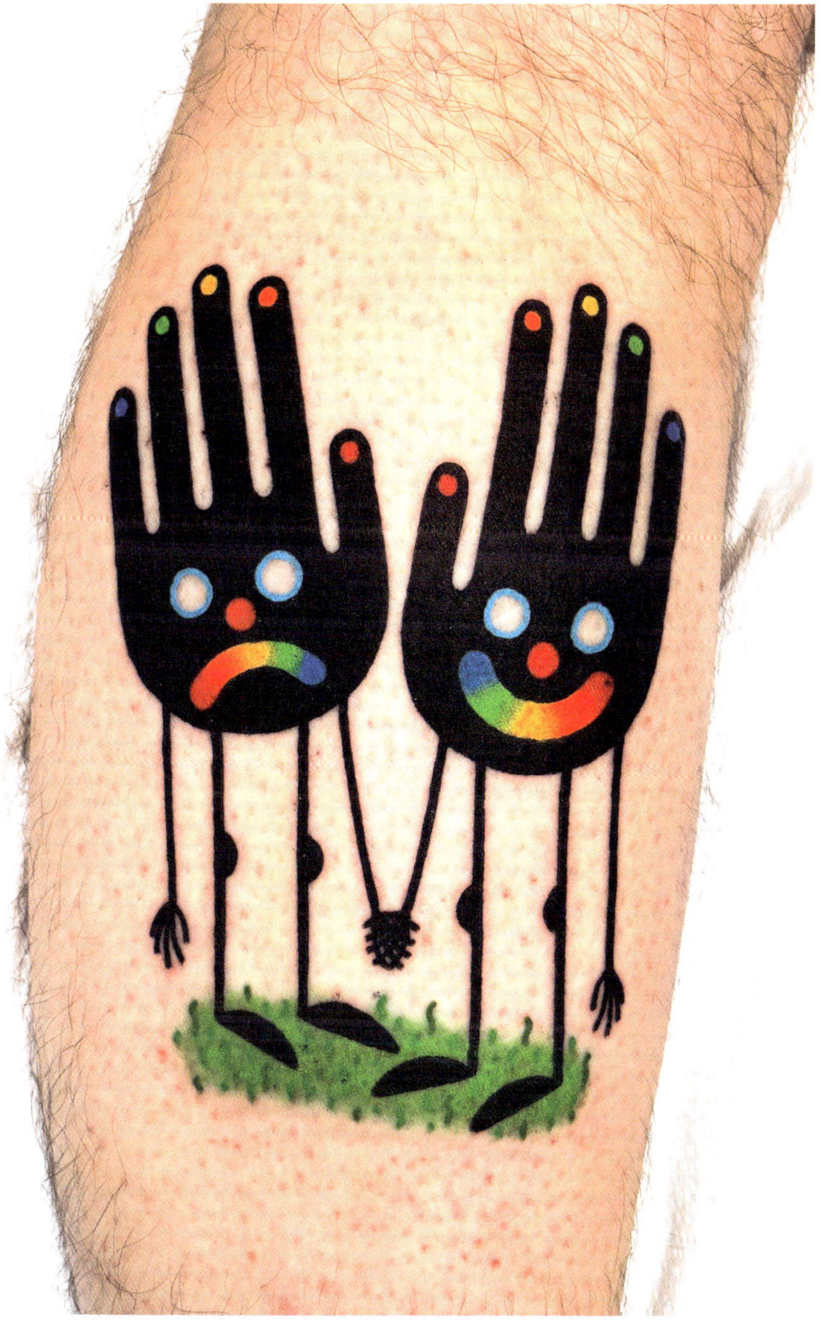

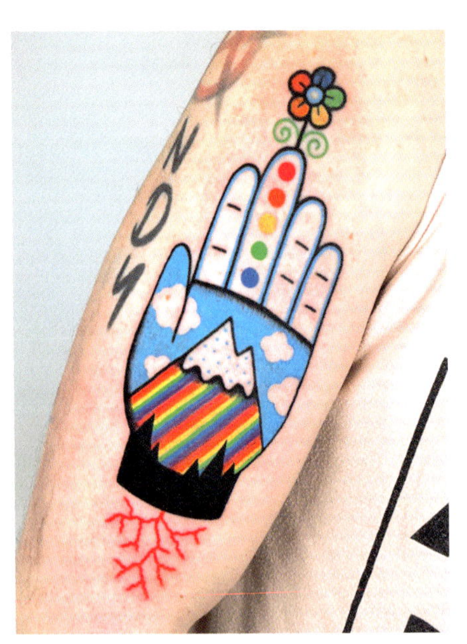

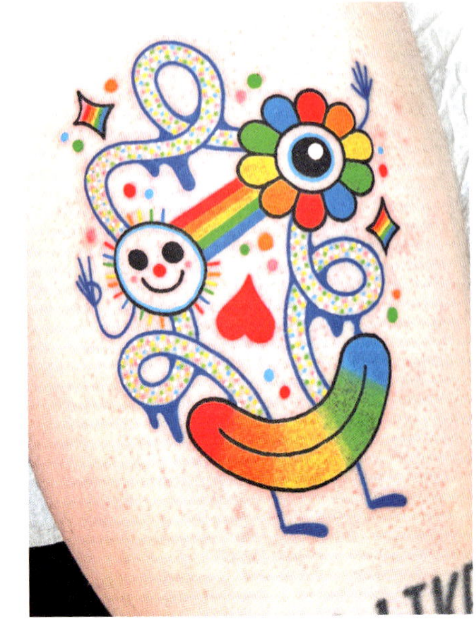

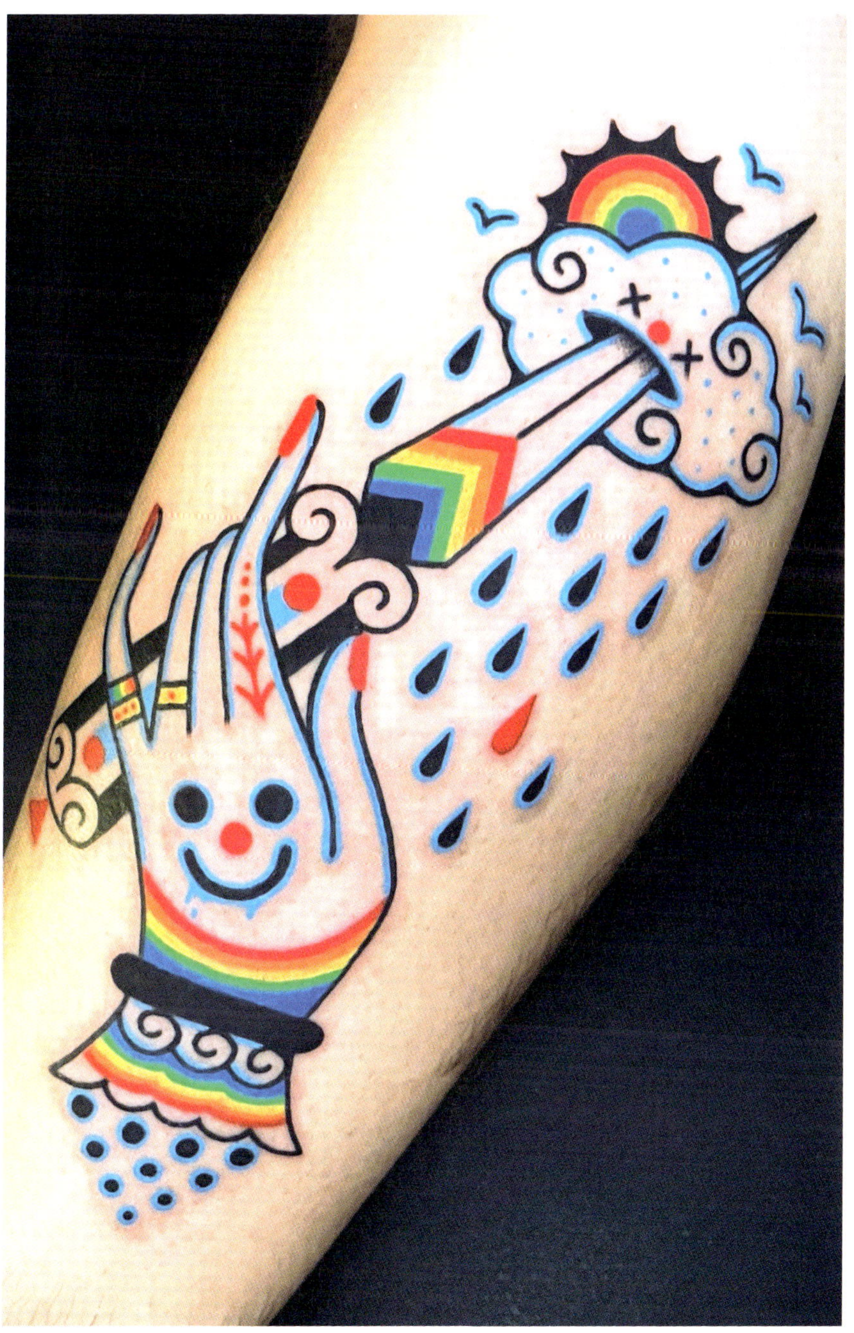

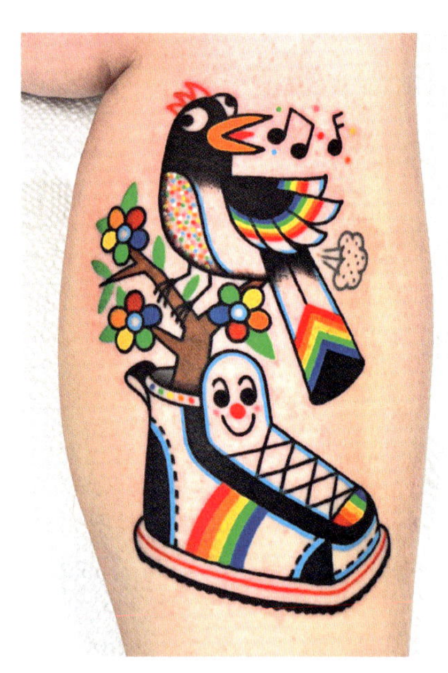

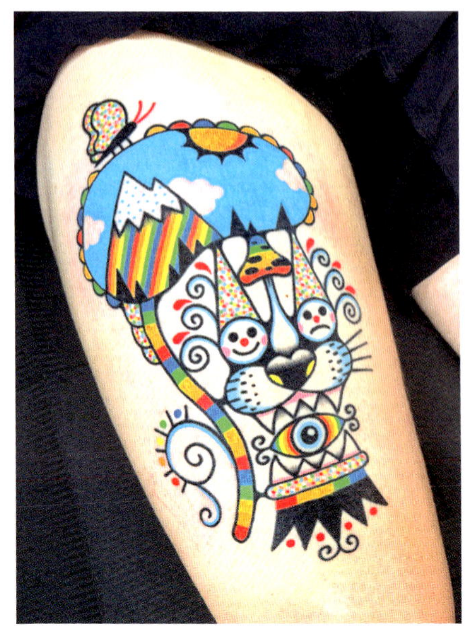

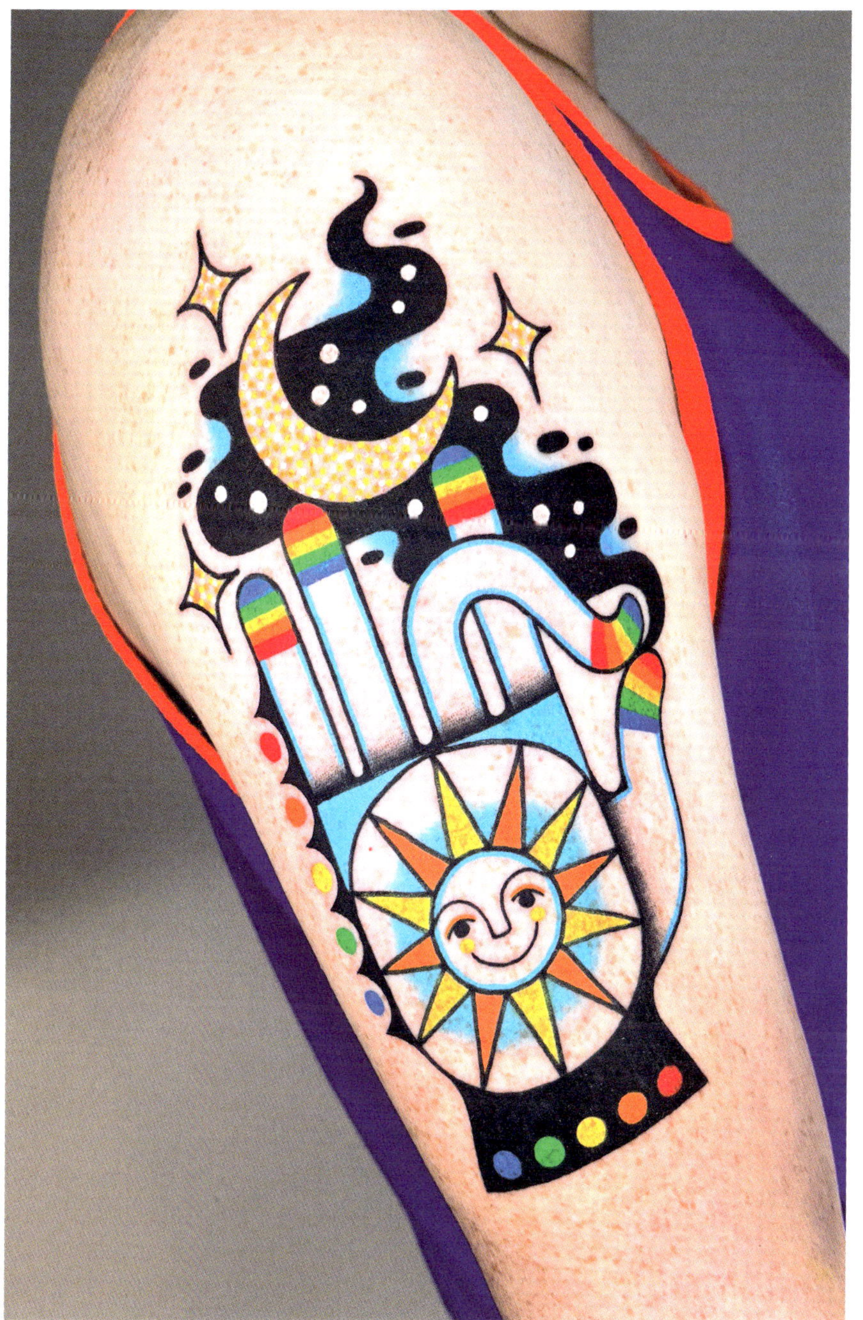

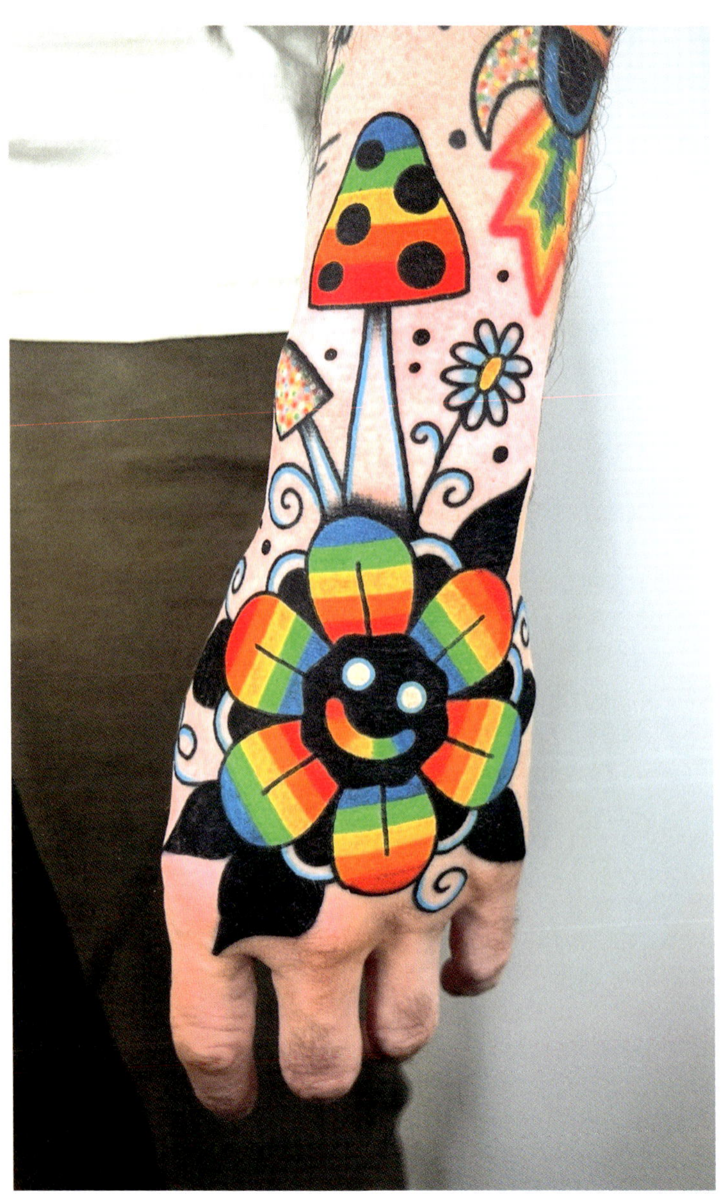

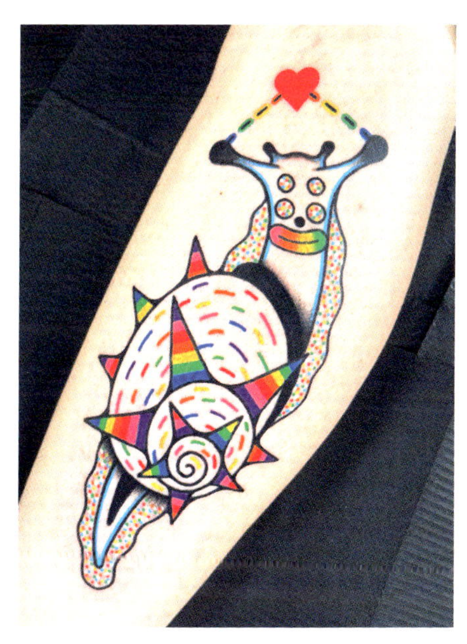

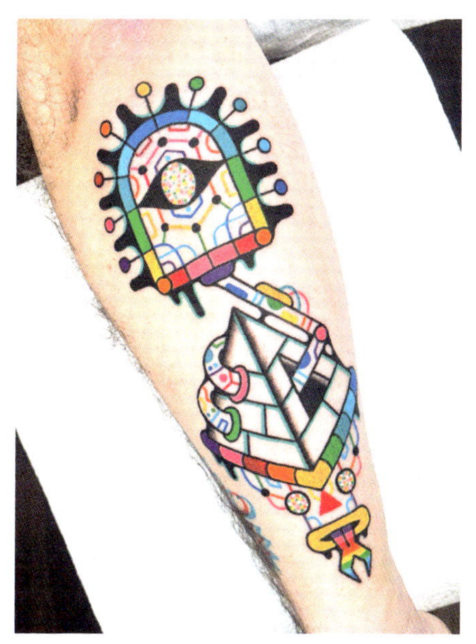

WOOZY MACHINE

London, UK

Based in London, UK, Woozy Machine is a tattoo artist with a background as a gallery artist, musician and even a zookeeper - leading a life as colourful and unconventional as his work. His art embraces simplicity and emotional depth, using humour as a way to disarm and connect with people on a deeper level. For Woozy, drawing is a means of expressing unspoken thoughts and intangible feelings, often following an internal logic beyond conscious understanding.

His journey into tattooing began 20 years ago, when he bought a coil machine from eBay and started tattooing his own artwork onto himself. Though initially self-taught, he fully committed to the craft professionally in 2017. Before tattooing, he studied Fine Arts at Chelsea College of Arts and the Royal College of Art, later exhibiting work in gallery shows and releasing records under his real name.

Now a resident artist at Parliament Tattoo in London, Woozy continues to develop his unique artistic voice, blending his eclectic life experiences with a passion for creating tattoos that are both fun and deeply resonant.

25.

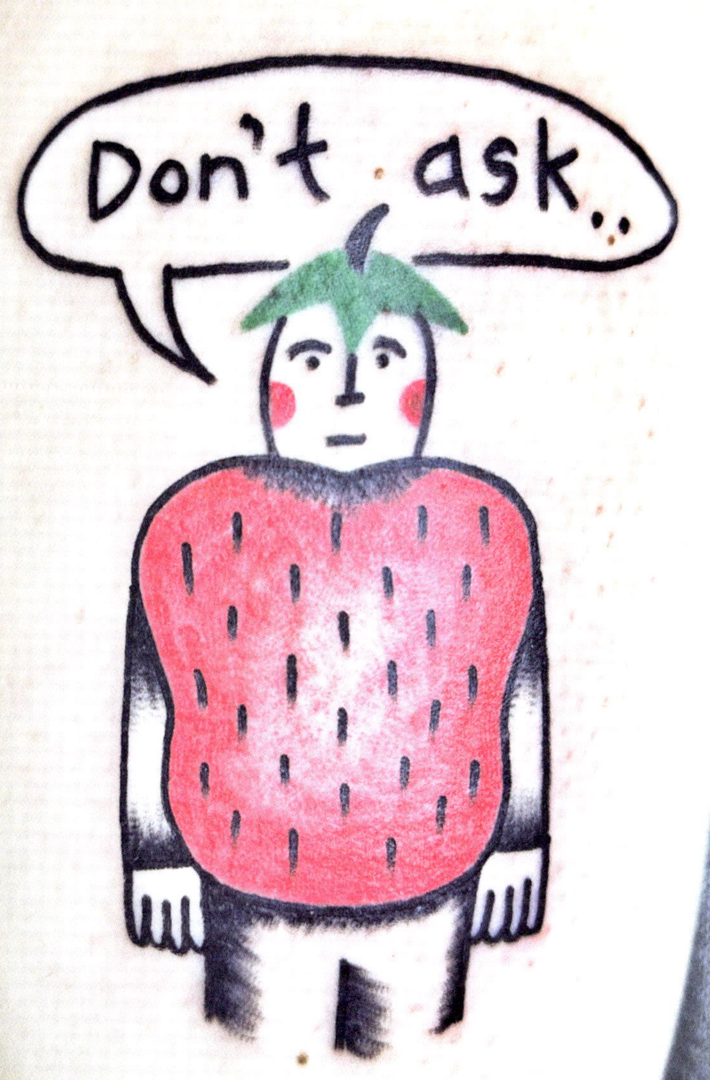
Don't ask..

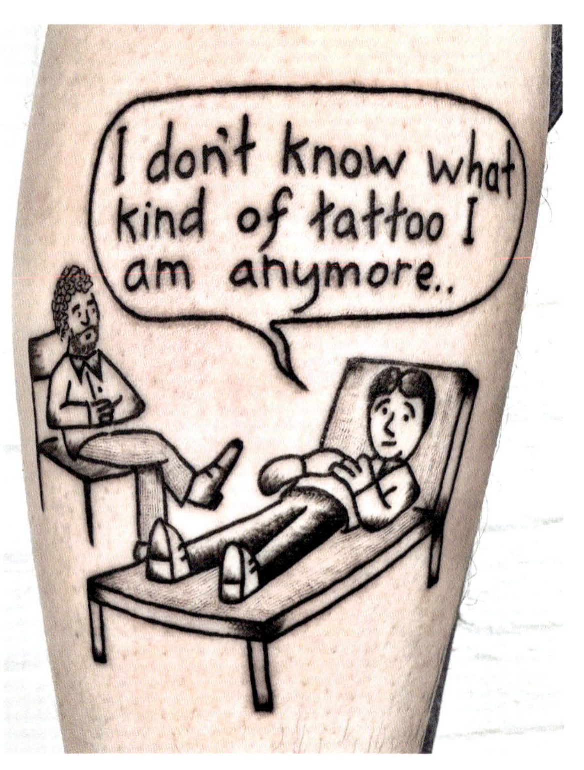
I don't know what kind of tattoo I am anymore..

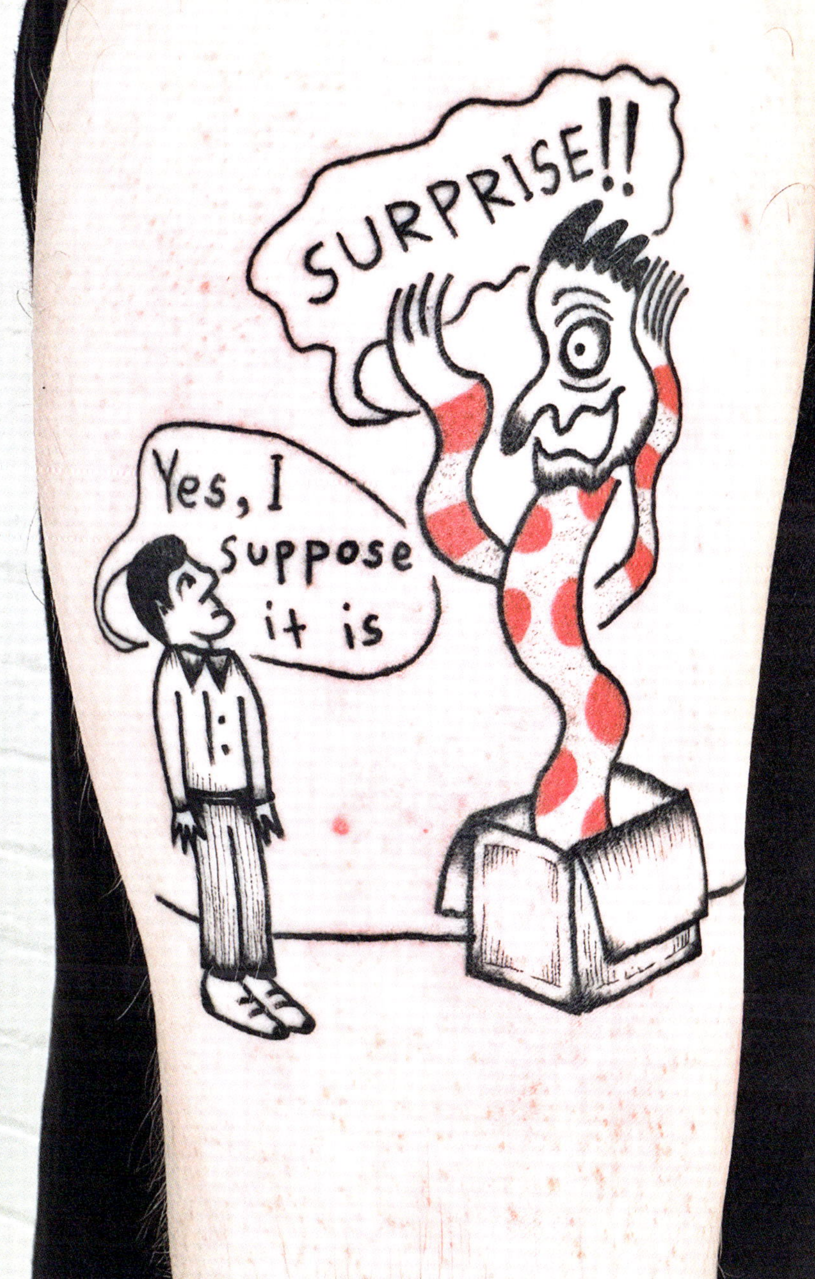
SURPRISE!!
Yes, I suppose it is

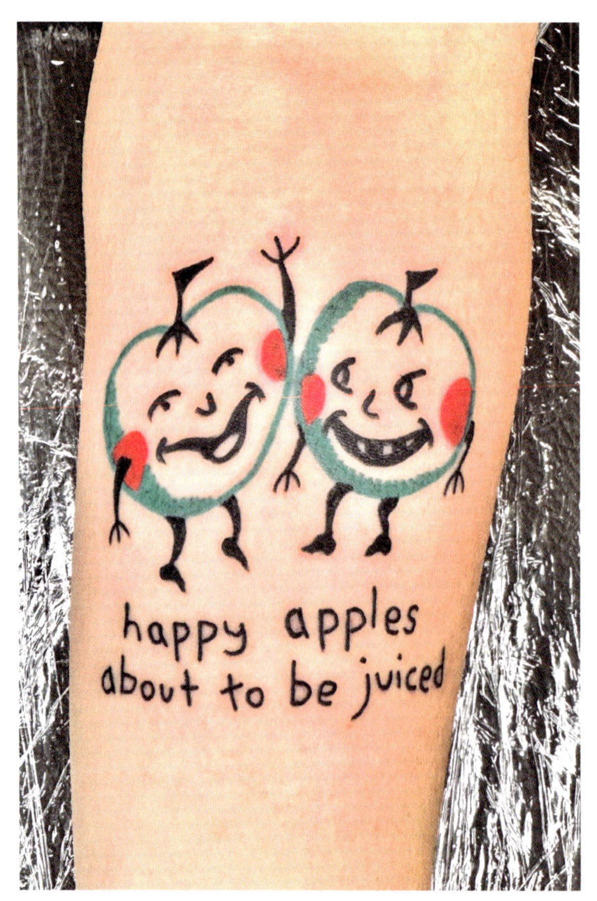
happy apples
about to be juiced

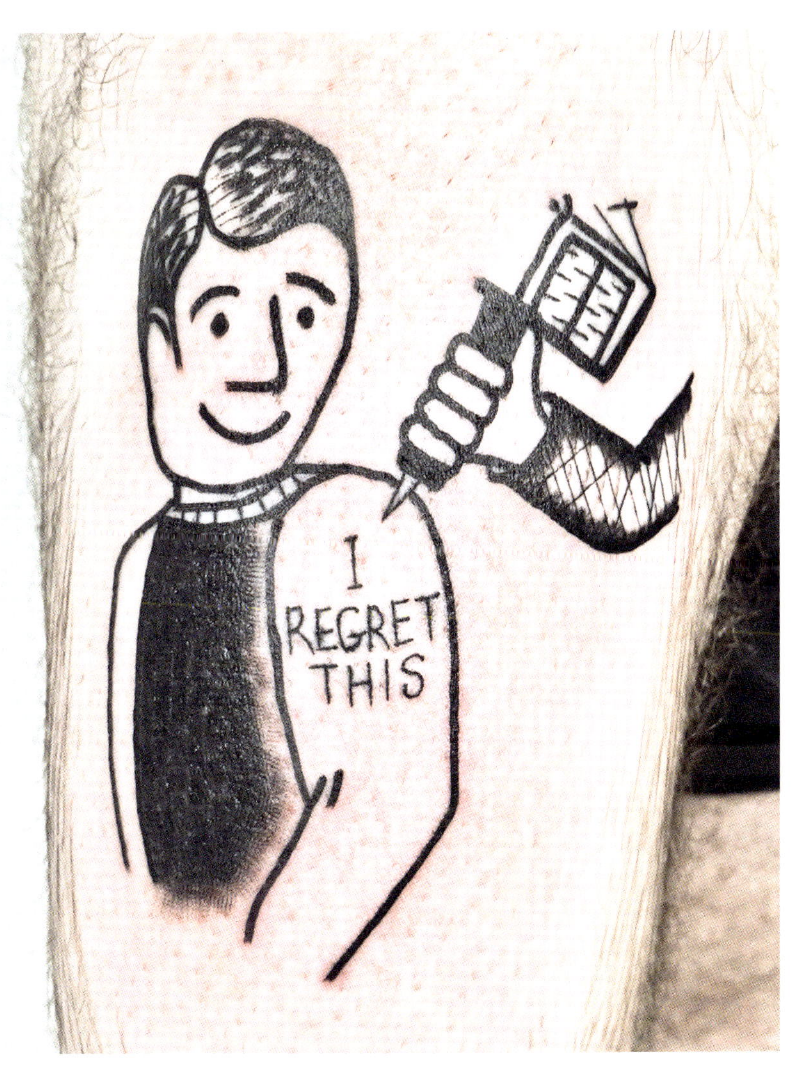
I
REGRET
THIS

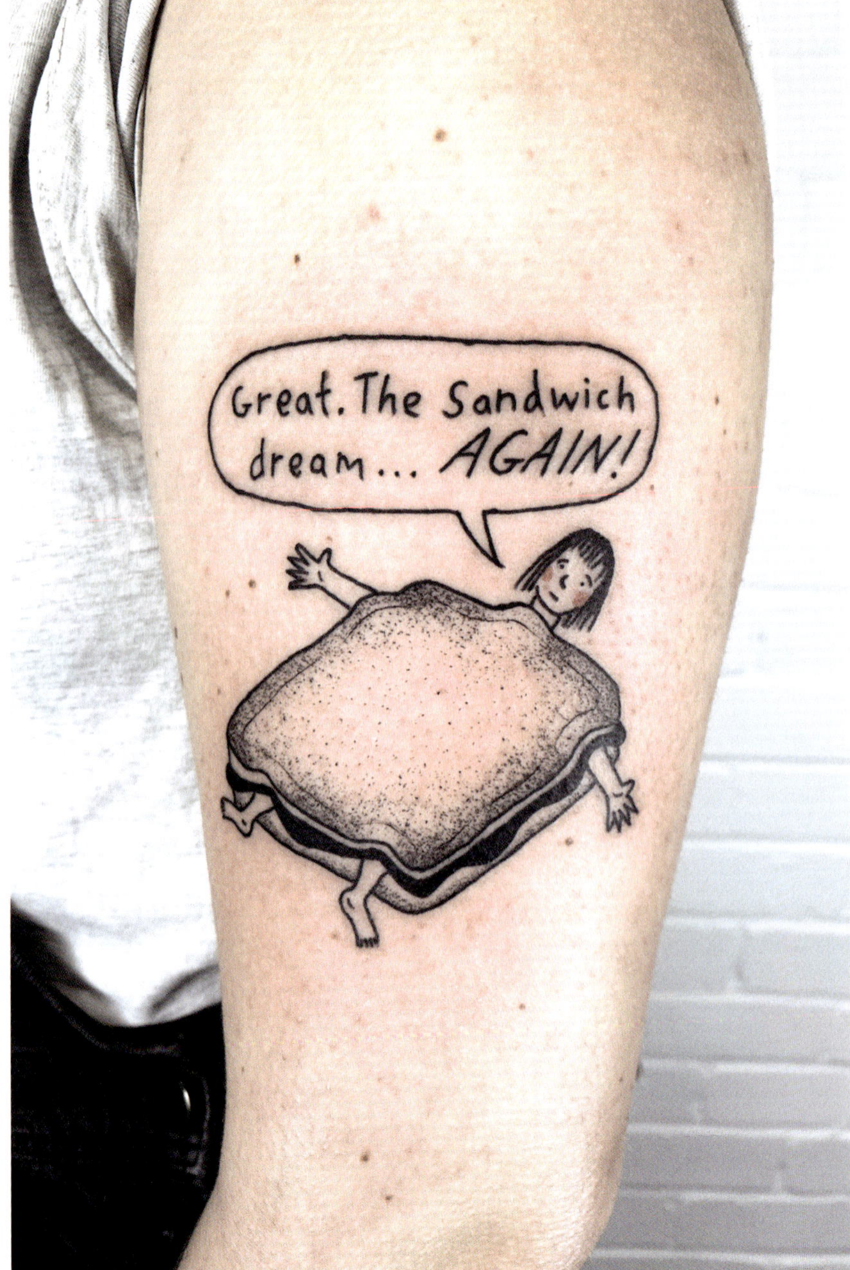
Great. The Sandwich dream... AGAIN!

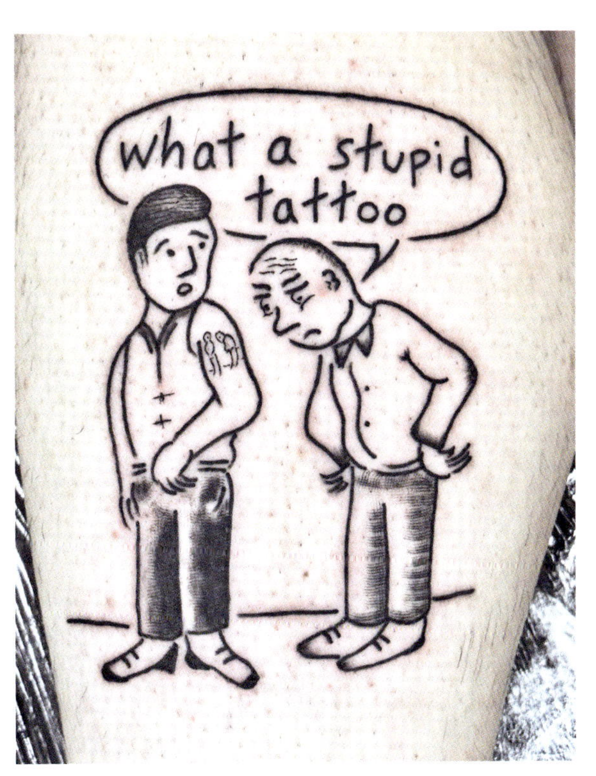
what a stupid tattoo

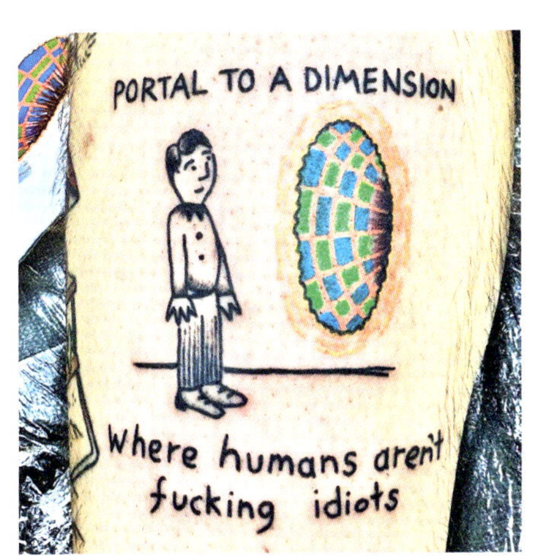
PORTAL TO A DIMENSION
Where humans aren't fucking idiots

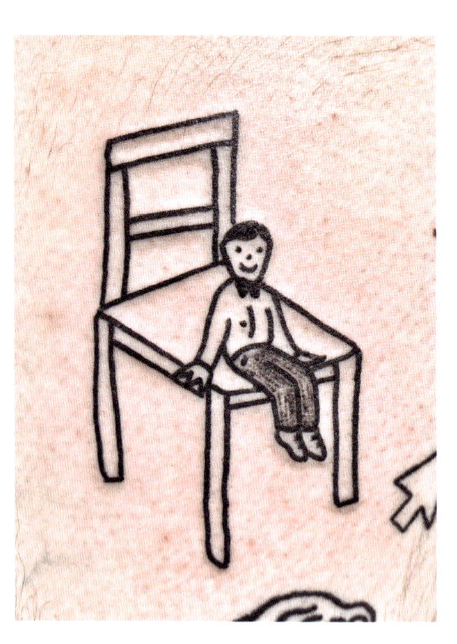

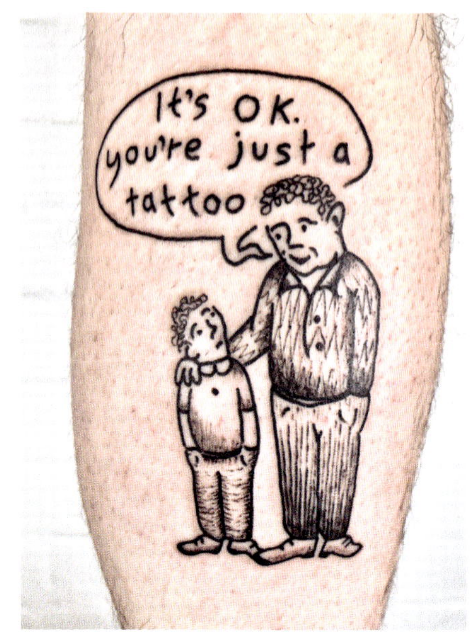
It's OK. you're just a tattoo

— INTERVIEW

What's the story behind your artist name?
In 2007 I had an exhibition at Sonia Rosso Gallery in Turin and one of the works was a collection of a few hundred drawings that I called 'woozy machine', reflecting my idea of a human. Like a machine that is woozy, which - of course - machines can't be.

How did your journey into tattooing begin?
I bought a coil machine from eBay about twenty years ago and just started tattooing myself. It was such a revelation that you could decorate your own body with your own imagery. I had no idea what I was doing and it was just an on-off hobby until 2015 when I decided to take it seriously and got obsessed with learning.

What three things make you happy besides tattooing?
Comics, UFOs, meditation.

Do you think there's a downside to being a tattoo artist?
The fact it relies so much on social media to sustain a decent career.

Did you go through a traditional apprenticeship to learn tattooing?
No, I'm self-taught. I learnt via tips from the internet, practising on myself a ton, then on friends, and then strangers.

If you weren't tattooing today, what would your job be?
I was a gallery artist for years and I was also a musician making records. So maybe I would do one of those, or make comics.

Can you describe the first tattoo you ever gave and what that experience was like for you?
If you don't count the stick and poke ones I made with a sewing needle and Indian ink on my arms, the first machine tattoo I made was a guy coming out of a stool holding up a plus and a minus sign. I made it upside down on my thigh. How did I feel? I was drunk but excited about the new chapter.

What is your main source of inspiration?
The fact my heart keeps beating.

How do you collaborate with clients during the design process?
I have a Dropbox with over a thousand drawings in that I constantly add to and delete from. They mostly choose from there or I do variations of my past tattoos.

Are there any types of tattoos or themes you absolutely won't do?
Anything that is hateful.

What kind of experience do you hope to give your clients during a tattoo session?
I want them to leave feeling positive about the time they had getting tattooed. It doesn't really matter about the image – tattooing is about the transformative process first, image second.

In what other creative areas do you express yourself beyond tattooing?
Music, comics, documentary art, dreaming.

What's your hope for the next generation of tattoo artists?
For them to tattoo with a relentless tinnitus of love.

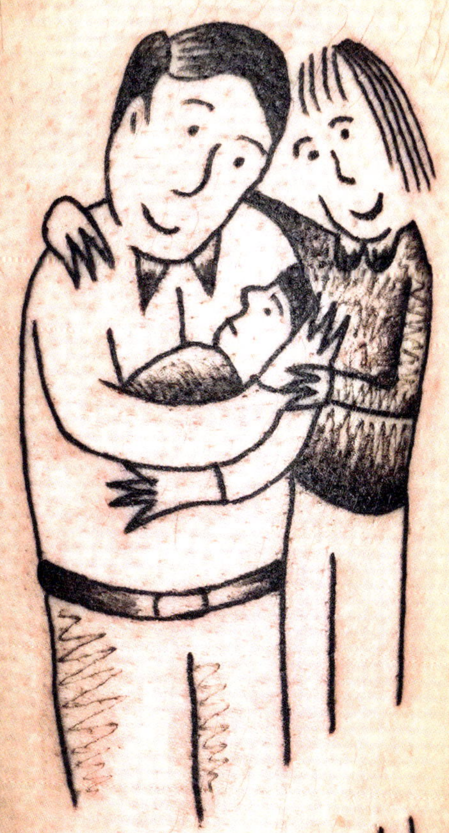
A new tattoo

INDEX

www.lannoo.com
Sign up to our newsletter for updates on our latest publications on art, interior design, food & travel, photography and fashion, as well as exclusive offers and events.

Texts
Ti Racovita
Sven Rayen

Copy Editing
Heather Sills

Image Selection
Ti Racovita
Sven Rayen

Book Design
Freek Lukas (Repress Design)

Typesetting
Stef Lantsoght (Keppie & Keppie)

Photography
All imagery is courtesy of the artists.
Imagery on the cover: © Sven Rayen
Imagery on the belly band:
Happy Fishhead (top left), Mr Heggie (top right),
Woozy Machine (bottom left), Linda Flowers (bottom right)

If you have any questions or comments about the material in this book, please do not hesitate to contact our editorial team: art@lannoo.com

D/2025/45/179 - Thema: AKT / AKL
ISBN 9789020975390